HOW TO SPOT YOUR CHILD'S POTENTIAL

CW01636201

CE [illegible] nalist. Her acc [illegible] *of the Red La* [illegible]

DF [illegible] cian at the Hc [illegible] is, one of Fra [illegible]

Overcoming Common Problems Series

The ABC of Eating
Coping with anorexia, bulimia and compulsive eating
JOY MELVILLE

Beating the Blues
SUSAN TANNER AND JILLIAN BALL

Beating Job Burnout
DR DONALD SCOTT

Being the Boss
STEPHEN FITZSIMON

Birth Over Thirty
SHEILA KITZINGER

Body Language
How to read others' thoughts by their gestures
ALLAN PEASE

Bodypower
DR VERNON COLEMAN

Calm Down
How to cope with frustration and anger
DR PAUL HAUCK

Comfort for Depression
JANET HORWOOD

Common Childhood Illnesses
DR PATRICIA GILBERT

Complete Public Speaker
GYLES BRANDRETH

Coping with Anxiety and Depression
SHIRLEY TRICKETT

Coping with Depression and Elation
DR PATRICK McKEON

Coping with Stress
DR GEORGIA WITKIN-LANOIL

Coping with Suicide
DR DONALD SCOTT

Coping with Thrush
CAROLINE CLAYTON

Coping Successfully with Your Child's Asthma
DR PAUL CARSON

Coping Successfully with Your Child's Skin Problems
DR PAUL CARSON

Coping Successfully with Your Hyperactive Child
DR PAUL CARSON

Coping Successfully with Your Irritable Bowel
ROSEMARY NICOL

Curing Arthritis Diet Book
MARGARET HILLS

Curing Arthritis – The Drug-free Way
MARGARET HILLS

Curing Coughs, Colds and Flu – the Drug-free Way
MARGARET HILLS

Curing Illness – The Drug-free Way
MARGARET HILLS

Depression
DR PAUL HAUCK

Divorce and Separation
ANGELA WILLANS

The Dr Moerman Cancer Diet
RUTH JOCHEMS

The Epilepsy Handbook
SHELAGH McGOVERN

Everything You Need to Know about Adoption
MAGGIE JONES

Everything You Need to Know about Contact Lenses
DR ROBERT YOUNGSON

Everything You Need to Know about Your Eyes
DR ROBERT YOUNGSON

Everything You Need to Know about the Pill
WENDY COOPER AND TOM SMITH

Everything You Need to Know about Shingles
DR ROBERT YOUNGSON

Family First Aid and Emergency Handbook
DR ANDREW STANWAY

Feverfew
A traditional herbal remedy for migraine and arthritis
DR STEWART JOHNSON

Fight Your Phobia and Win
DAVID LEWIS

Overcoming Common Problems Series

Getting Along with People
DIANNE DOUBTFIRE

Goodbye Backache
DR DAVID IMRIE WITH COLLEEN DIMSON

Helping Children Cope with Divorce
ROSEMARY WELLS

Helping Children Cope with Grief
ROSEMARY WELLS

How to be a Successful Secretary
SUE DYSON AND STEPHEN HOARE

How to Be Your Own Best Friend
DR PAUL HAUCK

How to Control your Drinking
DRS W. MILLER AND R. MUNOZ

How to Cope with Stress
DR PETER TYRER

How to Cope with your Child's Allergies
DR PAUL CARSON

How to Cope with Tinnitus and Hearing Loss
DR ROBERT YOUNGSON

How to Cure Your Ulcer
ANNE CHARLISH AND DR BRIAN GAZZARD

How to Do What You Want to Do
DR PAUL HAUCK

How to Enjoy Your Old Age
DR B. F. SKINNER AND M. E. VAUGHAN

How to Improve Your Confidence
DR KENNETH HAMBLY

How to Interview and Be Interviewed
MICHELE BROWN AND GYLES BRANDRETH

How to Love a Difficult Man
NANCY GOOD

How to Love and be Loved
DR PAUL HAUCK

How to Make Successful Decisions
ALISON HARDINGHAM

How to Move House Successfully
ANNE CHARLISH

How to Pass Your Driving Test
DONALD RIDLAND

How to Say No to Alcohol
KEITH McNEILL

How to Spot Your Child's Potential
CECILE DROUIN AND ALAIN DUBOS

How to Stand up for Yourself
DR PAUL HAUCK

How to Start a Conversation and Make Friends
DON GABOR

How to Stop Feeling Guilty
DR VERNON COLEMAN

How to Stop Smoking
GEORGE TARGET

How to Stop Taking Tranquillisers
DR PETER TYRER

Hysterectomy
SUZIE HAYMAN

If Your Child is Diabetic
JOANNE ELLIOTT

Jealousy
DR PAUL HAUCK

Learning to Live with Multiple Sclerosis
DR ROBERT POVEY, ROBIN DOWIE AND GILLIAN PRETT

Living Alone – A Woman's Guide
LIZ McNEILL TAYLOR

Living with Grief
DR TONY LAKE

Living Through Personal Crisis
ANN KAISER STEARNS

Living with High Blood Pressure
DR TOM SMITH

Loneliness
DR TONY LAKE

Making Marriage Work
DR PAUL HAUCK

Overcoming Common Problems Series

Making the Most of Loving
GILL COX AND SHEILA DAINOW

Making the Most of Yourself
GILL COX AND SHEILA DAINOW

Managing Two Careers
How to survive as a working mother
PATRICIA O'BRIEN

Meeting People is Fun
How to overcome shyness
DR PHYLLIS SHAW

The Nervous Person's Companion
DR KENNETH HAMBLY

Overcoming Fears and Phobias
DR TONY WHITEHEAD

Overcoming Shyness
A woman's guide
DIANNE DOUBTFIRE

Overcoming Stress
DR VERNON COLEMAN

Overcoming Tension
DR KENNETH HAMBLY

Overcoming Your Nerves
DR TONY LAKE

The Parkinson's Disease Handbook
DR RICHARD GODWIN-AUSTEN

Say When!
Everything a woman needs to know about alcohol and drinking problems
ROSEMARY KENT

Self-Help for your Arthritis
EDNA PEMBLE

Sleep Like a Dream – The Drug-Free Way
ROSEMARY NICOL

Solving your Personal Problems
PETER HONEY

Someone to Love
How to find romance in the personal columns
MARGARET NELSON

A Step-Parent's Handbook
KATE RAPHAEL

Stress and your Stomach
DR VERNON COLEMAN

Trying to Have a Baby?
Overcoming infertility and child loss
MAGGIE JONES

What Everyone Should Know about Drugs
KENNETH LEECH

Why Be Afraid?
How to overcome your fears
DR PAUL HAUCK

Women and Depression
A practical self-help guide
DEIDRE SANDERS

You and Your Varicose Veins
DR PATRICIA GILBERT

Your Arthritic Hip and You
GEORGE TARGET

Overcoming Common Problems

HOW TO SPOT YOUR CHILD'S POTENTIAL

Cécile Drouin and Dr Alain Dubos

translated by Dinah Livingstone

SHELDON PRESS
LONDON

First published in France in 1984 as *Votre Enfant est Doué* by
Sylvie Messinger éditrice, 24 rue de l'Abbé Grégoire, 75006 Paris.

This edition first published in Great Britain in 1989 by
Sheldon Press, SPCK, Marylebone Road, London NW1 4DU

© Éditions Sylvie Messinger 1984
Engish translation © Dinah Livingstone 1989

All rights reserved. No part of this book may be reproduced or transmitted in any form or by any means, electronic or mechanical, including photocopying, recording, or by any information storage and retrieval system, without permission in writing from the publisher.

British Library Cataloguing in Publication Data

Drouin, Cecile
Spot your child's potential.
1. Children. Aptitude. Children's aptitude.
Assessment of parents
I. Title II. Dubos, Alain III. Series IIII. Votre enfant est doué et vous ne le savez pas. *English*
649'.68

ISBN 0-85969-599-9

Typeset by Deltatype, Ellesmere Port, South Wirral
Printed in Great Britain by Biddles Ltd, Guildford and Kings Lynn

Contents

PART I

1

What does 'Gifted' Mean?

Gifted or not, that is the question. First, what do we mean by 'gifted'? According to the dictionary, a gift is a natural advantage with which you are born.

We often think that there are not very many truly gifted people. This is not so. Nearly all of us have some gift, but perhaps we have not discovered it so it has not been developed.

Imagine a country where everybody, with a very few exceptions, is blind. Sight then would be a gift possessed by a privileged few. Then imagine that these people are simply those who have discovered the knack of opening their eyelids, while everyone else keeps their eyes closed. This is what we mean by *discovering* a gift. Then all we have to do is learn how to use the gift, and this means developing it.

Many people have a gift but do not know it; it does not bother them because they do not know about it. But wouldn't they be a lot happier if they were able to use their talent? What would you think of someone who lived in poverty but had a fortune stashed away in the house? This is why it is so important to discover a gift, and to discover it in time.

Some gifts need to be nurtured from babyhood. But fortunately this is not the case with all gifts. Some late-discovered gifts can still develop and flourish. (The famous primitive painter Henri Rousseau did not discover painting until he had retired.)

It is a pity when someone discovers a gift as an adult and cannot put it to use, either because it is too late to develop it into anything more than a hobby (for example, playing the piano, dancing, acrobatics) or because commitments to a profession, family etc. make it impossible to change course. How often we hear people saying, 'I could have done something else . . . unfortunately . . .', betraying a lifetime's regret.

We hope this book will help you discover your children's talents and gifts, which are often hidden. The method we have chosen is play. But remember an answer to a test is like an instant photograph. It captures a fleeting moment. It does not record unchanging truth.

2

Twenty Questions Parents Ask

1. *At what age can you tell whether a child is gifted?*

There is no definite age for this. Everything depends on the child's development and behaviour. It also depends on how carefully the child is being watched. From their very first weeks, some newborn babies have truly astonishing powers of communication with their surroundings. They use their eyes, their hands and even smile. For the neutral observer such children have an astonishing rapport with others. Of course it is not possible to predict from this that they will always have this talent. But at least the parents' attention can be drawn to the need to stimulate and encourage their child's wish to make contact with the outside world. And of course this advice goes for all parents, whatever their baby is like.

We should look carefully at the way in which a child may be above average – precocious – apart from early family influences. It is important to know what we mean by 'precocious'. Observation by neutral witnesses who do not belong to the family is probably the ideal way to support the parents' impression of their child's capabilities, which are obviously likely to be very favourable.

Sometimes the child becomes less precocious as it grows older. There are many reasons for this – familial, social, cultural or medical. But it should be possible to keep a gift if it is nurtured properly. Albert Camus's father, for example, was illiterate. It was one of his son's teachers who nurtured the future Nobel prize-winner's gift for writing.

A gift is not miraculously revealed from one day to the next. Growing a particularly fine plant, for example, needs daily care, the right environment, constant attention. The same goes for a child's gift. Of course we can say that a six- or seven-month-old baby who grabs a spoon, lifts it to its mouth and empties it without spilling too much has a certain manual dexterity. The parents may be amused or proud but they know it is only a small skill. Compared to others this baby has a good spatial feeling for its own body.

A child who crows when she hears music shows that she enjoys it and wants to listen to it. But she must hear the same tune quite often to recognize and anticipate the feelings listening to it produces.

We cannot speak of a gift until later when the child has shown that this is what she wants and her musical apprenticeship is underway.

To take another example: Karine was standing at six months and trying to climb out of her cot. Three months later her mother found her on top of a bookshelf, and she is still wondering how she could have got up there. At two years Karine decided to climb over the balcony and fell from the second floor, fortunately without hurting herself. Karine is now seventeen and training at the National Circus School. She developed into adulthood a gift she showed from infancy, the gift of physical coordination and suppleness. This needed a long apprenticeship, during which there were times of doubt and discouragement. It also needed family support to go along with the child patiently and tolerantly – in a word, to stimulate her. A gift is never just there. The initial 'capital' always has to be improved on.

2. *Can a child be equally gifted in several directions or is there always one obviously outstanding gift?*

Some children have various talents which may sometimes amount to real gifts. The talents may be physical, intellectual, manual, artistic etc. The child may start with a certain number of aptitudes (showing an interest in the world, mental or motor precocity, manual dexterity, definite tastes, etc). And some of these aptitudes are likely to develop more than others.

The child's interests will turn in a certain direction. When the child seems to have made a firm choice, then you have to foster this aptitude, nurture it as much as possible, always remembering that even in the best conditions nothing is ever certain. The child may still choose to reject this choice, for all sorts of reasons, one of which might be in order to develop a different talent.

John is now seventeen. He is just finishing school and wants to study political science. From early childhood he was considered extremely gifted at the piano. He dropped it because his overstrict mother pushed him too much, forcing him to go in for competitions against his will when all he wanted was to study on his own or with his teacher. Now John is perfectly capable of playing for his own pleasure or to entertain his friends, but of course his mother's dream of seeing him as a concert pianist has been shattered. This musically gifted child also developed an early taste for reading, particularly history books, with an understanding well above average. John is now thinking about a career in which he will use his gift for reading.

This is a good example of having to choose between two talents. It is up to the parents to enable a gifted child to make this choice, whether final or not. When this happens the parents should support the change.

3. *What happens when a child who feels he has a gift he wants to use is thwarted?*

Everything depends on the child's age. Before the age of nine or ten a child is adaptable to his environment in a way that decreases later. Thus it is easier to turn a child away from a goal he has fixed for himself and push him in another direction. It all depends on the personality of both the child and his parents. Some children are very determined from a very young age about what they want to do. Most of these children, however much they were thwarted when they were young, whatever the choices that were made for them without respecting their own wishes, will still feel the same drive and certainty when they are grown up. If possible they will come back to what they originally wanted to do as a child.

This means they have stood out against their parents; even if they did not show it, they have been in conflict with them. This conflict is a major issue. For the child everything depends on how he settles the problem of his own frustration. He will either submit completely to what is demanded of him (and nothing more is said) and forget the conflict. Or he will put it to the back of his mind, knowing that some day he will be able to take it up again.

In the past a rigid educational system must often have given rise to such situations. But today a better understanding of children, greater willingness to listen to their wishes, in other words treating children as small independent persons with judgement and free will, has fortunately decreased the number of such wasted talents. Of course the ideal would be never to hear disappointed remarks such as 'I had a gift for so and so but I was not allowed to express it . . .'. Better informed parents will, we hope, achieve this goal.

4. *Should you try to develop all a child's gifts if he has several?*

In the education system and vocational training it is quite usual to concentrate more on one particular talent, both for the student's own best development and to make it easier to find a job later on. But before this happens it is important that the child should have the chance to try out many different subjects and activities. Many children engage in all sorts of cultural, sporting, artistic and leisure activities both at home and at school.

Of course it is sensible not to overwhelm the child with too many activities at once, and to suggest things when the child seems to show the inclination. Doctors are familiar with children who are pushed into doing too many things. They feel got at and worn out and are likely to become disgusted with all these activities and end up refusing to do anything.

So if a child appears to have a number of gifts, a choice has to be made. It is of course most important that the child agrees with this choice. Parents must listen to the child, discover preferences, help him or her choose what to do without being too dominant. Respect for the child is essential. Many parents dream of their children developing gifts that they would have liked to possess themselves, so caution is always wise. Children must never be forced to put some activity first which they rank second or third among their talents, as they are likely to get bored. It is vital to listen to the child with patience and understanding. There is no harm in trying to interest the child in a particular subject, but in the end it is up to the child to decide.

On the other hand it is important not to jump to the conclusion that this is a real gift every time the child shows the slightest inclination to engage in some activity. Our society goes in for 'crazes' that may change every six months and children may want to try something just because it is 'trendy' – they have seen it on television or 'all their friends are doing it'. This 'trend-hopping' simply reflects the child's inability to make up her own mind; she/he may have some gift which is not always easy to assess. But fortunately it is not uncommon for it to be discovered sooner or later.

Once again, patience and listening as well as talking to the child are crucial.

5. *If a gifted child is ill should she give up practising her gift until she is better?*

Everything depends on how long the illness lasts and what the particular gift is. For short periods of one to three weeks, the vast majority of cases, the child should rest from her usual activities or do something else. The sick child in bed wants coddling. She likes to be made a fuss of. During this time children may become involved in reading and games. Some discover new pleasures for the first time, maybe reading, drawing or listening to music.

These enforced rest periods may be very positive for discovering a new interest or developing it. The problem is quite different when it is a long illness, lasting whole terms or even years. I am thinking of chronic articulatory disorders, muscular, cardiac or respiratory disorders, which mean the child has to have a complete change of lifestyle. A child with one of these diseases needs suitably adapted schooling and to learn to cope with the disease. Any gifts such a child has should be investigated and supported as strongly as possible. Everything should be done to help the child develop as fully as possible and react positively to the disease. A child who is very keen on sport, for example, but unable to develop this gift because of heart or rheumatic trouble, must find other activities – passions even – instead.

Isabel did competition gymnastics. When she was eleven she had to stop because of heart trouble following severe rheumatoid arthritis. During many months of enforced rest, she spectacularly developed a gift she had previously relegated to second place, which was designing clothes. This new turn her life took seemed to suit her. At thirteen Isabel follows a school curriculum adapted to her needs and she now wants to become a professional fashion designer. This example shows that one gift may sometimes hide another.

Thus a long illness in a child may actually lead to unforeseen blossoming. Family support is essential because with such an illness there may be many setbacks and periods of discouragement. The family must take care to control their distress about the illness and not be overprotective. If illness stops a gift developing it is vital to turn the child's energies and will in another direction.

Some illnesses actually seem to favour the development of certain gifts. Take asthma, for example. Because victims suffer from breathlessness, which may even take the form of suffocation attacks, and general muscular weakness, they are forced to turn inwards. The effect of this may be negative but sometimes it helps the development of intellectual talents, such as reading, drawing, music, and even dramatic talents.

This interesting side to illness should be borne in mind as part of the treatment. The best known example of this symbiosis between illness and artistic creation is Marcel Proust, whose very special search into his past probably would never have happened without the terrible bouts of illness that kept him imprisoned indoors.

6. *What happens if the child's gift is not discovered and the child is also unaware of it?*

Literature, especially English literature of the eighteenth and nineteenth centuries, is full of child characters who are thwarted from the beginning of any chance to develop. These heroes and heroines have to create a life for themselves when nobody has recognized they have any talents at all.

They are neglected at home and at school. No one takes any notice of them and they are constantly humiliated. These children's gifts are not discovered because no one has bothered to look out for them. If the child is also unaware of any gifts she may have, then of course these gifts have very little chance of developing.

It is quite easy for a child to have a gift and be completely unaware of it. It happens frequently. That is why it is important for parents to seek it out. It should never be assumed that a child has *no* gifts. This is extremely uncommon. Usually when children do not seem to take an interest in anything, it is because they have not discovered what they are good at. So it is really important to give a child every opportunity to try things out.

To arouse a child's interest, the subject should be presented in an attractive way. The parents should be enthusiastic, even if it is not a subject that really interests *them*. Sometimes a very gifted child may be able to overcome all kinds of obstacles, but another equally gifted child, who is less sure what she wants and perhaps shy by temperament, needs a lot of moral support and family involvement.

To sum up, I would say that most children who do not appear to be gifted in any way have simply not been pointed in the right direction.

7. *What should be done when a child has a gift and refuses to develop it?*

We need to redefine what we mean by a gift. Children who refuse to follow a course to which others think they are ideally suited are probably being pushed in the wrong direction. This happens quite often if the child is pushed too hard without being allowed to make up his own mind. The child has reasons for refusing and probably simply lacks the motivation to pursue a particular course. All children are sometimes offhand, lazy or scatterbrained.

Parents, faced with long-term refusal on the child's part to follow a course they propose, should examine themselves. Parents often project onto their children wishes of their own that never came true. These frustrations, which may go back a long time, create a need to have a second chance through their children. I know some parents –father or mother or maybe both – who literally force their children to learn to play the piano or violin, because they themselves love these instruments and did not get the chance to play them when they were children. Some children seem to cope quite well with this, but the majority sooner or later violently reject the parents' wishes.

These unfortunate projections are quite frequent. They explain many failures because a child feels, 'I am being made to do something which is not really "me".' They become aware of the selfish nature of the pressure being put on them and try to escape from it.

It may be some consolation to disappointed parents that such behaviour also occurs within 'artistic' families, although they are literally swamped with culture. This only goes to show that some children are clearly not gifted in certain fields, even if the environment seems ideal.

But refusal can also be a way of expressing conflict either within the child or between the child and the family, or within the family itself. Rejection of the parents' wishes then becomes a powerful weapon for the child. Failure and setbacks of this kind often happen with the coming of adolescence, between the ages of twelve and fifteen. At this age young people often have a poor self-image or refuse to try and create a good one. They therefore choose to fail and thus create a situation in which they are bound to feel bad. A wise way of dealing with this behaviour is just to be patient, try to understand what is bothering the child, without being too harsh. Sometimes psychological investigation into this problem shows that the child's refusal to develop a gift is caused by an overpowerful parental image. When children feel crushed by the too dominant personality of father or mother, they may deliberately take refuge in failure so that they do not have to measure up to a person who is too strong for them.

So the reasons why a child refuses to develop a gift concern the family as a whole. The whole family must be involved, examine itself, perhaps, and take responsibility for each child growing up well-balanced and developing individual gifts.

8. *Does comparison with others stimulate a gifted child?*

This can cut both ways. Competition with other children, particularly at school, may stimulate a child into making an effort. But systematically devaluing the child by comparing her unfavourably with the parents or an unattainable model can have a very damaging and negative effect, the opposite of what was intended. It will inevitably cause feelings of failure and withdrawal in children who are sensitive to this sort of pressure.

The child must be certain that the comparison may turn out in her favour. The model must be attainable and surpassable. The atmosphere must be one in which the child can learn and also teach, at her own level of course. If the child is put together with those more advanced than she is and also with beginners who have not yet reached her level, she will be stimulated. She can cheerfully and freely take her place on such a ladder. In many different fields – games, art, sport, study – the child needs to be able to make comparisons to see how far she has progressed and how far there is still to go.

If she is truly gifted progress will be rapid, first out of a wish to copy and then through a taste for competition and winning. It will also make her realize the need to work hard and not give up, which is especially important for those who are perhaps less gifted than others and take longer to learn, but who may still end up among the best.

Rubinstein, for example, was a true virtuoso on the piano as a child. But this would not in itself have been enough to make him the best pianist of his day. He had to disregard the fact that he was a prodigy and work hard for many years. An educated public is able to distinguish between the supergifted pianist who has no trouble at all with technical difficulties, and the 'plodder', who may be far less imaginative but just as good a musician. This proves that people with unequal gifts may both reach the top of their art, and long hard work can get you as far as a superb gift and apparent facility.

Before reaching the top, of course, the child has to serve an apprenticeship in which competition has a part to play. Competitions can be a good thing as long as the child has room to develop, but they become stultifying if they do not give the child space to improve his performance.

For example, the tennis player Manuel Santana was one of the best players in the 1960s. He began as a ball boy in Madrid, then found he had a gift for tennis and with help worked untiringly to overcome setbacks, disappointment and moments of discouragement. He was certainly gifted but he was also a stubborn slogger, with a supreme goal that he finally reached.

In summary, I think a child, particularly a gifted child, must be free to set his own standards. If he believes he is first rate he must keep going but always remember that somewhere somebody will be better than him. This can do him good. It is up to family and teachers to help him take the final steps to the top. This may mean sometimes offering criticism when the child himself asks for comparisons and judgements. I am sure that a feeling like jealousy can if used correctly be a strong impetus. A child should never be pointlessly humiliated by being told: 'You can't do that' or 'It is too much for you', but 'If you work hard you should be able to do it'. Pointless challenge and unequal comparison do nothing but harm if the child does not have it in himself to improve. Such challenges are only valuable at a later stage when the child is used to working hard and has firmly decided where he wants to go.

9. *Are there children with no particular talent?*

Not at all, except perhaps for the very severely mentally retarded or children with insuperable learning difficulties. *Every child has a talent*, which can be discovered and nurtured. Even severely handicapped children – those with Down's syndrome, for example – often show a taste for music. They are deeply moved by it and find it soothing; listening to music makes them happy and is a great help to them. Autistic children are often so withdrawn that they are completely cut off from the outside world; such children cannot be expected to show talent in the ordinary way. But here too music can be a vital link with the outside world. And in some fortunate cases this love of music can be the first sign of a possible cure.

Apart from these extremes, it is fair to say that every 'normal' child has some skill or talent. If this does not show up, the most likely explanation is that no one has bothered to draw it out. Children subjected to massive physical, intellectual and emotional deprivation can reach a rock bottom point where they simply run wild. There are well authenticated historical accounts of such child 'savages'. But even these wild children have succeeded in adapting to their natural environment, which means they must have some practical intelligence and necessary skills for basic survival.

10. *If a gift is not developed early enough does it disappear?*

With gifts it is the same as with anything else. If a skill, an organ or a limb is not used for a long while, it takes a great deal of work and energy to get it going again.

On an eight-year-old child's hand, for example, the finger movements and joints are completely different from the same person's hand as an adult. Exercising a high level skill – playing the piano or guitar, for example – requires daily practice, sticking to a routine and not letting up. For some artists a fortnight's holiday away from their instrument means they have to put in a lot of extra practice when they get back to work. And the longer time is spent without playing the longer it will take to get back into it.

Nowadays hobbies are regarded as a good thing but we also tend to idolize top professionals. If someone has a skill that is discovered late, everything depends on how much development is possible. Certain manual skills for playing a piano, guitar or violin must nearly always be acquired as a young child, or else it is too late. Music teachers know how different it is teaching a child of seven or eight with supple, malleable and tireless fingers, and even a gifted adult, whose hands will be much stiffer and find some movements much harder to pick up.

On the other hand, the 'gift' of writing or painting can come to light at any age. The primitive painter Rousseau is a perfect example. But in sport, which is very different, competitive swimming, for example, especially for girls, or gymnastics – as they are taught at the moment – must be started very young. The Soviet bloc countries have developed scientific training techniques, about some of which we might have reservations, in order to produce 'child champions', whose career lasts for just one Olympiad – that is, four years at the most.

At any rate someone who has a potential gift for swimming who only begins doing it at the age of twenty or twenty-five will find their scope for development considerably reduced. If this person had been put into the water as a child, and given the right encouragement, they might have been a medal winner! Gifts of this kind shrivel away if they are not developed in good time.

Adolescence seems to be the time when athletic gifts may be discovered. The individual's rapid physical growth may produce a future champion, provided of course they can endure the hard training discipline required. Here too, teachers and parents must act promptly and wisely to help the child develop the gift.

For others, the vast majority, who will not become prodigies, there is still the huge pleasure to be gained by exercising a skill for its own sake.

11. *Are gifts hereditary?*

For years this has baffled geneticists, psychologists, doctors and sociologists (to name but a few experts!). Probably the truth lies somewhere between those who hold that heredity is all, so that an individual's genetic make-up explains and excuses everything, and those who hold that environment is more important. Nature or nurture?

Eye colour, mouth shape and temperament, for example, are coded in some way in the chromosomes. Thus each of us come into the world with a given package of qualities, that we may or may not get the chance to unpack and use.

One thing that strikes us in paediatrics is that tiny babies are all very alike. Of course some are unusually precocious in using their hands or communicating, for example. But in most cases until about the age of four months, most babies behave very much alike. Only after that do differences begin to appear and the baby's environment clearly show its effect.

Some children are brought up in special environments (with musicians, painters, scholars, writers etc.). Some are thrust into an environment where they are continually being talked to. Heredity may also take the form of a family tradition in which small children are rapidly involved. Generations of musicians are a good example of this, where talent which may be inherited also provides the child's cultural environment.

12. *Is it possible to go about developing a gift in the wrong way and destroy it?*

There is no doubt that this can happen. We have already seen that it all depends on the gift, what the child wants, and what happens at home, for better or worse. Each child and each home is different so there can be no hard and fast rule. It can only be said that regular practice is necessary to develop the gift; this must be made clear and the child must accept it.

We must always remember that the gift belongs to the child and is part of a secret self. A child can perfectly well want to read or write, for example, with no family pressure. These are solitary activities and the parents are not involved. In fact it is wiser for the parents not to interfere or try to bully the child. It is essentially the child's business and he can be left to get on with it within the normal demands of family life.

Encouragement is the main thing. It could almost be thought of as good medicine, to be administered regularly in variable doses, according to the child's mood, energy state and other factors at home or at school.

The child should not be told off for disturbing others by his gift. A budding violinist, for example, should not be discouraged from making horrible noises at the beginning. The parent's presence during music or gym practice, warmly attentive without interfering, will help the child improve. And if one day the child asks the parent not to be there, there may well be good reasons for this and the parent should accept them.

At adolescence, the child needs freedom. New relationships in the family should take this into account. This is a tricky time during which the child must learn how to become an adult and needs space but also some control. The parents should be neither too strict nor too laid back. Either way the child may become discouraged and give up developing a gift.

13. *What should you do if a child thinks she has a gift but has not?*

Let the child take her time to find this out for herself. The result will probably be she will give it up and turn to something else. The child must be offered the choice from the beginning and the chance to have a go. A time limit can be set – quite long, about a year or eighteen months.

During this time the child should be encouraged exactly as if she had a real gift. She should not be tricked. Then if she gets no results after a while she will realize she has made a mistake. Meanwhile this apprenticeship can only do her good. We all need our special creative moments. Enjoyment is the main thing. And progress should not just be judged from the outside. What the child feels about it is also crucial.

The teacher is very important. If the gift does not blossom this time devoted to it must not be felt as wasted. If the child has spent time creatively but abandons this particular activity one day, she will still not forget the experience. And this is important.

The problem may be what facilities to offer the child. Some parents do not want to 'pay out for nothing', which is understandable. But fortunately there are many free courses available, which should be explored.

Buying a football or judo kit, or a musical instrument means the child must make a commitment for a certain period. Children should not flit from hobby to hobby with the parents' vague support. If they do not put enough into an activity the result will be discouragement and boredom. They will get more enjoyment if there is some discipline.

14. *If a child has the same gift as father or mother, should this parent be the only one to develop the child's gift?*

Of course a gift is often developed because one parent wants it to be. Sometimes this is taken to excess. For example, Beethoven's father passing the evening with little Ludwig's teacher sometimes woke the poor boy up in the middle of the night to have a lesson! The future creator of the Fifth Symphony had a lot to put up with. But his love of music and will to go on was stronger than his father's eccentricities.

Mozart was another example of a child under pressure from a dominating parent. His father hawked him round from salon to salon, from one European court to another, to show off his prodigious talent. Many children would have rebelled against such treatment. In fact, it has probably put an end to many promising careers! But the genius of both Mozart and Beethoven flowered very early in life and vigorously enough to resist such offputting experiences. A parent's authority is irreplaceable up to a certain age. Then the parent has to hand over and trust both the child and new teachers. This requires a certain humility on the parent's part. It is tempting for a parent to judge – sometimes wrongly – a teacher's competence and thus keep control of the child's progress. But is is essential to take notice of what the child wants. Meanwhile parents and teachers should together be able to find ways to see how the child's gift is developing.

In the past passing on a particular skill or trade was a necessity. The parent's authority was exercised over gifted and ungifted children alike. The child's wishes did not come into it and he was obliged to follow the path mapped out for him in advance. Today parents still have authority but in a different way. The child has other role models besides mother and father. He may decide he is not interested or refuse to do what the parents want. Parents who want to have a part to play in their children's education must not be too heavyhanded or the result may be counterproductive and the child will turn away and choose other role models.

15. *If a child seems at first to be very gifted in one way and it turns out that he is not, what should be done?*

The most important thing is whether the child enjoys carrying on. Parents must be careful not to push the child to become professional. Many parents, with the best will in the world, imagine their child pursuing a profession or artistic career they would have liked for themselves. If the child is pushed too far in the wrong direction, he is unlikely to want to go further.

Parents should be careful about transferring hopes on their children in this way. If the child reaches some limit, this will be because for all sorts of reasons connected with the child himself and his environment, it is time to stop, at least for a while. Pushing the child now will lead to a block. But it is also a pity to give up altogether and not allow the child a chance to return to what may be a true passion, which has simply been laid aside for the moment.

The right thing to do is to suggest something else. This means that the parents have to give up their own wishes, temporarily or for good. This may not be easy but it is right.

A little 'twinkletoes' will not automatically become a star dancer. All kinds of obstacles may arise, even when the environment is perfectly geared to success. But if the little 'twinkletoes' still enjoys dancing in adolescence and uses her body's suppleness to keep fit through gymnastics, all her efforts will not be in vain. Even if they do not lead to a professional career, hobbies that are enjoyed add a lot to the quality of life.

So if a child hits a peak, the choice is simple. Does she enjoy the activity and want to go on? Well then, let her. If she is bored and discouraged and wants to give up, then the time has come to offer other possibilities. The parents can hope that she will develop in a different field or even come back one day to the abandoned one.

16. *If a child develops a sudden block, what should be done?*

The first thing to do is look at the situation carefully. A block does not necessarily mean a final refusal to go on. Maybe the child is just examining himself and his situation.

There are various reasons for such blocks. School problems and being unsettled in class should be discussed with the teachers. Sometimes ill health is a reason. Eyes, hearing and growth should all be carefully tested. Sometimes children get blocked because a physical inferiority – or even superiority – makes them feel uncomfortable. This is not necessarily a bad thing for the development of a gift, because the child may engage in compensatory activities. Lack of selfcare, or too much television, may also be other reasons for a child's failure to progress. Many children become lethargic at around thirteen or fourteen, either because most of their energy is taken up in their own rapid physical and mental transformation, or because they look at what they are getting in return for their efforts and find it is not enough. This is the time when children give things up, have long periods of inertia which it is very difficult to do anything about. The child's apparent idleness should be investigated. Sometimes children hear different things at school and at home. This is when teachers' help becomes very important.

But as well as getting help from the teachers, the parents should also give it. To do this the family must make an effort. Many blocks are caused by family dramas. Children are helpless witnesses of their parents' quarrels and have to express their anxieties and fears in one way or another: problems at school, behaviour problems, perhaps even running away from home . . . It is therefore important, though it may be difficult, to avoid letting these dramas affect the child as much as possible and try to provide a 'shelter', particularly for the child to go on developing his gift.

17. *In order to stimulate a child who is quite gifted, is it a good idea to let them think they are* very *gifted?*

Parents should always be encouraging, even when they know their child's limitations. The child should be able to get praise from people round him. He needs to be reassured about his talents and pleased by the progress he makes, even if it is quite modest.

A four-year-old who can read music before knowing the alphabet should be admired and congratulated, because even at that age the embryonic practice of an art is an indescribable pleasure. Of course some children are supergifted and this is evident from when they are very young. But most children are not. The majority are 'normally gifted' at something and need the chance to express this gift creatively. Once again the temptation to push the child towards being professional should be firmly resisted and dreams of glory kept in check. This does not mean the child will not make surprising leaps – on the contrary. As well as the 'geniuses', there are many hard workers who can go very far. If this is kept in mind and the child stimulated in the right way, this will happen. The child must choose, because freedom is essential.

18. *In the development of a gift should the child's rhythm be borne in mind or should the child be pushed to adapt to others?*

This notion of rhythm is essential. Every child has his own, which he adapts as well as he can to the constraints of school. The majority of pupils adapt fairly well. But it is more difficult for the 'exceptions' who are partially or severely retarded. It is essential to respect these children's individual rhythms. Balance is necessary and the child must not be pushed too hard or exhausted. Parents who have invested too much hope in their child often set their sights too high.

Moderation is needed. The child is not a consumer product in competition with others. Of course competition is possible, but not to the detriment of a child's individual rhythm.

A child who is physically or mentally behind his peers must be able to find forms of expression that suit him. The smallest in a group of large children should not be bullied for his small size. Often it is these odd ones out who compensate for it in the most astonishing ways. A child who runs less fast than others may be able to find a personal space in games – chess or computer games, for example – or art, where he can shine.

There is therefore no reason to think a 'backward' child has no gifts or talents. The child needs reassurance because in some ways he is behind the others. It is up to parents and teachers to give the child other things to do, where he can do as well or even better than others. But it is also important not to spoil the child by over-protection and separating him from his peers. Many children are labelled 'delicate' and treated as such by their parents. These parents are strongly advised to go against their own mollycoddling inclinations – not always easy.

19. *If a child shows a gift about which the parents understand nothing, should parents try to take an interest in this gift, or is it enough just to give the child the means to express it?*

There is something to be said for both.

Parents should have the patience – which is also a gift – to listen to their child, respect him and take an interest in what is on his mind. If they cannot share the child's passion for something that surprises them, it is up to them to provide, to the best of their ability, the means for the child to develop this gift.

And it is important not to forget that children like being able to teach their parents things. Ours is the computer and electronic age. Generations who have not grown up with this technology often do not understand it, and children have an advantage.

Ideally the parent should make the effort to catch up with the child, which is sometimes too difficult even for real intellectuals. If parents cannot keep up with the child's activities, they must keep listening to the child and try to help him in material ways, with subscriptions to specialist periodicals, extra teaching, etc.

A family's interest in a child's progress is just as important as the resources put at the child's disposal. Some parents who think they have done all they can simply by paying for lessons may find themselves reproached one day for not having listened to the child with loving attention.

Ignorance is no obstacle. There is always something to be learnt from a child. This affectionate exchange of knowledge can bring a lot of mutual satisfaction.

20. *Can a child appear completely ungifted in a field and then suddenly develop a gift for it a few years later?*

This happens much more often than one might expect. Some children develop very slowly, which does not mean they will not go far later on. They just need more time to get going. Albert Einstein is a good example. The future inventor of the theory of relativity was a mediocre student, bad at chemistry, and did not look set for a glorious future. We know the rest of the story.

A child who develops very slowly may disappoint his parents in a field where as an adult he will be brilliant. It can only do harm to brand the child as a failure. It is vital to have faith in the child.

There are countless children who get down to work late, before or during their adolescence. If they have enough determination, they can reverse a worrying situation in a few months, because at last they have the motivation.

Motivation is essential and the child must always be given the chance to acquire it. Chance can do a lot but parents can make use of it to awaken their child's interest. As always, patience, listening and love are the indispensable ingredients in this exciting 'adventure' of the development of a human being.

Above all it is important not to be too rigid. For it is simply not possible to make final judgements about a child at a particular stage, because development is what childhood is about. Therefore the tests offered here are intended only to give certain indications and make no claim to judge personalities that are as diverse as there are children in the world.

PART II

Tests to Determine your Child's Gifts and Abilities

3
Introduction to Tests

Before starting any test, try to forget that this is your own child. A child is a human being in his or her own right. Even if he or she has your eyes and grandfather's aquiline nose, the child is not you and not your father. Whatever likenesses there may be to other family members, this child is different.

Johann Sebastian Bach had many children, all musicians. They had inherited this gift from their father, but each of them had their own personal approach to music, which was not the same as their father's. It is even possible (but we can never know now) that some of Bach's children were even more gifted at something other than music.

People are not necessarily gifted at just one thing (think of Leonardo da Vinci). It is quite possible to have several gifts but only develop one. In such a musical atmosphere, Bach's children were bound to develop their gift for music. Was this ideal? Perhaps they might have been happier in another discipline? We may well ask this question because none of the children became as famous as their father. Parents all have a tendency to imprison their children within their own world, project their dreams, tastes, inclinations, regrets and rejections onto them. Most of the time this is done subconsciously.

'I like the violin, so my son will play the violin' or 'I would like to have played the violin but did not have the chance. Luckily my child will be able to.' This is too often the way the parents think. If the child is gifted at the violin, so much the better. But if the child does not have this talent, what a waste of effort, time and money, all of which are liable to have a bad effect on the child who could have developed in another direction.

So do not jump to the conclusion that your child is a failure. Try to find out what he is really good at. Give the child a chance to find his own level, even if it is not yours. A good plumber is much happier with his gift than a bad doctor. What's more, a bad doctor can do harm! All this is so obvious that perhaps you might wonder why it is necessary to state it. But oddly enough, what parents lack more than anything else is simple commonsense. All too often they do not see their children as they are but in a dream. They do not separate the child from themselves. So, first and foremost, forget that this is your child. Imagine it is a friend's child entrusted to you for a little while.

These tests designed for your child will also test you indirectly. Are you capable of being objective and lucid with your child? Are you capable of discovering the child's talents and helping the child go this way, even if it is not the way you wanted? Are you capable of enabling your child to become a happy and successful person, and not just a good child who is well brought up, clean and studious. Can you help your child to develop his real self? You love your child, otherwise you would not have bought this book.

How to use these tests on your child

For maximum success follow these rules.

1. Treat the tests as a game.
2. Do not do all the tests on the same day, especially if the child is very young. Spread them out.
3. Never help your child. He must do the test on his own. If he gets muddled or makes a mistake and corrects it when he sees your reaction, only count the first answer.
4. Don't worry if the result is not what you hoped for. Do not tell your child off. The child has done no wrong by failing a test.
5. Every child is developing. Note the results and keep them. When your child has reached the next age bracket, you can give him the tests for his age and compare the results. If the child gets lower marks in similar tests, it means there is something wrong with his education. There should always be some progress, even if it is only slow.
6. Do all the tests in a lighthearted atmosphere. It is not an exam. Of course the tests should not be given to the child on a day when he is ill, tired or in a bad mood.
7. The results should help you discover your child's abilities. But they are not infallible. When you have discovered which way your child's talents lie, you can help him develop them. A child must follow his bent but always go forward. For example, if your child has a wonderful memory, you can help him to develop it and use this talent. But if your child has a poor memory, it should always be remembered that memory can improve with practice.
8. If your child has very poor results in one area, do not insist on trying to push him on in this area alone. You can help him make a

little progress, of course, and it is a good thing to help him. But do not make an issue of it. Time and energy spent on trying to turn a child with no gift whatever for music into a musician are time and energy wasted for both the child and for you. The same time and energy spent on something the child is really gifted at will help the child become a happy and successful human being.

9. These tests are for normal children with no severe physical or psychological problems. If your child has serious problems or is disturbed, you should consult a doctor or child psychologist.
10. Sometimes it is easier for an outsider to give these tests. Everything depends on your relationship with the child. If you think you may have difficulties, ask someone your child likes and is at ease with to give the tests.
11. These tests are mostly for children from the ages of three to fifteen. Some are divided up according to age brackets. Others are suitable for the whole age group, with perhaps just one or two questions that are different. There is also a third set of tests that are not intended for your child. They are for you to answer and your replies will help you make discoveries about your child. Think carefully about each question and never answer too quickly because it seems easy. If in doubt, ask your partner or someone who knows your child well to help you.
12. Sometimes different tests may give results which appear contradictory. Do not be surprised. This simply means that your child has a double personality, of which you must be aware. For example, a child may have a sociable side to his nature and another side which needs solitude. This means the child needs both in turn, which should be respected. This child can only find a balance by being able to satisfy both sides of his nature. Of course, that does not make things easier for you but such complexity can be of great value in a personality and make for generosity of spirit. Most psychologists, psychoanalysts, writers and artists have been children with two or even multiple sides to their personalities.

4

Does your Child have a Good Memory?

There are two main kinds of memory: aural and visual. Certain jobs or hobbies need a lot of memory, very specific memory. Others do not. This is why it is interesting to determine what your child's memory is like so as not to guide him towards a field in which he has little chance of success.

Of course memory can be developed. But even if with great efforts you manage to improve a poor memory, you will still never be someone who naturally has a remarkable memory.

Table 3, at the end of this book, gives a list, which is not complete, of jobs that need a lot of memory and jobs that manage quite well without it.

These tests are the same for children of quite a wide age range. That does not affect their reliability. However, we advise you to give a very young child of three or four a bit more time and expect a five or six-year-old to be quite quick. A child can have a good immediate memory, but lack a long-term or lasting memory. You need both kinds to have a really good memory.

Tests for children from three to six

Immediate aural memory

First test

Put the child on a chair and blindfold him so that he can concentrate better on the sounds rather than your actions.

Tell the child: 'I am going to make five different noises. Listen carefully. I will tell you what each noise is. Then I will make the same noises again without telling you what they are. Do you think you can guess what they are?'

First noise: You shut the door.
Second noise: You strike a match.
Third noise: You pour water into a glass from a jug or bottle.
Fourth noise: You kiss your hand.
Fifth noise: You open the window.

After making each noise tell the child what it is.

Chat for a little while (about ten minutes for a very young child and about five minutes for a five- or six-year-old). Empty the glass you filled. Then make the same noises again and ask the child to guess what they are. Make each noise again in the same order and in exactly the same way. Give the child one mark for each correct answer.

Let about the same length of time pass and empty the glass. Tell the child you are going to make the same noises again but not necessarily in the same order and ask her to guess what they are. Make all the noises backwards:

First noise: You open the window.
Second noise: You kiss your hand.
Third noise: You fill the glass.
Fourth noise: You strike the match.
Fifth noise: You shut the door.

Let the same length of time pass (of course during these intervals you can take off the blindfold and let the child move about, especially if she is very small). Empty the glass. Make the same noises again but mix up the order.

First noise: You fill the glass.
Second noise: You kiss your hand.
Third noise: You shut the door.
Fourth noise: You strike the match.
Fifth noise: You open the window.

Ask the child to guess again. Give one point for each correct answer.

The next test should be done much later. It is difficult for a young child to concentrate for long and the previous test requires quite enough effort.

Second test

Take a record or cassette that the child does not know. Be careful to avoid all the current hit tunes on the television and radio and also the records and cassettes you already have. Choose carefully. It does not matter whether you use a classical or modern piece of music, but it should be without words.

Ask the child to listen very carefully. Put on the record and stop it after three or four minutes. Ask your child immediately to hum the first few bars.

If he hesitates and gets it wrong or if he hums the last few bars he has just heard rather than the beginning, be sure not to help him by humming yourself. Play the record again in exactly the same way and ask the child to hum the beginning of the music again. If the child still cannot get it right there is no need to do it a third time.

If the child got it right first time count five points. If he does it at the second attempt count two points. If not count zero.

Now you can add up the marks.

RESULTS

17–20 points: The child has a remarkable immediate aural memory.
13–16 points: The child has a good immediate aural memory.
10–12 points: The child has an average immediate aural memory.
5–9 points: The child has problems with his immediate aural memory.
Under 5 points: The child has a very bad immediate aural memory.

Long-term aural memory

Two days later, if the child is three or four, four days later if he is five or six, do these tests again in the following conditions:

For the first test do not start by making the noises and telling him what they are. Sit the child down in the same place, blindfold him in the same way and begin immediately with the second stage. Make the five noises in the following order:

First noise: Door shutting.
Second noise: Match striking.
Third noise: Glass being filled.
Fourth noise: Hand kissing.
Fifth noise: Window opening.

For each correct answer give one point. Then go on to the next stage: the same test the other way round.

First noise: Window opening.
Second noise: Hand kissing.
Third noise: Glass being filled.
Fourth noise: Match striking.
Fifth noise: Door shutting.

Give one point for every correct answer.

Finally do the test again with the order mixed up:

First noise: The glass.
Second noise: The kiss.
Third noise: The door.
Fourth noise: The match.
Fifth noise: The window.

Give one point for each correct answer.

Note: It is very important to redo the tests in exactly the same order as you did it two or four days before.

Additional test of long-term aural memory

Later you can ask the child: 'Do you remember the record I played you a few days ago? Can you hum the tune from the beginning of the music?' If the child hums it at once without any hesitation, count five points. If he hesitates, makes mistakes but finally gets the tune right without help, give him two points. Otherwise, give no points.

Now you can add up all the points.

RESULTS

17–20 points: The child has a remarkable long-term aural memory.
13–16 points: The child has a good long-term aural memory.
10–12 points: The child has an average long-term aural memory.
5–9 points: The child has problems with his long-term aural memory.
Under 5 points: The child has a very bad long-term aural memory.

Immediate visual memory

First test

Take five sheets of different coloured paper. It does not matter what colour they are as long as they are different.

On each sheet do a drawing, which should be as simple as possible:

Draw a house on the white sheet.
Draw a tree on the blue sheet.
Draw a cat on the yellow sheet.
Draw a flower on the red sheet.
Draw a little man on the green sheet.

Your drawings must be recognizable. Do not say: 'Look, this is a cat, this is a little man. . . .' If you do you are also involving the aural memory, which is not what the test is for.

When you have finished your drawings, show them to the child and ask her to look at them carefully. After a short while, a bit longer for the three- to four-year-olds than the five- to six-year-olds, hide the drawings.

Take five other sheets of paper of the same five colours and ask the child to do the same drawing on each coloured sheet, trying to remember which drawing went with each colour.

Do not help at all. You must not answer the child's questions or make things easier for him. He has got to do it for himself.

Give him enough time to suit his age: about average for a child of three or four would be half an hour; for a child of five or six, a quarter of an hour.

For each correct drawing on the right colour, give one point. Of course you ignore whether the drawing is like yours. It is only what it represents that counts.

Second test

Take five common objects which do not take up too much space, for example: a pair of glasses, a bag, a cup, a book and a pen. Put them all on the table and tell your child you are going to hide each thing in a place where it does not usually go.

Do not say anything else. Make sure you do not say. 'Look I am hiding the glasses in the fridge. . . .' Your child must just watch what you are doing. If he asks questions, say: 'Shh. This is a game with no talking. I am not allowed to say anything.'

Hide the objects in unusual places. For example:

Hide the glasses in the fridge.
Hide the bag under the bed.
Hide the cup in the clothes cupboard.
Hide the book in the food cupboard.
Hide the pen in a saucepan.

Then blindfold the child or tell him to stay in a room where you have not hidden anything until you fetch him. Take out the five objects and hide them again using the same hiding places but putting different objects in each. For example:

Hide the glasses in the saucepan.
Hide the bag in the fridge.

Hide the cup under the bed.
Hide the book in the clothes cupboard.
Hide the pen in the food cupboard.

Take off the child's blindfold or go and fetch him. Tell him you have changed the things round, that the hiding places are the same but there are different things in them. Then ask the child to put each thing back where he saw you hiding it the first time.

Do not help the child by saying things like: 'Do you remember where the pen was?' just say: 'See if you can find the five things and put them back where I hid them the first time when you watched me.'

If the child is three or four give him ten minutes. If he is five or six, five minutes should be enough. If he makes a mistake, leave it.

For everything found and put back in the right place, give one point.

Third test

Take a pack of cards. Ask the child to choose five cards and look at them carefully. Write down which cards they are on a piece of paper. Put the cards back and shuffle the back. Let ten minutes go by if the child is three or four, five minutes if he is five or six.

Ask the child to find his five cards in the pack. For every correct card give one point. Now you can add up all the points.

RESULTS

17–20 points: The child has an exceptional immediate visual memory.
13–16 points: The child has a good immediate visual memory.
10–12 points: The child has an average immediate visual memory.
5–9 points: The child has problems with his immediate visual memory.
Under 5 points: The child has a very bad immediate visual memory.

Long-term visual memory

Two days later if the child is three or four, and four days later if he is five or six, do the tests again in the following conditions:

First test

Take five sheets of different coloured paper, exactly the same as the ones you used before.

Give them to the child and ask him to do the same drawing on each sheet that he did before. Do not forget to tell him that the drawings have to go on the same coloured paper as before.

Give him a quarter of an hour if he is five or six, half an hour if he is three or four.

For each correct drawing on the right coloured paper give one point.

Second test

Take the five items you hid on the previous occasion. Put them on a table jumbled up with fifteen other items. These can be anything provided they are different. Do not add another pair of glasses, even if they are not the same colour, or another bag or book.

Ask your child to pick out the five items from the previous test and put them back where you hid them while he was watching.

If the child is very young, explain carefully: 'Do you remember I took some things and hid them while you were watching me? These things are on the table. Can you find them? Now can you put them back where I hid them while you were watching?'

Never say what the things are or name the hiding places.

If the child makes a mistake with one item, do not interfere, let him go on. Give a quarter of an hour to a child of three or four, ten minutes to a child of five or six. For each correct object hidden in the correct hiding place, give two points.

Third test

Take the same pack of cards. Ask the child to find the five cards he chose before and give them to you. Give a child of three or four ten minutes and a child of five or six five minutes.

Give one point for each correct card.

Now you can add up all the points.

RESULTS

17–20 points: The child has an exceptional long-term visual memory.

13–16 points: The child has a good long-term visual memory.

10–12 points: The child has an average long-term visual memory.

5–9 points: The child has problems with his long-term visual memory.

Under 5 points: The child has a very bad long-term visual memory.

Tests for children from seven to ten

Immediate aural memory

First test

Buy or borrow a record or cassette that you have not already got. Choose a song that is *not* a current hit and not often played on the radio and television.

When the child is not there, listen to the song and write down its words. Then ask the child to listen to the song very carefully. Play the record twice.

Let half an hour go by. Take your paper and make sure that the child cannot read what is on it. Choose a phrase at random, which is neither the first nor the last in the song. Say this phrase to the child and ask:

(a) What phrase comes before this one in the song?
(b) What phrase comes after it?

Give one point for each correct answer. If there is a mistake in the phrase do not give a point. Do the same thing four more times, choosing four different phrases.

This makes five phrases and ten answers given by the child in all, with a total maximum possible ten points.

Second test

Read the following text to the child and ask him to listen carefully. Read it only once, but slowly and carefully. Do not let the child read it.

> The Congo terrier is a very special dog. These strange dogs appear for the first time on the Egyptian pyramids and were discovered by Jean François Champollion, who deciphered the mysterious hieroglyphs. But until the last century no one had seen this dog alive. It comes from tropical Africa, where it is to be found most frequently in the Congo valley, Zaire and Southern Sudan.
>
> The Congo terrier or Basenji is a hunting dog, which tracks and catches game in the bush and savannah. Africans sometimes call it the 'jumping dog' because of its strange habit of jumping on tufts of grass to find its way in the bush. One special characteristic is that it does not bark. It just growls and when it is

very excited it gives out a sort of whistle and snort. So as not to lose it, its owners hang all sorts of bells or wooden rattles round its neck.

The Congo terrier was only introduced into Europe at the beginning of this century, but those that were imported quickly died. The dog was only acclimatized and bred in Europe in the 1930s.

The Congo terrier is about 40 centimetres high and weighs 10 to 12 kilos. Its hair is short, smooth and hard. It is honey coloured or brown, reddish or black and sometimes has white spots. Its tail is quite short, set high and curved over its back.

After half an hour ask the following questions:

1. Where did the Congo dog appear for the first time?
2. As its name says the Congo dog comes from the Congo. But in what other tropical African countries is it found?
3. It has another name and a nickname. What are they?
4. When does it emit a sort of whistle and snort?
5. How much does it weigh?
6. How tall is it?
7. When did it become acclimatized and bred in Europe?
8. All sorts of bells and what else are hung round its neck?

The correct answers are:

1. On the Egyptian pyramids.
2. Zaire and Sudan.
3. Basenji and 'jumping dog'.
4. When it is very excited.
5. 10–12 kilos.
6. About 40 centimetres.
7. In the 1930s.
8. Wooden rattles.

Count 1 point for each correct answer. But as questions 2 and 3 are double questions, count one point for Zaire and one point for Sudan, one point for Basenji and one point for 'jumping dog'. The maximum total is ten points.

Now add up all the points gained in the two tests.

RESULTS

17–20 points: The child has an exceptional immediate aural memory.
13–16 points: The child has a good immediate aural memory.
10–12 points: The child has an average immediate aural memory.
5–9 points: The child has problems with his immediate aural memory.
Under 5 points: The child has a very bad immediate aural memory.

Long-term aural memory

One week later repeat these tests under the following conditions:

First test

Do not let the child listen to the song again. Take your paper with the words written on it. Do the same as on the previous occasion. Choose a phrase and ask the child to tell you:

(a) What is the phrase that comes before this phrase?
(b) What is the phrase that comes after it?

Give one point for each correct answer, a maximum total of ten points.

Second test

Do not read the text about the Congo terrier again. Ask exactly the same questions. Give one point for each correct answer.

Now add all the points gained in both tests.

RESULTS

17–20 points: The child has an exceptional long-term aural memory.
13–16 points: The child has a good long-term aural memory.
10–12 points: The child has an average long-term aural memory.
5–9 points: The child has problems with his long-term aural memory.
Under 5 points: The child has a very bad long-term aural memory.

Immediate visual memory

Test 1

Make the child read carefully the test below, taking plenty of time. Do not allow the child to help his memory by reading aloud.

The English greyhound is directly descended from the greyhounds of ancient Egypt. King David said their movements were as graceful as horses and women. This dog has always been used for deer and wolf hunting. In the sixteenth century they began to be selectively bred for racing, which is what they are still used for today. The first official race took place in the reign of King Henry VIII of England. The greyhounds either race freely in pursuit of a live hare (in which case they are always raced in pairs and followed by a judge on horseback); or they are raced on a track, 350 to 500 metres long, in pursuit of a mechanical 'hare', which nowadays is remote-controlled. A good greyhound can reach a speed of 50 to 60 kilometres an hour, but of course this requires serious training. The dogs go into training from the age of six months and their racing careers then last until they are seven or eight years old.

Wait for half an hour. Then show the child the test on the next page, in which certain words are missing. Ask her to fill in the missing words in pencil, so that they can be rubbed out later. Take no notice of spelling mistakes. Every correct word inserted gets one point.

The English greyhound is directly descended from the greyhounds of ancient Egypt. King . . . . said their movements were as graceful as horses and . . . . This dog has always been used for deer and . . . . hunting. In the . . . . century they began to be selectively bred for racing, which is what they are still used for today. The first official race took place in the reign of King Henry VIII of . . . . The greyhounds either race freely in pursuit of a . . . . hare (in which case they are always raced in pairs and followed by a . . . . on horseback); or they are raced on a track, 350 to . . . . metres long, in pursuit of a mechanical 'hare', which nowadays is . . . . A good greyhound can reach a speed of 50 to 60 kilometres an hour, but of course this requires serious training. The dogs go into training from the age of . . . . months and their racing careers then last until they are seven or eight years old.

Test 2

Ask your child to read the following test very carefully, without reading aloud:

1. People from Holland are called Dutch.
2. People from Ireland are called Irish.
3. People from France are called French.
4. People from Guatemala are called Guatemalan.
5. People from Lebanon are called Lebanese.
6. People from Greece are called Greek.
7. People from Angola are called Angolan.
8. People from Iceland are called Icelandic.
9. People from Pakistan are called Pakistani.
10. People from Wales are called Welsh.

After half an hour give the child the following game in which she has to give the right answer to each question:

1. People from Holland are called:

☐ A. Deutsch

☐ B. Dutch

☐ C. Ducks

2. People from Ireland are called:

☐ A. Irish

☐ B. Irelandan

☐ C. Irelandic

3. People from France are called:

☐ A. Frogan

☐ B. French

☐ C. Frantic

4. People from Guatemala are called:

☐ A. Guacamolan

☐ B. Guatemalan

☐ C. Guatemali

5. People from Lebanon are called

☐ A. Lebanoni

☐ B. Lebanonish

☐ C. Lebanese

6. People from Greece are called:

☐ A. Greek

☐ B. Grecian

☐ C. Greekish

7. People from Angola are called:

☐ A. Angolese

☐ B. Angoli

☐ C. Angolan

8. People from Iceland are called:

☐ A. Icelandic

☐ B. Icy

☐ C. Icelandish

9. People from Pakistan are called:

☐ A. Pakistanic

☐ B. Pakistani

☐ C. Pakistanish

10. People from Wales are called:

☐ A. Waley

☐ B. Walish

☐ C. Welsh

The correct answers of course are:
1B; 2A; 3B; 4B; 5C; 6A; 7C; 8A; 9B; 10C.

Give one point for every correct answer. Now add the marks from both texts.

RESULTS

17–20 points: The child has an exceptional immediate visual memory.
13–16 points: The child has a good immediate visual memory.
10–12 points: The child has an average immediate visual memory.

5–9 points: The child has problems with his/her immediate visual memory.
Under 5 points: The child has a very bad immediate visual memory.

Long-term visual memory

First test

One week later, do the test on the English greyhound again. Rub out the words written in pencil by the child. (Of course you will not let the child re-read the whole text. You give him the text with the ten words missing.) Ask the child to write in the missing words again.

Give one point for each correct word put in its right place.

Second test

One week later, do the second test on the names of people from different countries again. Rub out the answers written in pencil by the child the week before. Do not let the child re-read the first part of the test. She must just fill in the answers to each of the ten questions.

Now add up all the marks from both tests.

RESULTS

17–20 points: The child has an exceptional long-term visual memory.
13–16 points: The child has a good long-term visual memory.
10–12 points: The child has an average long-term visual memory.
5–9 points: The child has problems with her long-term visual memory.
Under 5 points: The child has a very bad long-term visual memory.

Tests for children of eleven to fifteen

Immediate aural memory

Ask the child to listen very carefully. Then read the following text loudly and clearly, taking plenty of time. (The child must *not* see the text.)

> The Arab horse was selectively bred a thousand years before other breeds. Some people maintain that it has lived wild in the

deserts of Arabia for thousands of years. Others say that prehistoric horse bones have never been found in the desert. This seems to be confirmed by the fact that the Arab is not among the twelve breeds mentioned by the Romans and there is nothing about it in pre-Roman history. The Muslims believed that Allah had created the Arab horse with a fistful of south wind.

In fact, like all horse and pony breeds, the Arab comes from prehistoric wild horses which lived on the plains and steppes of Europe and Asia long before civilization, and which looked very like the tarpans and wild horses of Mongolia that exist today.

The Bedouin have gone in for selective breeding of Arab horses at least since the time of Mahomet (sixth century AD) and it is likely that they did so thousands of years earlier. The bedouin took great care to keep the breed pure. Unless a horse was recognized as 'asil' (pure) it could not mate with a pure bred ('asil'), however perfect its conformation. This together with the exceptionally hard climatic conditions of the desert combine to create the most graceful and magnificent horse in the world. Food was scarce in the desert. Grass only grew in winter and at the beginning of spring. The rest of the time the horses lived on camel milk, dried dates, grasshoppers and dried camel meat. Mahomet was firmly convinced of the military importance of these tough desert horses. He bought them from the nomadic tribes and paid for them with slaves. Mares were preferred and used for battle and pillage.

Arab horses were probably introduced into Europe during the invasion of the Western Mediterranean basin by the Moors.

These horses are sometimes called 'wind drinkers' because they are so fast.

Let an hour go by. Then ask the following questions:

1. How long before other breeds were Arab horses selectively bred?
2. How many horse breeds did the Romans recognize?
3. Where are tarpans found?
4. In which century did Mahomet live?
5. What does 'asil' mean to a Bedouin?
6. At what time of the year does grass grow in the desert?
7. Arab horses were fed by Bedouin on dried dates, dried camel meat, camel milk and what else?

8. How did Mahomet pay for the horses he bought?
9. Who did he buy them from?
10. What were the mares used for?
11. Who probably introduced Arab horses into Europe?
12. On what occasion?
13. What nickname is given to Arab horses?
14. What did the Muslims believe Allah had created the Arab horse from?
15. Where did prehistoric horses live in Europe and Asia?

The right answers are:

1. A thousand years.
2. Twelve breeds.
3. Mongolia.
4. Sixth century AD.
5. Pure.
6. In winter and spring.
7. Grasshoppers.
8. Slaves.
9. Nomadic tribes.
10. Battle and pillage.
11. The Moors.
12. When they invaded the Western Mediterranean basin.
13. 'Wind drinkers'.
14. A fistful of south wind.
15. Plains and steppes.

Give one point for each correct answer, the maximim total number of points is fifteen.

Second test

Buy or borrow a record or cassette which you have not got. Choose three songs, sung by the same singer, which are not current hits or heard on radio or television.

When the child is not there listen to these songs and write down their words on a separate piece of paper for each song.

Then ask the child to listen very carefully to the songs. Tell him the title of each song very clearly. Only let him listen to the songs once. Let an hour go by. Take your sheets of paper and make sure your child cannot read them. Choose five phrases at random from the three songs. Ask your child which song each phrase comes into.

Give him a point each time he gives exactly the right title for the song with the phrase in it. The maximum total number of points is five.

Now add up all the points obtained from both tests.

RESULTS

17–20 points: The child has an exceptional immediate aural memory.
13–16 points: The child has a good immediate aural memory.
10–12 points: The child has an average immediate aural memory.
5–9 points: The child has problems with his immediate aural memory.
Under 5 points: The child has a very bad immediate aural memory.

Long-term aural memory

One week later do these tests again under the following conditions:

First test

Do not re-read the text about the Arab horses, but ask exactly the same questions. Give one point for each correct answer; this gives a maximum total number of fifteen points.

Second test

This test should also be done again one week later. Do not let the child listen to the songs again. He should not have heard them again since the first test.

Get out the papers with the words written on them and choose five phrases from the three songs. These phrases can be different from the first set. Ask the child which song each phrase comes from.

Give one point for each correct answer, making a maximum total of five points.

Now add up all the points obtained in both tests.

RESULTS

17–20 points: The child has an exceptional long-term aural memory.
13–16 points: The child has a good long-term aural memory.
10–12 points: The child has an average long-term aural memory.
5–9 points: The child has problems with his long-term aural memory.
Under 5 points: The child has a very bad long-term aural memory.

Immediate visual memory

Test

Make the child read the text below. Tell him to read carefully taking plenty of time, but do not allow the child to help himself by reading aloud.

The chimpanzee is an anthropoid four-handed tailless monkey. They give delight to children and grown-ups and few zoos are without them.

Its face is very prognathous, its ears are large and its nostrils of average size.

The torus or visor is very marked and the forehead is receding. The sagittal crest of the skull only exists in old males and it is relatively unprominent.

The body is covered with fairly sparse black hairs, but the face is hairless. The mouth is wide and the lips thin, the eyes are very expressive. The forelimbs are long and muscular. Breast and shoulders are wide. The lower limbs are short and end in a true hand, whose thumb can be opposed to the other fingers.

The chimpanzee is a tree dweller but is also at home on the ground. It walks slightly obliquely, supporting itself with the palms of the hind hands and the outside of the first joints of the fore-hands.

This monkey is mainly vegetarian and lives on leaves, buds, fruits, shoots and grains. But it also likes honey, eggs and insects.

Chimpanzees cover a great distance every day in order to feed themselves. They are nomads and only set up temporary camps for one night at a time. These nests consist of crude platforms set in the forks of trees.

They live in bands under the leadership of a male. The band consists of younger males, females and babies.

Chimpanzees have exceptional intelligence and a good memory. They are capable of making and using tools to enable them to reach something they want. For example, they can fit bamboo canes into one another to make a long enough pole to reach something with.

Hide this text and after an hour give your child the following text, in which twenty words are missing. Ask your child to write in these words (in pencil so that they can be rubbed out later). Disregard spelling mistakes; each correct word in the right place gains one point.

The chimpanzee is an anthropoid . . . . tailless monkey. They give delight to children and grown ups and few zoos are without them.

Its face is very . . . . , its ears are large and its nostrils of average size.

The torus or . . . . is very marked and the forehead is receding. The sagittal crest of the skull only exists in old males and it is relatively . . . .

The body is covered with fairly sparse black hairs, but the face is . . . . The mouth is wide and the lips thin, the eyes are very expressive. The fore limbs are long and muscular. Breast and shoulders are wide. The . . . . limbs are short and end in a true hand, whose thumb can be . . . . to the other fingers.

The chimpanzee is a . . . . but is also at home on the ground. It walks slightly . . . . supporting itself with the palms of the hind-hands and the outside of the first joints of the fore-hands.

This monkey is mainly . . . . and lives on leaves, ... , fruits, ... and grains. But it also likes . . . . , eggs and insects.

Chimpanzees cover a great distance every day in order to feed themselves. They are . . . . and only set up temporary . . . . for one night at a time. These nests consist of crude . . . . set in the . . . . of trees.

They live in bands under the leadership of a male. The band consists of younger males, females and babies.

Chimpanzees have exceptional intelligence and a good memory. They are capable of making and using . . . . to enable them to reach something they want. For example they can fit . . . . canes into one another to make a long enough pole to reach something with.

RESULTS

17–20 points: The child has an exceptional immediate visual memory.

13–16 points: The child has a good immediate visual memory.

10–12 points: The child has an average immediate visual memory.

5–9 points: The child has problems with his immediate visual memory.
Under 5 points: The child has a very bad immediate visual memory.

Long-term visual memory

A fortnight later take the chimpanzee text again. Rub out the words written in pencil by the child. (Of course you do not let the child re-read the complete text. You just give him the text with the twenty words missing in it.) Ask the child to fill in the missing words again. Give one point for each correct word put in its right place.

RESULTS

17–20 points: The child has an exceptional long-term visual memory.
13–16 points: The child has a good long-term visual memory.
10–12 points: The child has an average long-term visual memory.
5–9 points: The child has problems with his long-term visual memory.
Under 5 points: The child has a very bad long-term visual memory.

5

Is your Child Observant?

The gift of observation (so essential to spies, for example!) is not an absolute requirement in many professions. Nevertheless it is still a great asset. For the gift of observation you have got to have an excellent visual memory together with an acute awareness of the slightest changes. Very few people have this gift, which makes it all the more precious to those who have.

Test for children from three to six

Put the child in a room and tell her not to follow you when you go to change. Ask her to look carefully at what you are wearing. Then tell her: 'I am going into the bathroom (or bedroom) and will change just one thing at a time. I'll do this several times and you have got to guess what I have changed. All right?'

You then proceed to make ten changes, one at a time. For example:

First change

You have no parting in your hair and you make one. Or you have a parting and you get rid of it. You go back in: What have I changed? Only accept one answer each time.

Second change

You put on different shoes, as like the ones you were wearing before as possible. You go back in: What have I changed? Note whether the child's answer is right or wrong.

Third change

If you are a woman, take off your necklace or your stockings, or put some on. If you are a man or are wearing trousers, change your socks. You go back in: What have I changed? Right or wrong answer?

Fourth change

Take off your watch, or put one on. You go back in: So what have I changed this time?

Fifth change

Take off or put on a belt.

Sixth change

Put an elastic band round your wrist.

Seventh change

If you are a woman take off a brooch or put one on. If you are a man, take off your tie or put one on.

Eighth change

Take off your watch and put it back on the other wrist. If you took it off in the fourth change, put it back on, but not on the usual wrist.

Ninth change

Come back in bare feet.

Tenth change

Change your shirt or jumper.

These are just ideas for change. But of course you can adapt them. The important thing is that there should be *ten* changes. For each correct answer count two points.

RESULTS

18–20 points: The child has an exceptional gift of observation.
14–16 points: The child has a good gift of observation.
10–12 points: The child has an average gift of observation.
6–8 points: The child is not gifted at observation, but she can certainly improve with practice.
2–4 points: The child has no gift for observation. Perhaps she is a dreamer or finds it hard to concentrate.

Test for children from seven to ten

Take ten common objects and put them on the table in a very precise order, for example:

A pair of glasses at one corner.
An ashtray at another corner.
A box of matches at the third corner.

A watch at the fourth corner.
A bracelet in the centre of the table.
A photo near the glasses.
A folded napkin near the ashtray.
A cake of soap near the match box or lighter.
A sheet of folded paper near the glasses.
A bottle of aspirin near the bracelet.

Let the child look at all the objects without saying anything for three minutes. Carefully write down the position of all the objects. Take all the objects off the table and put them in a basket.

Wait for quarter of an hour. Then give the child the basket and ask him to put the objects back on the table in exactly the same place as they were before.

Every object put in its correct place gets two points.

RESULTS

18–20 points: The child has an exceptional gift of observation.
14–16 points: The child has a good gift of observation.
10–12 points: The child has an average gift of observation.
6–8 points: The child is not gifted at observation, but she can certainly improve with practice.
2–4 points: The child has no gift for observation. Perhaps she is a dreamer or finds it hard to concentrate.

Test for children from eleven to thirteen

Take twenty common objects, for example: an ashtray, a lighter, a cake of soap, a bracelet, a watch, a book, a tie, a ring, a saucer, a cup, a handkerchief, a wallet, a diary, a packet of pills, a comb, a brush, a pair of scissors, a packet of cigarettes, a pen, a key.

Put all the objects on a table if it is big enough, otherwise put them on the floor in a very precise order, so that the objects are touching one another and form a cross.

Ask your child to look at this cross for five minutes. Then ask her to go into another room. Write down the exact position of each object. Take all the objects away and put them in a basket.

Wait for half an hour and then give your child the basket. Ask her to put the twenty objects back on the table or the floor in exactly the same order as before. Each object correctly placed gets one point.

RESULTS

17–20 points: The child has an exceptional gift of observation.
13–16 points: The child has a good gift of observation.
10–12 points: The child has an average gift of observation.
5–9 points: The child is not gifted at observation, but she can certainly improve with practice.
Under 5 points: The child has no gift for observation. Perhaps she is a dreamer or finds it hard to concentrate.

6

Does your Child have Willpower?

There can be no success in any field without willpower. Three things are needed for success: a certain talent in the chosen field, an interest in the field and a lot of willpower. The latter is so important that it can change a moderate gift into a major one. And without willpower no gift can come to fulfilment.

In other words, if your child has a small gift for something and a lot of willpower, she may well succeed. And on the other hand, if she has a great gift but lacks willpower, she has very little chance of developing her gift.

Some champions and very successful people only had a minor gift for the discipline in which they were so successful. But they were motivated by strong willpower.

One example of this is René Lacoste, the tennis champion. In his biography of him, Gauquelin writes:

> René Lacoste was not very gifted at tennis, in his own opinion. But he had decided to become a champion. Every day he studied all his actions in the mirror. On the court he repeated the same stroke up to a hundred times in order to attain automatic perfection. He put a handkerchief down in one corner and forced himself to make the ball land on it. He invented a machine to send the ball to exactly the place and angle he wanted so that he could practise hitting it back. He kept careful account in a little notebook of his progress, and the reasons for his victories and defeats. A few years later Lacoste won the prestigious Wimbledon championship.

This is a good example of the importance of willpower.

So here is a test of your child's willpower. This is not a test for your child to do. It is for you. Some questions are connected with patience, which should come as no surprise. Willpower without patience does not get you very far.

Test for children from three to fifteen

This is a test for you to do.

1. When your child learnt to walk:

☐ A. He struggled to walk without any pushing on your part and wanted to walk all by himself without your help.

☐ B. He made efforts to walk when you helped him but gave up as soon as you stopped helping.

☐ C. He made no effort to walk and you had a difficult time with him.

2. When you cook something he does not like:

☐ A. You know that whatever you do he will not eat it. He will stay for hours without eating it rather than give in.

☐ B. He gives in in the end but you have a fight.

☐ C. He eats it if you tell him to.

3. When he has free time:

☐ A. He always finds something to do that interests him without your help.

☐ B. With your help he finds something to do that interests him.

☐ C. He is capable of day dreaming for hours without doing anything.

4. His chin:

☐ A. Has a strong shape (square or rectangular) and sticks out.

☐ B. Is normal.

☐ C. Small and receding.

5. If he makes a mistake when he is doing something he usually:

☐ A. Begins again to try and put the mistake right if possible.

☐ B. He only begins again if he feels like it.

☐ C. Gives up.

6. When he wants something you don't want to give him:

☐ A. He nags you continually till he gets it.

☐ B. He keeps on about it until you get angry.

☐ C. He does not insist.

7. If he does not get what he wants from you:

☐ A. He tries to get it from someone else.

☐ B. He gives up for a little while and then tries again.

☐ C. He says no more about it.

8. In a game with his friends he is:

☐ A. Nearly always the leader.

☐ B. Sometimes the leader.

☐ C. Never the leader.

9. If you explain something he does not understand, he:

☐ A. Goes on asking for explanations until he has understood.

☐ B. Asks for explanations if the subject interests him.

☐ C. Does not ask for any explanation.

10. He is capable of saving up for something very much wanted:

☐ A. For a very long time.

☐ B. For quite a long time.

☐ C. He spends everything at once and is incapable of saving.

Note: For children under seven ask the following question instead of question 10:

When he wants a toy and does not get it:

☐ A. He is still thinking about it a week later.

☐ B. He thinks about it for two or three days and then forgets about it.

☐ C. He forgets about it the very next day.

11. When your child is asked what he wants to do later, he:
☐ A. Answers at once and does not change from day to day.
☐ B. Answers at once but gives a different answer on different days. Or wavers between several answers.
☐ C. Hasn't the slightest idea.

Note: For children under 7 ask the following question instead of question 11:

If you tell your child you are going to give him a toy, he:
☐ A. Tells you immediately what he wants.
☐ B. Thinks for a moment before telling you what it is.
☐ C. Dithers a long time before choosing.

12. You notice that your child's ideas are much too fixed:
☐ A. Often.
☐ B. Sometimes.
☐ C. Never.

13. If you give your child a toy (or present) he has been wanting for a long time:
☐ A. You know that this toy (or present) will give him pleasure for a long time.
☐ B. You know that this toy (or present) will give him pleasure until it is replaced by a new one.
☐ C. You know he will get bored with it very quickly.

14. You think your child is:
☐ A. Much too spiteful.
☐ B. Fairly spiteful.
☐ C. Not at all spiteful.

15. Your child can sulk:
☐ A. For a very long time.

☐ B. For a fairly long time.

☐ C. He never sulks or only for a very short time.

16. If he is engrossed in doing something and is interrupted, he:

☐ A. Hates being interrupted even for a good reason.

☐ B. Does not like it but accepts it if there is good reason.

☐ C. Does not mind.

17. After this interruption he:

☐ A. Goes on doing what he was doing before.

☐ B. May or may not continue depending on circumstances.

☐ C. Does something else; does not feel it is worth continuing as he has been interrupted.

18. When he is hurt he:

☐ A. Hardly ever complains.

☐ B. Sometimes complains but not excessively.

☐ C. Makes a big fuss.

19. The games he prefers are:

☐ A. Games requiring patience and reflection, puzzles, cards, model-making, etc.

☐ B. Games on television.

☐ C. Games with others which do not require much concentration, such as forfeits, 'it', blind man's buff, hide and seek etc.

20. When he loses in a game he:

☐ A. Tries to get better at it and practises until he is the best.

☐ B. Tries to get better at it when the occasion arises but does not push at it.

☐ C. Either because he doesn't care or because he is annoyed, he refuses to play that game again.

Count the ticks for each letter.

RESULTS

15–20 As

Your child has an exceptionally strong will. This is a very good thing, even though it may make him a difficult child to live with and educate. Carefully look out for what interests him. You will find that any gift he has, however small, he will persevere with and may go very far. His willpower is so strong that he could easily double the gift as long as it is a real interest.

15–20 Bs

Your child has a strong will, combined with a capacity to adapt. The will is only exerted when he is sure about the choice made and chances of success. He does not want to succeed just for the sake of it. What counts is finding fulfilment. He is quite capable of changing course if this seems necessary. These qualities make the child a person with enough willpower to succeed but also an opportunist with a certain sense of tactics. If he finds the right direction he could go far.

15–20 Cs

Your child has no willpower. He goes along with things at random and does not try to influence how they go. He is totally dependent upon others and needs to find a field of activity (and there are many) requiring an effort to adapt and be sociable, but where he will not need to struggle or assert his personality. However, this child is pleasant, easy to live with, kind and capable of being content with little.

6–14 As and 6–14 Bs

Your child has a strong willpower but does not use it when it seems unnecessary. All his energies are concentrated on what interests him and there is no interest in competition in areas where he has no motivation to succeed. He does not feel the need always to come first but is quite capable of doing so if he sets his mind to it. If the child seems to lack willpower, this is because he has not yet found something to engage his interest.

6–14 As and 6–14 Cs

Your child is erratic. He seems to have willpower but he lacks patience and gets discouraged very easily. However, he is capable of making a special effort and can do remarkably well if asked to do this for particular occasons. Avoid long-term sustained efforts, long-term projects and in general anything that only shows results after a long time. Confined to the present and immediate future this child is capable of strong willpower.

6–14 Bs and 6–14 Cs

Your child has not got much willpower but is capable in certain circumstances of showing courage and stubbornness. Do not expect him to make constant efforts – this would be too much to expect – but ask the child to struggle for what really interests him. Well-motivated and supported, this child can show the necessary willpower to become, if not the best, at least excellent. It is important not to discourage the child by asking him to show willpower in things that do not much matter, because then the child will not see the importance of willpower for what really matters.

Under 7 each of As, Bs and Cs

Your child has a lot of willpower in general but also moments of weakness and discouragement. The child must be allowed to follow his own rhythm. Forcing the child to show willpower in negative phases will not lead to anything. The child has enough positive periods for the good side to win. So do not worry if the child seems erratic. These are just unimportant brief phases.

7

Is your Child Interested in her Environment?

As we have just seen, it is not only the gift but also the willpower to pursue it that matters. The third indispensable element is interest. Although it may seem strange, it is possible to be very gifted for a certain activity without being interested in it. Interest is of prime importance. Without it both the gift and the willpower count for nothing.

A child may have a number of interests and have to choose between them. Interests usually begin to emerge fairly late. It is not always possible to see what they are in early childhood. They are fluid at ten years old but begin to take shape at thirteen or fourteen. That is why this test is only for children between eleven and fifteen.

Interests arise from a combination of the child's experiences and approach to life. Watching what goes on around her, reading, watching television the child gradually discovers the world and becomes more and more involved. The child is then attracted to jobs and activities that seem to correspond to what she can expect from life. There is an undeniable correlation between intelligence and success at school and likewise also between interest and professional success. Without interest in the job professional success is impossible. So it is very important to know what an adolescent or pre-adolescent is interested in. These interests are important for the choice of studies and later profession. It is vital not to force a child to get involved in an activity for which she feels no interest. The following test is very important and must not be omitted.

Test for children between eleven and fifteen

In Table 1 below there are four columns listing various jobs. In each column your child should mark the job or jobs that she would most like to do. Or if she would not really like to do any of them, the job she would dislike the least. There are no 'best' answers. Any answer is good if the child is answering sincerely. The first answer that comes into her head is the one to mark. Count the number of jobs chosen in each column.

Table 1 Job chart

A	B	C	D
Journalist	Scholar	Banker	Actor
Explorer	Chemist	Business person	Singer
Mountaineer	Astronomer	Politician	Model
Sailor	Librarian	Sales person	Tennis player
Parachutist	Poet	Shopkeeper	Photographer
Racing driver	Doctor	Advertising	Producer
Messenger	Publisher	Lawyer	Interpreter
Pilot	Painter	Restaurant manager	Lecturer
Stuntperson	Vet	Jeweller	Tourist guide
Police officer	Writer	Factory manager	Dress designer
Fire fighter	Secretary	Garage owner	Bar person
Acrobat	Records clerk	Hotel manager	Press attaché
Footballer	Accountant	Tax inspector	Decorator
Animal tamer	Watchmaker	Plumber	Hairdresser
	Inventor	Architect	TV presenter

RESULTS

More than ten jobs in column A

Your child absolutely must have an active job. She is overflowing with energy and would never put up with a routine job in an office. She enjoys taking risks, making quick decisions, and needs to be physically active. She hates finicky tasks and activities involving sitting still and staying indoors. Diplomacy would not suit her either because this child likes to speak out and finds it hard to understand the subtleties of politics and human relationships. She tolerates discomfort well and recovers quickly.

Suitable activities: As a general rule, everything involving exploring, adventure, travelling. The armed services would also suit the child well and all activities requiring more muscle than subtlety. Manual activities outdoors or in a fairly open space would also suit.

More than ten jobs in column B

Your child is a dreamer, an introvert who communicates fairly poorly with those around her. This child dislikes large noisy meetings, detests having to elbow for position. She prefers to work in a quiet intimate place, does not like the unexpected and needs to organize and live life in accordance with her own rhythm.

Suitable activities: All calm, contemplative activities requiring patience, precision, meticulousness and reflection, and jobs requiring concentration and perseverance are suitable. Very delicate manual tasks requiring great care and finesse are also suitable.

More than ten jobs in column C
Your child likes money and is perfectly capable of making a fortune, if she wishes and is sufficiently motivated. She enjoys activities offering the chance to make many contacts and also to dominate others. The child is well able to get what she wants and has an acute sense of communication. She enjoys company and needs it to mobilize her energy. But she only feels at ease in a dominant role or in a job where she is her own boss.

Suitable activities: Self-employed jobs, and all jobs in which it is possible to make a lot of money quickly.

More than ten jobs in column D
Your child needs to 'perform'. She attaches enormous importance to appearances and finds other people's opinions very important. This child can shine in society, as she is graceful and charming. She dislikes solitude and needs many social contacts. She is often disorganized and not very punctual in keeping appointments. This character is subtle and knows very well how to make use of others.

Suitable activities: Diplomatic jobs, politics, all careers in which she can be an intermediary and get her way by charm. Artistic professions which offer contact with the public are equally suitable. Manual activities requiring a certain artistic sense may also suit.

Six to ten jobs in column A and six to ten jobs in column B
Your child's preference for calm and meticulous activities is combined with a taste for quick decision-making and energetic solutions. She is not particularly good at social contacts as she is outspoken and often rather brusque. But beneath her rather bluff manner lies a kind heart and intellectual honesty, which will win friends later.

Suitable activities: All jobs that require both great precision and a lot of commonsense. She may also be suited to being a doctor, technician or farmer.

Six to ten activities in column A and six to ten activities in column C
Your child has a taste for risk, adventure and likes making quick decisions. She is attracted to money and likes exercising authority. This gives her the qualities particularly suited to a leader or organizer.

Suitable activities: Creating and directing an enterprise of any kind. All military careers in which she will gain rapid promotion.

Six to ten activities in column A and six to ten activities in column D
Your child's taste for adventure and risk is combined with an enjoyment of social contacts. She is particularly at ease in 'society'. She will enjoy belonging to clubs and associations. She is a good public speaker and may become involved in and lead mass movements. This child is brilliant and will easily become a 'leader'.

Suitable activities: All political activities, law and political science, high administrative and teaching posts. Manual activities in which she can do the designing as well as executing are also suitable.

Choice mixed between column B and column C
Your child is calm, reflective and cautious. She has a rich inner life but is also realistic. She is capable of choosing a job considered non-lucrative and making a fortune from it. When motivated she is highly responsible and capable of great discipline. She is not afraid of hard work provided it pays, but she has a horror of uselessness and needs an objective in order to work well.

Suitable acitivities: Self-governing jobs not requiring team spirit. This child needs to earn money without being too dependent on others. Even if it takes time, the necessary patience will be forthcoming. This child is good at choosing what suits her and is not easily influenced, particularly if badly guided.

Choice mixed between column B and column D
Your child has a double personality, being both inward-looking and secretive and capable of shining in society. She enjoys times of being alone to develop herself but then seeks the company of others because she needs them to confirm her in her view of herself.

Suitable activities: Those needing both solitary work and public performance. This child can blossom in a creative or artistic activity which will be practised alone but then performed in public. She cannot be happy unless the gift is shown in public.

Choice mixed between column C and column D
Your child wants both to be admired and to earn a lot of money. These are her chief ambitions and she is not fussy about the means. She seeks competition but wants it to be lucrative. She is sure of herself and does not engage in self-questioning. If you really want her to excel herself, just say that this is what she is capable of.

Suitable activities: Any activity, provided it allows the child to shine and be applauded. Let the child choose. She will instinctively go where stardom is possible.

Choice mixed between three or four columns.
Your child is a bit too young for this test. At any rate she is immature and does not yet know what she likes or is suited to. These contradictory interests may make her waver for quite a while still between varying aspirations. This child needs time to find herself, and possibly also help. If she gets involved too lightly in a set career, she may feel uncomfortable and have a sense of failure, even with above average aptitude for it.

This child must not be pushed into choosing a career too quickly.

8
Is your Child Logical?

A logical mind is indispensable for certain things. Lawyers, economists, managers, accountants, officers in the police or armed forces, for example, all require a logical mind.

A child will show a logical mind very early, so these tests can be done on very young children.

Test for children from three to six

Test 1

Show the child the five pictures below and opposite. Each of these pictures shows a particular setting.

Ⓐ

Ⓑ

Ⓒ

Ⓓ

Ⓔ

Now show the child the five people wearing different clothes suitable for the settings in the pictures (see page 66). Ask the child to put each person in the right setting. Give him three minutes. Be careful not to interfere if you see him making a mistake.

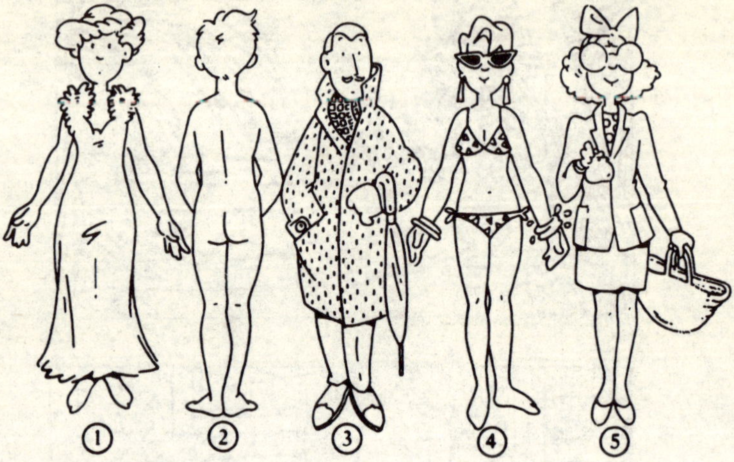

The correct answers are:

Person 1 belongs in setting D.
Person 2 belongs in setting E.
Person 3 belongs in setting A.
Person 4 belongs in setting C.
Person 5 belongs in setting B.

Give two points for each correct answer, then move on immediately to the next test.

Test 2

Show your child the items in the drawings opposite and the people in the drawings on pages 67–8. Each item goes with a particular person. Ask your child to give each person the right item. Allow three minutes for this test.

The correct answers are:

Object 1 belongs to person C.
Object 2 belongs to person D.
Object 3 belongs to person E.
Object 4 belongs to person A.
Object 5 belongs to person B.

Give two points for each correct answer. Now add up all the points.

①

②

③

④

⑤

Ⓐ

Ⓑ

(C)

(D)

(E)

RESULTS

16–20 points
Your child has a gift for logic. This gift, which will certainly develop with age, means that later he can go for the appropriate activities listed in Table 3, page 133. But even if he chooses something else, his logical mind will always be useful.

10–14 points
Your child can be logical but it does not come naturally and requires quite an effort. However, as he is still very young the gift for logic may well develop if he is with people who can help create a taste for this kind of thinking.

Under 10 points
Your child's mind is not at all logical. He is a daydreamer, does not concentrate or perhaps is not interested. But do not worry, logic is only indispensable in certain very precise activities and it is quite possible to succeed without it.

Test for children from seven to ten

Show your child the table below, which has four words on each line. Three of them have something in common and the fourth does not. Ask your child to mark which is the odd one out. Allow five minutes for this test.

1. Horse	Saddle	Field	Stable
2. Soap	Toothpaste	Shampoo	Comb
3. Meat	Wine	Lemonade	Water
4. Painting	Carpet	Rug	Floor
5. Ladle	Salad bowl	Knife	Saucepan
6. Overcoat	Mackintosh	Jacket	Tie
7. Umbrella	Walking stick	Sunshade	Parasol
8. Biro	Pencil	Pen	Ruler
9. Chicken	Duck	Turkey	Pheasant
10. Tennis	Volleyball	Football	Table tennis

The correct answers are:

1. Field (saddle and stable do not exist without the horse).
2. Comb (not used for cleaning the body).
3. Meat (not a drink).
4. Painting (not necessarily on the ground).
5. Knife (not a receptacle).
6. Tie (not a coat).
7. Walking stick (does not protect from the weather).
8. Ruler (does not write).
9. Duck (the only swimmer).
10. Football (the only game not using a net).

Give two points for each right answer.

RESULTS

16–20 points
Your child thinks very logically. This precious gift will certainly be useful to him in the future.

10–14 points
Your child can be logical when he makes the effort, but it does not come naturally. He will be able to do a job requiring minimum logical skills, but not too rigorous or he will get discouraged.

Under 10 points
Your child is not into logic. Sometimes he actually rejects it. Any discipline requiring a logical mind will quickly discourage him and it would be better to direct him towards activities he would enjoy more.

Test for children from eleven to fifteen

First test

In each group below ask your child for the two words with a common idea which the other words lack. Allow five minutes.

1. (a) Ostrich (b) Seal (c) Chaffinch (d) Horse (e) Whale
2. (a) Nose (b) Ear (c) Eye (d) Forehead (e) Cheek
3. (a) Leaf (b) Flower (c) Tree (d) Stem (e) Root
4. (a) Sword (b) Catapult (c) Pistol (d) Gun (e) Club
5. (a) Bicycle (b) Wheelbarrow (c) Cart (d) Car (e) Lorry

The right answers are:

1. (b) and (e): These two animals are sea creatures.
2. (a) and (d): A face has only one of them.
3. (b) and (c): Both are complete plants.
4. (c) and (d): Both are firearms.
5. (d) and (e): Both are motor vehicles.

Count two points for each correct answer.

Second test

Try this test immediately after the last one. Ask your child to tell you which of the following statements are true or false and why. Allow ten minutes.

1. To increase a locomotive's speed all you have to do is increase its wheels' diameter.
2. Sometimes a child can say: 'I am not my father's son.'
3. Forgotten memories are the saddest.
4. There are words that do not exist.
5. A man can legally marry his widow if he remarries.
6. Some objects can go forward without moving.
7. Some keys do not open any doors.
8. Days follow one another and are unalike.
9. You cannot sell a bearskin before you have killed the bear.
10. The more money you earn the more you spend.

The right answers are:

1. False. Speed does not depend on wheel diameter.
2. True if it is a girl speaking.
3. False. Forgotten memories are no longer memories.
4. False. Impossible or they are not words.
5. False. Impossible since he is dead.
6. True. A watch, for example.
7. True. The musical key of G, for example.
8. True, obviously.
9. True. Also obvious.
10. False. It is by no means obligatory.

Give one point for each right answer. Then add up the marks from both tests.

RESULTS

16–20 points
Your child has an extraordinary gift for logic and must also have a mathematical mind. He is realistic, aware and full of commonsense. Try to guide him towards an activity requiring this sort of mind and he will do wonders if he enjoys it.

10–14 points
Your child can be logical on occasion, but it is not his real bent. An activity requiring a little logic may suit him but avoid directing him towards an area where he will need to use it a lot because he will quickly be put off.

Under 10 points
Your child is not at all attracted to logic. He even dislikes it. Do not nag and try to force him to be logical in spite of himself. He will be much more comfortable and happy if he is guided towards activities that do not require logic.

9

Is your Child Skilled with her Hands?

Many people do manual work for lack of anything better or because they did not manage to study to qualify for something else.

Likewise in the so-called 'intellectual' professions or office work there are many people who are out of place and doing a job that does not suit them. Middle-class people often make the serious mistake of believing they must force their children into any job whether or not they are suited to it provided it is not manual work. Without realizing it, these parents are storing up trouble for their children, who will never have a happy future.

Obviously a manual job done by someone who enjoys it makes life much more interesting than an 'intellectual' job she does not like and therefore does badly.

Many manual jobs, particularly craft work, require creativity, research, imagination and are similar to the artistic professions. You need to be really gifted to do these jobs. It is wrong to turn a child away from a gift that will enable him to blossom out, make him happy and also make it possible to earn a living at it later on.

Those who think you need less intelligence to do a manual job than an intellectual job are wrong. You have to be intelligent to succeed in any profession but there are different kinds of intelligence.

It will be a great step forward when people realize that handwork is just as challenging and worthwhile as brain work.

In work of any kind satisfaction depends on the relation between the worker and the task. If the worker is not in control, the work will dominate him and he will feel devalued.

Test for children from seven to fifteen

A child under seven is too young to test. In any case this is not a test to give your child; you yourself should answer the following questions, ticking your chosen answer.

1. Your child drops things:

☐ A. Very seldom.

☐ B. Sometimes.

☐ C. Often.

2. Your child breaks things:

☐ A. Very seldom.

☐ B. Sometimes.

☐ C. Often.

3. When she breaks an object or a toy she:

☐ A. Tries to mend it and often succeeds.

☐ B. Tries to mend it but only occasionally succeeds.

☐ C. Does not try to mend it.

4. Your child takes things to pieces to look inside and see how they work:

☐ A. Often.

☐ B. Sometimes.

☐ C. Never.

5. When she does this she can put it back together again:

☐ A. Often.

☐ B. Rarely.

☐ C. Never (tick this answer if she has never taken an object to bits).

6. When she sees someone doing household repair jobs she:

☐ A. Is interested and tries to get involved.

☐ B. Is interested but does not try to get involved.

☐ C. Is not interested.

7. On the whole you think she is:

☐ A. Very good with her hands.

☐ B. Fairly good.

☐ C. Clumsy.

8. Her sight is:
- ☐ A. Excellent.
- ☐ B. Fairly good.
- ☐ C. Bad.

9. If you give her a model ship or aeroplane:
- ☐ A. She is thrilled and assembles it by herself.
- ☐ B. She is thrilled but needs help to assemble it.
- ☐ C. She is not interested.

10. Her school books are:
- ☐ A. Very neat.
- ☐ B. Fairly neat.
- ☐ C. A mess.

11. Her writing is:
- ☐ A. Very legible.
- ☐ B. Fairly legible.
- ☐ C. A scribble.

12. She can draw a straight line (if you are not sure, ask her to try):
- ☐ A. Perfectly without a ruler.
- ☐ B. Perfectly, but with a ruler.
- ☐ C. Even with a ruler she finds it difficult.

13. When a picture is crooked she:
- ☐ A. Notices and puts it straight.
- ☐ B. Notices but does not straighten it.
- ☐ C. Does not notice.

14. She borrows your tools:
- ☐ A. Often.
- ☐ B. Sometimes.
- ☐ C. Never.

15. She finds drawing:
☐ A. Very easy.
☐ B. Fairly casy.
☐ C. Hates it.

16. She makes things:
☐ A. Often.
☐ B. Sometimes.
☐ C. Never.

17. For Mothers' Day:
☐ A. She often gives something she has made.
☐ B. She sometimes does.
☐ C. She never does.

18. In your opinion being a Girl Guide:
☐ A. Would give her a lot of pleasure.
☐ B. Would give her a certain amount of pleasure.
☐ C. She would not enjoy it at all.

19. If you said 'you are too clumsy to do that' about something quite difficult to do:
☐ A. She would be annoyed and try to prove you wrong.
☐ B. She would be annoyed but not try to prove you wrong.
☐ C. She would not be annoyed and agree with you.

20. When something interests her:
☐ A. She absolutely must touch it.
☐ B. She looks at it very carefully.
☐ C. She glances at it admiringly.

Count the number of As, Bs and Cs.

RESULTS

15–20 As
Your child is very gifted with her hands. If she is not interested in intellectual or abstract work, you should definitely encourage her to do manual work. Otherwise she has the choice. If later on she chooses an intellectual job, she can always find a hobby to practise her manual skills.

15–20 Bs
Your child is gifted with her hands provided she really feels motivated. That means she is not fascinated by all manual activity but she can be attracted to a particular discipline and shine at it. Of course the thing is to find which; this can only be done by trial and error.

15-20 Cs
Your child is not gifted with her hands. Even if you think this a pity do not force her; she is obviously not made for it. Her world is elsewhere.

6–14 As and 6–14 Bs
Your child may do remarkably well at working with her hands provided it is her own choice. Just provide the necessary equipment. You will find she will get on fine. Do not push her into one single area. Let her try things out even if they do not get very far; in this way she will find what suits her best.

6–14 As and 6–14 Cs
Paradoxically your child is both gifted at working with her hands and totally unsuited to it. Her brain pushes her towards it but her body responds badly. She would like to be gifted with her hands but she is too clumsy to get good results. Do not let her choose a manual job without trying to tell her this. On the other hand a hobby would suit her perfectly and enable her to fulfil this aspiration to which she is only half suited.

6–14 Bs and 6–14 Cs
No, your child is not suited to working with her hands. From time to time she has slight urges in this direction but is quickly discouraged. She is right. This is not for her and she would be wasting her time.

Later she can always do a bit of do-it-yourself, which is the most that can reasonably be expected from her. So let her find satisfaction in doing something else.

Under 7 points of any kind

Your child can become competent at do-it-yourself but do not guide her towards a job with her hands. Skilful or clumsy according to circumstances, she can use her manual gifts for her own personal satisfaction but certainly not professionally. She is too uneven. But she can use her manual gifts to complement other talents in certain professions that do not just involve manual work.

10

Is your Child Imaginative?

All artistic jobs as well as certain 'creative' manual jobs need imagination. The creative intellectual professions, writing or research, for example, also require it.

Before guiding your child towards these areas, try to find out how imaginative she is.

This is not a test for your child to do. The questions are for you to answer about your child.

Test for children from seven to fifteen

1. Does your child often have nightmares?
   YES NO
2. Has she ever had tetanus spasms?
   YES NO
3. Does she often need reassuring?
   YES NO
4. Does she cry easily?
   YES NO
5. Does she love animals?
   YES NO
6. Does she love reading?
   YES NO

Note: If she is under seven substitute the following question:
Is she very attracted to picture books?
YES NO

7. Can she play quietly for hours on her own?
   YES NO
8. Does she need times on her own?
   YES NO
9. Does she love music?
   YES NO
10. Does she tell lies easily?
    YES NO
11. When she tells lies, does she sometimes not know whether they are true or not?
    YES NO

12. When she repeats a story she has been told, does she tend to change it, either consciously or unconsciously?
    YES NO
13. Does she like drawing?
    YES NO
14. Do some things which she finds obvious seem strange to you?
    YES NO
15. Does she easily fall in love with someone or something?
    YES NO
16. Is she easily afraid?
    YES NO
17. Ask if she dreams in colour or black and white. Does she answer that she dreams in colour?
    YES NO
18. Does she like playing on her own?
    YES NO
19. Does she sometimes invent games?
    YES NO
20. When she does not want to do something she is supposed to, does she nearly always find a good excuse?
    YES NO
21. Does she ask a lot of questions about all sorts of things?
    YES NO
22. Does she often ask questions you do not understand?
    YES NO
23. In general does she ask a lot of questions about everything?
    YES NO
24. Do you get the impression that she never accepts things as they are and always wants to change them?
    YES NO
25. Does she sometimes criticize a film, a comic or a book because she does not like the story or the end and does she make up her own version?
    YES NO

Count the number of YES and NO answers.

RESULTS

20–25 YES answers

Your child is very imaginative. Do you know this is quite a rare gift? You must help your child to develop her imagination, which is exceptionally good. She should be directed towards creative activities of any kind she enjoys. It is also essential not to repulse her if she asks too many questions, even though this may be irritating or exhausting. Make an effort always to give an answer. If you do not know the answer, say 'I don't know. Let's try and find out, shall we?' Finally, a very imaginative child often tells more lies than other children. This is the other side of the coin. Try to teach her to tell the truth without making an issue of it. (She often finds it difficult to distinguish between what is real and what is imaginary and she is much less to blame than you think.) When she tells a lie your reaction should be: 'It could have been like that. But I don't think that's quite right. What else could it be? Tell me the other possibilities and which is right. This is the one I want to hear.' This attitude should lead the child to understand when the truth is necessary without damaging her imagination. The more imagination a child has, the more vulnerable she is, so treat her with care.

14–19 YES answers
Your child has a lot of imagination. Everything in the above paragraph also applies to her but to a lesser extent. She is less vulnerable, less inclined unconsciously to mix up the true and the false, closer to reality and easier to deal with. She will adapt better to social constraints and whatever you want her to do.

6–13 YES answers
Your child has a normal imagination. She is not necessarily very creative but has enough imagination to do any job that does not require an extraordinary amount. She is much less vulnerable than a very imaginative child and is thoroughly capable of adapting to life's realities, and perfectly able to distinguish between true and false. When she tells lies she does it very lucidly.

Under 6 YES answers
Your child is very unimaginative. She should be directed towards practical things. She has a horror of everything abstract and likes keeping her feet on the ground. She is not highly strung or excessively vulnerable, but open, sincere and steady. She is probably a particularly easy child to bring up because she freely accepts discipline and constraints when she can understand their usefulness.

11

Is your Child Sociable?

It is a gift to be sociable! Not everyone is. In general, extroverts are sociable and introverts find it much more difficult.

A sociable child may appear superficial, more scatterbrained, than a child who is not, but he has the ability to adapt, and an instinct for making contact which will come in very useful when he grows up. Some jobs, particularly those in which there is contact with the public (tourism, hotel work, journalism, sales, political and trade union work, social services, public relations or personnel work etc.) can only be done well by sociable people.

Try to find out how sociable your child is.

Test for children from seven to fifteen

Under seven, the child is too young to test. Of course he will have tendencies but these may or may not be confirmed later. This test is for you. Tick your answers.

1. Your child prefers to play:

☐ A. Alone.

☐ B. With a friend.

☐ C. With several friends.

2. He lends his things:

☐ A. Grudgingly.

☐ B. It depends on what toy or thing it is.

☐ C. Generously.

3. He confides:

☐ A. With great difficulty.

☐ B. Fairly easily but only to certain people.

☐ C. Easily in everyone.

4. He is:
☐ A. Rather taciturn.
☐ B. Not talkative but expresses himself easily and freely.
☐ C. Talkative.

5. He listens to other people's confidences:
☐ A. With difficulty. He is not interested.
☐ B. It depends on who is speaking and what they are talking about.
☐ C. He loves to hear others tell about themselves or telling stories.

6. When you are entertaining someone he dislikes:
☐ A. He goes to his room.
☐ B. He stays but does not take part in the conversation.
☐ C. He makes the best of it and takes part cheerfully in the conversation.

7. When he was small he:
☐ A. He hated having to kiss people.
☐ B. He kissed them spontaneously if he felt like it.
☐ C. He kissed everybody indiscriminately.

8. When he was small:
☐ A. He tended to 'cling to mother's apron strings'.
☐ B. He clung to mother in unfamiliar surroundings but when he was somewhere familiar he would run off.
☐ C. He always ran off.

9. He can ask his way in the street:
☐ A. With difficulty because he is very shy.
☐ B. Fairly easily as long as he can choose who to ask.
☐ C. Ask anyone with no problem.

10. He has:

☐ A. Just one or two friends.

☐ B. A few friends.

☐ C. Loads of friends. ✓

11. He is:

☐ A. Distrustful.

☐ B. Neither distrustful nor credulous. ✓

☐ C. Credulous, he can be made to believe anything.

RESULTS

15–20 As

Your child is not at all sociable. He is introverted and shy and much prefers being by himself to being with others. He has no team spirit and team games do not suit him. He should aim for activities (and later a job) he can do on his own. There are plenty that do not suit more sociable people at all.

15–20 Bs

Your child is normally sociable. He needs contact with others but it is not a pressing need. He is selective and will not choose just anyone to be sociable with. He may well choose a job needing social skills but may also choose something else.

15–20 Cs

Your child has a great gift of sociability. He has a great need for others, whoever they are and finds it hard to be on his own. He will be very unhappy unless he can engage in communal activities and later in a profession requiring a lot of contact with others. He is likely to be highly successful in such a job.

7–14 As and 7–14 Bs

Your child is not obviously sociable but he can make efforts from time to time. Everything depends on the context. He will not be at all sociable if he grows up in an environment which is too different from his personality. On the other hand if those round him have the same tastes and aspirations as himself he may become sociable but only with those people. At any rate he should not be directed towards activities or a profession in which a social gift is a necessity, as he will not feel comfortable.

7–14 As and 7–14 Cs

Your child is very erratic. He can be very sociable with certain people and at certain times. But when he has had enough he may become brusque and withdrawn, even with the same people in the same context. He is unpredictable and needs these changes. He tires of everything quite quickly and something he enjoys one day he may grow tired of the next. The ideal would be a job in which he could organize his own time, see people when he feels like it and stay at home or in his office when he is not feeling sociable. There are such jobs and they suit people with this temperament very well. Many artists are in this category, and also many creative people.

7–14 Bs and 7–14 Cs

Your child is extremely sociable and orientated towards the outside world. He needs others, but can also cope with moments of solitude provided he has sought them himself and they are not imposed on him. His social gift should not be undervalued.

None of the above scores

Your child does not have the gift of sociability but he can be sociable in a discriminating way. It is not an absolute need and he can quite well do without others. He is selective and will be sociable or solitary as it suits him. In fact he organizes things very well to suit his personality.

12

Is your Child Creative?

There are two ways of being creative – in the intellectual or scientific field, or the artistic. Of course, it is perfectly possible to succeed without being creative in a profession that does not require creativity.

Being creative means being able to find new solutions, different from the existing ones. It is thanks to creators of all sorts that we progress, society evolves and we are no longer in the stone age. If your child is creative, she has a rare gift and should be guided towards activities where it can develop. Avoid pushing her into ready programmed activities which take no account of the individual.

Tests for intellectual creativity

These tests are based on association of ideas. You start with a cue word or theme and quickly have to find the largest possible number of associated words. The words do not have to be linked strictly logically to the cue, but by association.

Test for children from three to six

Ask your child to think of as many words as possible that have something to do with eating. Allow five minutes, watch in hand, and note down the words.

Accept all foodstuffs (bread, cheese, meat, fish, poultry etc.) and also drinks (milk, water, wine etc.) because a child of this age does not distinguish between them.

After five minutes do not accept any more words and count the ones you have written down.

RESULTS

More than 18 words
Your child has an exceptional capacity for intellectual creativity. You must be sure to give her the chance to use it.

12–15 words
She has a high capacity for intellectual creativity. If well guided this talent can help her succeed.

7–11 words
Her intellectual creativity is normal, neither above nor below average.

Under 7 words
She is not intellectually creative. But never mind, this is only a handicap in a few particular jobs to which she is unlikely to be attracted.

Test for children from seven to ten

The same process is in force here. But ask the child to write down as many words as possible connected with something round. This idea will conjure up images of objects such as a balloon, a sphere, the earth, a plate, a circus etc. Allow any words connected with the idea of round. After five minutes, watch in hand, count the words the child has written and cross out the invalid ones.

RESULTS

Over 20 words
She has exceptional intellectual creativity, with which she could go far.

15–20 words
She has high intellectual creativity. This will be an advantage later if she chooses a job in which she can use this gift.

9–14 words
She has average intellectual creativity. This will always come in useful but she should not go for a job where this gift is of great importance.

Under 9 words
She is not intellectually creative. She must be guided towards activities where this is not needed (most jobs).

Test for children from eleven to fifteen

The same process is in force here. But this time the theme is the colour white. All the words the child writes must be connected with this colour, for example: whitewash, an egg, wedding dress, the white of the eye etc.

After five minutes count the number of acceptable words written down.

RESULTS

Over 20 words
The child has remarkable intellectual creativity and could go far.

15–20 words
The child has high intellectual creativity, which will lead to success later if she chooses a profession needing this gift.

9–14 words
The child has average intellectual creativity, neither greater nor less than normal.

Under 9 words
The child is not intellectually creative. This will not matter provided she chooses a profession that does not need this facility.

Tests for artistic creativity

Test for children from three to six

Give your child four different coloured pieces of plasticine. Ask him to model with them, making one or more things. Give him half an hour. Take no notice at all of what his model represents or how like it it is. If necessary ask him what it is meant to be.

RESULTS

(a) With the four bits of plasticine he has made several models in mixed colours and grouped them in a sort of set.

For example: he has made a brown house with a red roof; beside the house runs a blue river with a brown bridge, shaded by a green tree with red fruits on it.

It all makes a whole picture. Take no notice of how the whole fits together but only of the fact that your child has tried:

(a) to link the models;
(b) to mix the colours in one or more models.

If you are not sure it is a whole, ask your child whether he intended the models to go together. If the two elements noted above are present then your child has an extraordinary artistic creativity, which he really must develop because it is rare.

(b) Your child has made one single model with the plasticine but has used all four colours.

For example he has made a yellow house with a red roof, brown chimney and green shutters. Take no notice of what he has tried to represent. The essential point is that he has made a single model using all the colours.

Your child has a great capacity for artistic creation, which can take him far provided he wishes to use it.

(c) With the plasticine your child has made several models, with no connection between them and each model is only one colour.

For example, he has made a yellow house, a red lion, a green table and a brown car.

Your child has an average capacity for artistic creation. This is quite sufficient for most jobs but not enough for certain artistic careers.

(d) Your child has not used all the pieces of plasticine, but only one, two or three.

There are two possibilities:

The model or models he has made are in various colours (for example a red house with a yellow roof and a brown man with a red hat). He has weak potential for artistic creation but it can be developed.

The model or models he has made are single-coloured (for example, a yellow house and a brown man). This means he has no capacity for artistic creation. He should be directed towards other activities.

Test for children from seven to fifteen

Give the child four different coloured pieces of paper (for example: blue, red, green and orange), scissors, glue and a white card.

Ask him to cut out the coloured paper into people, plants, or other items as he likes, and stick them on the white card. Give him a pencil to draw the shapes before cutting. Allow him an hour.

RESULTS

Take no notice of what items he has cut out or how alike they are. Ignore the quality of drawing and choice of colours (for example, if the sun is green this has no importance).

(a) He has made a whole picture and every element is linked to the others.
(If you are not sure, ask him what he has tried to do.) He has used the four colours and all or some of the elements in the picture are made up of more than one colour.

For example: there is a blue sea on which there is a red boat with orange sails; by the sea there are green trees with red fruit, under which there is an orange person with a red hat.

Your child has remarkable and rare artistic creativity and he must certainly be helped to develop this gift.

(b) He has made a picture consisting of one element but has used all the four colours.
For example: he has drawn a clown with an orange face, blue and red costume and a green hat.

Your child has great potential for artistic creativity. He will go far with it if he wants to.

(c) He has done several things with no relation between them and each is only one colour.
For example: he has drawn a red house, a green boat, an orange dog and a blue vase. He has used all four colours.

Your child has average artistic creativity, which he can develop if he wishes.

(d) He has done several things with no connection between them but all or some of them use several colours; he has used all the colours he was given.

Your child has fairly good potential for artistic creativity but this potential needs developing. Everything now depends on your child's motivation and how attracted he feels to this work.

(e) He has not used all four colours but with the colours he has chosen he has done either one thing with several colours, or several things with two or three colours.
At the moment your child's artistic creativity potential is weak. But the potential exists and can be developed, provided your child wants it to be.

(f) He has not used all four colours and he has done one or more things, each with one colour.
For example: he has drawn a red house and an orange sun.

Your child's potential for artistic creativity is practically nil. It would be better to direct him towards activities that do not require artistic skill.

13

Is your Child Musical?

The gift for music is innate but it is essential for it to be developed. Gipsies say that you should begin in pregnancy. When a woman is pregnant a gipsy well known for being a good musician plays the violin as close as possible to the expectant mother's stomach. According to them, the fetus can hear it (and nowadays doctors confirm this). If the child has a gift for music it is important to begin as young as possible.

One thing is certain, which proves that a musical gift must be inborn – you cannot make a child who does not enjoy music and cannot hear it correctly into a great musician. But a musical gift still needs developing. Studies have proved that if a child (whatever his potential) has not heard any music before the age of six, he will never be able to become a musician, even a mediocre one.

So it is clear that a child needs to grow up in an environment where music is important if his talent for music is to be developed. But even deprived children, brought up by parents who are not at all interested in music, benefit from music on radio and television nowadays. Few if any children now never hear any music before the age of six. But the problem is that there is very little musical education today except in certain schools that have made a special effort to teach it.

This is a pity because, as we have seen, a child's musical education needs to begin as early as possible. Obviously it is impossible in a book like this to conduct a test to determine whether a child really is musically gifted. This test must be done by a competent music teacher with the help of musical instruments.

However, the test below will help you discover whether your child has a chance of being musically gifted and further investigation is required.

Test for children from three to fifteen

Part 1

Turn back to the test on long-term aural memory. If the child got seventeen to twenty points in that test, give him five points in the musical test. If he got thirteen to sixteen points for long-term aural memory, give him three points in the music test. Below that, give no points.

Part 2

Can the child sing in tune?

Don't just trust your own judgement. Ask other people. If necessary play a song to the child in front of four people and ask your child to sing it. It does not matter if he does not know the words. He can hum it. The important point is to try and find out whether your child can sing in tune. Of course for this part of the test, if possible, it is best to find four people who love music even if it is not their profession or hobby.

For every person who says the child is singing in tune (including yourself) give one point. Thus the maximum possible is five points.

Part 3

Choose a song on a record or cassette. It should be as simple as possible, preferably a song the child knows, particularly if he is young. Let him listen to it a few times. Then write the words on a piece of paper and ask him to sing the song. If the child is too young to read he should simply sing the tune.

The child must begin singing at exactly the same time as the record begins. This is essential for the test.

Tell him that he must sing exactly in time with the singer on the record. Towards the middle of the song, lower the volume so that the child can no longer hear it but keep the record going. Of course you will have warned the child that you are going to do this, so that he does not panic and continues to sing normally. Let him sing alone without support from the record until you see the song on the record is coming to an end. Then turn up the sound again. Where is the child? Has he kept time with the singer on the record or not? Has he sung too quickly or too slowly?

If the child is exactly in time with the singer, give him ten points. This is a rare and excellent result.

If he is just a little out of time with the singer – not more than three words out (judge from just the tune if your child is too young to sing the words), allow five points.

If he is four or five words out, allow two points.

If he is further out, give no points. If your child did not get ten points, you can try the test again. If he is perfectly in time with the singer the second time, add three points. If he is not more than three words out, add two points. Other results get no points. Do not bother to do the test a third time. Add up all the points.

RESULTS

15–20 points
There is a very good chance that the child is musically gifted. You must have him tested by a competent teacher. If he proves to be really gifted, help and encourage him to develop this gift.

9–14 points
The child is quite musical. Perhaps he will not be a great musician but will enjoy music if you help him develop.

Under 9 points
The child is probably not musically gifted. Never mind. He is not alone in this and is probably gifted in other ways.

14

Is your Child Good at Sport?

To be good at sport you need not only the physical aptitude but plenty of willpower and endurance. But even if your child is not really gifted, the practice of a sport is one of the best ways of keeping him healthy and developing well. Of course you must choose the right sport, not take it to excess, and never force a child to practise a sport. If he rejects it outright this is because this sport is not for him.

Sport can develop physical and mental qualities, whose results will show in daily life and in the future. Some sports can be practised all through life and learned at any age. You can only find out whether someone has a gift for a sport by seeing him do it – on the field.

The test below will only help you discover whether your child is mentally suited to sport and has the necessary physical endurance. A talent for sport also requires a certain aggressiveness (intelligent, well-directed aggression is a plus) and a taste for action.

You will find Table 2 after this test, which shows sports to choose from to suit your child's personality.

After the test turn back to the tests on willpower (page 53) and sociability (page 82). If your child has a strong will, this is a plus for sport. If he is sociable, make him practise a team sport. If not, a sport that can be done alone will suit him better.

Test for children from seven to fifteen

The following questions are for you to answer:

1. Is your child hardy?
   YES NO
2. Does he like violent games?
   YES NO
3. Do you find him physically exhausting?
   YES NO
4. Does he need to move about even when he is ill?
   YES NO
5. Does he often run for no reason?
   YES NO

6. Does he hate sitting still?
   YES NO
7. When he is tired does he recover quickly?
   YES NO
8. Does he drop off to sleep easily?
   YES NO
9. Is he seldom ill?
   YES NO
10. Is he reckless?
    YES NO
11. Is he seldom afraid?
    YES NO
12. Does he often fight?
    YES NO
13. When he loses a fight does he fight with the same person again?
    YES NO
14. Does he often attack much older or stronger children?
    YES NO
15. Does he love showing he can do something?
    YES NO
16. Does he hate overeating?
    YES NO
17. Does he stand up straight naturally without you having to tell him?
    YES NO
18. When he is interested in a game does he like to compare himself with others to try and be the best?
    YES NO

Count the number of YES answers.

RESULTS

15–18 YES answers
Your child probably has great talent for sport. You should let him try several to see which he is best at. Everything depends on his character but also his body and the way he uses it.

9–14 YES answers
Your child can probably become good at sport, perhaps not as a champion but an excellent amateur. Help him find the sport that suits him.

4–8 YES answers
Your child is certainly not gifted at sport. But practising a well-chosen sport which is not too demanding can help him develop harmoniously.

Under 4 YES answers
Is your child in good health? If he is, he is refusing all physical effort out of fear or some kind of block. He is an anxious nervous child and needs security. Before letting him practise a sport try to find out why he is so disturbed. Has he got problems at home or at school? You must help him to find a balance.

Table 2 Which sport suits your child?

Your child is	Sport recommended	Advantages	Restrictions
Unsociable, artistic	Figure skating	More than a sport Allows for self-expression	Quickly exhausting
Physically awkward	Trampoline	You learn to control your body in space	Be careful of minor injuries
A bit too reckless	Gymnastics	Disciplines impetuosity	Requires excellent teachers
Nervous and unstable	Fencing	Ideal sport to overcome nerves	Sabres are for the strong
Cerebral, finds it hard to move	Table tennis	Develops reflexes and agility	May cause tiredness

Temperamental and timid	Pony riding	Animal contact has a calming effect, teaches respect for others, gives confidence	Underexercised ponies may be frisky
Introverted and timid or too aggressive	Judo	Well organized with good teachers, channels aggression, teaches courtesy, trains the memory (to remember holds)	Needs complementing with fresh air sport
Restless, hyperactive	Swimming	As well as its other advantages swimming is calming	None
Aggressive or too introverted	Football	Uses up excess energy and develops team spirit	None

15

Is your Child an Actor?

To succeed in the theatre or cinema you need, of course, an excellent visual memory. Many actors cannot learn their lines except by reading them out loud.

But memory alone is not enough. If your child did well in the memory test and you want to know if she could be an actor, do the following test.

Test for children from eleven to fifteen

We purposely do not offer this test for children under eleven. In fact nearly all very young children have a gift for acting. But the talent may disappear with age. It is only from eleven onwards that one can tell whether the gift will remain.

You should answer the following questions yourself.

1. Does the child enjoy imitating people she knows or sees on television?
   YES NO
2. When she tries is she good at it?
   YES NO
3. Does the child enjoy dressing up?
   YES NO
4. Has the child got an expressive face?
   YES NO
5. Does she prefer plays and films on television?
   YES NO
6. Is she always wanting to go to the cinema?
   YES NO
7. Is she fascinated by actors and interested in everything they do?
   YES NO
8. When she sees a film does she criticize the actors?
   YES NO
9. Has your child told you she would like to be an actor?
   YES NO
10. If so has she said so often?
    YES NO

11. If she reads out loud does she do it well and with conviction?
    YES NO
12. In general does she articulate well?
    YES NO
13. Can she whisper and be heard clearly?
    YES NO
14. Does she often look at herself in the mirror?
    YES NO
15. Does she enjoy watching her own movements?
    YES NO
16. If she has (or had) a physical defect, such as standing hunched up or walking with her feet turned inwards, could she correct it easily?
    YES NO
17. When your child is with someone who speaks in a particular accent does she spontaneously pick up the accent?
    YES NO
18. When she wants to, is she capable of repeating the same gesture twenty times until she gets it exactly right?
    YES NO
19. Is she very emotional?
    YES NO
20. Does she love photography?
    YES NO
21. If she enjoys a film can she watch it several times?
    YES NO
22. Does she lie easily?
    YES NO
23. When she tells a lie is she convincing?
    YES NO
24. When she tells a lie can she look anyone straight in the eye without batting an eyelid?
    YES NO
25. Is your child very different when she thinks she is being watched and thinks she is alone?
    YES NO
26. Does she like to steal the show in public even among people she does not know?
    YES NO
27. At a meeting does she like to be the centre of attention?
    YES NO

28. Has she got a strong will?
    YES NO
29. When she gets an idea into her head is it difficult to make her change her mind?
    YES NO
30. Does she attach great importance to her appearance (even if she is not dressed up)?
    YES NO
31. When she likes someone does she spontaneously turn on the charm?
    YES NO
32. Does she want everyone to like her?
    YES NO
33. Does she smile easily?
    YES NO
34. Does she cry easily?
    YES NO
35. Does she easily arouse the admiration of her friends?
    YES NO
36. Does she sometimes confuse her dreams with reality?
    YES NO
37. Is she very imaginative?
    YES NO
38. Does she often have nightmares?
    YES NO
39. When she wakes up in the morning does she remember her dreams?
    YES NO
40. Does she speak aloud when she is alone?
    YES NO

Count the number of YES answers.

RESULTS

31–40 YES answers

Your child has a strong chance of being gifted at acting. If she wants to go in for it, encourage her. If she works hard she could succeed very well at it.

21–30 YES answers

If your child is determined to be an actor she could succeed because she is quite gifted. But if she is vague about it then it is pointless. She could only succeed at acting with great determination and effort.

Under 21 YES answers

Your child has no gift for acting, so it would be pointless to guide her in this direction. It is not her thing, but do not worry, something else will be.

16

Is your Child Gifted at Dancing?

Dancing is certainly one of the toughest professions. You need enormous determination, perfect health, endurance, discipline and hard work, as well as a gift for dancing. And all this for a future that may come to nothing.

A dancer has to retire at around 45 for a man or 40 for a woman, perhaps with no pension. If she wants to do another job she will have to start from the beginning. This should not be forgotten if you want to encourage your child to dance. It is extremely difficult to get into one of the top dance schools. How many of those who are accepted or rejected have a real vocation? Very few, it seems. It is usually the mother who has the vocation. So many mothers dream of becoming a professional dancer and push their child into it ferociously to fulfil their thwarted dreams. Many children suffer agonies for a vocation which is not their own. Television is also responsible. But this type of motivation does not generally survive the hard discipline required.

Some of the most painful cases of rejection from ballet school are for physical reasons. If at puberty a girl grows too big or a boy not big enough, if the muscles become too prominent or not prominent enough, that's it. You cannot be a dancer if you do not have the body for it. How can this be predicted so as not to engage in years of fruitless work? You can only try to limit the risks. Some hospitals for children can do 'size projections' so that those who are likely to grow too tall or remain too small will know this. 'Size projection' can be done at home, too.

Before letting your child go in for dancing (unless it is simply for pleasure and without a career in mind) study the test below.

Test for children from four to eight

The child must:

1. Have perfect health.
2. Have no physical or mental weakness.
3. Be very hardy and slow to tire.
4. Have a calm relaxed temperament.
5. Have a very strong will (see page 52).

6. Be capable of practising the same movement over and over again without becoming exasperated.
7. Be capable of great concentration.
8. Always be very attentive when she is interested in something (see test, page 59).
9. Be extremely supple.
10. Be able to stand pain.
11. Have a fervent and enduring desire to be a dancer.
12. Be long-limbed.
13. Be capable of following normal schooling.
14. Have a sense of rhythm (see test, page 103).
15. Have an ear for music (see test, page 92).
16. Have no tendency to put on weight.
17. Stand up perfectly straight without being told.

All the above criteria are essential. Unfortunately the absence or lack of even one of them is an insurmountable barrier. But if your child has all the necessary characteristics, give her the chance. Although many are rejected, some are chosen and why should she not be one of them?

17

Has your Child got a 'Head for Business?'

The most spectacular financial successes are people who are good at business. With a good head for business it is possible without teaching, without help and even beginning without money to have a spectacular career.

So if your chld is good at business you need not worry about his future. With very rare exceptions it is impossible to discover a gift for business in a very young child. That is why there is no test for children under eleven.

Test for children from eleven to fifteen

Here is a test for you to answer:

1. In general, when your child wants something you do not want to give him, instead of just asking for it can he produce convincing arguments as to why he should have it?
   YES NO
2. Is he interested in the price of things?
   YES NO
3. When he is given a present does he instantly realize its market value?
   YES NO
3. If he does not like a present, will he exchange it, either in the shop or for something he wants belonging to one of his friends?
   YES NO
5. Does he sometimes sell a present he has just been given?
   YES NO
6. Does he sometimes sell his belongings he no longer wants?
   YES NO
7. Does he tend to swap his belongings?
   YES NO
8. When he does swap things, is the exchange usually profitable for him?
   YES NO
9. Can he save up to buy an expensive thing that he wants?
   YES NO

10. Does he always know exactly how much money he has got, even if it is in a savings account?
    YES NO
11. Does he like advising you about what to buy?
    YES NO
12. Does he like looking round shops even if he cannot buy anything?
    YES NO
13. Does he discover discount shops for himself?
    YES NO
14. When he wants to buy something for himself can he shop around and find the shop where it is cheapest?
    YES NO
15. If you pay too much for something does your child reproach you?
    YES NO
16. Does he try to earn pocket money by doing small jobs?
    YES NO
17. Does he like the advertisements on television?
    YES NO
18. Does he sometimes comment on them with remarks such as: 'That ad won't sell much' or 'That's a good ad. It makes you want to buy'?
    YES NO
19. Does he sometimes criticize a shop, saying that the goods are badly displayed or the shop window is dull?
    YES NO
20. Is he good at figures?
    YES NO
21. In general would he rather be given money than a present?
    YES NO
22. If he is good at a subject at school, might he get schoolmates to pay him to do their homework?
    YES NO
23. Is he only interested in practical matters?
    YES NO
24. Did he start enjoying games like monopoly very young?
    YES NO

Count the number of YES answers.

RESULTS

19–24 YES answers
Your child definitely has a head for business. His practical mind, his realism, gift of persuasion, patience in getting what he wants and money all augur brilliant success in business. He is not one to let himself be pushed around and is well able to exploit what life has to offer in a practical way. He will go far in business.

11–18 YES answers
Your child is well able to manage a business provided it is not too big and does not require cunning, creativity or intense competition. A small business that is easy to run would suit him very well. He could also become a sales person in a business not his own. In general he will succeed in business as boss, manager or sales person provided he does not set his sights too high, does not get into too much debt or choose an area where the competition is very intense.

Under 11 YES answers
Your child is not at all cut out for business and if he tried to set up in business he would risk failing badly. He would be bad at selling and not at all motivated for this kind of work. If you have a shop or business and you want him to take over from you one day, give him intense training, and remember that failure is a real possibility and your child's happiness and success probably lie elsewhere.

18

Has your Child got the Gift of Communication?

Some modern jobs which are relatively new and interesting require the gift of communication if one wants to succeed.

In other words, you need to know how to approach people, make contact with them, get on with them and interest them, even in difficult circumstances. This gift is indispensable if you want to become a reporter, hostess, air hostess or steward, press attaché, high level sales person, work in public relations, advertising, or in general do any job which entails contact with the public.

Test for children from seven and fifteen

Under seven a child is too young to be able to judge whether she really has a gift for communication. Do not give your child this test. The questions are for you to answer.

1. Does your child smile easily?
   YES NO
2. In general has she got a happy nature?
   YES NO
3. Is she easy to live with?
   YES NO
4. Does she tend to look on the bright side?
   YES NO
5. Is she good at finding a quick answer?
   YES NO
6. Does she always find arguments to get what she wants?
   YES NO
7. Does she find it difficult to be on her own for long?
   YES NO
8. Does she enjoy team games?
   YES NO
9. Has she got a lot of friends?
   YES NO
10. Does she make friends easily?
    YES NO

11. Is she spontaneously outgoing?
    YES NO
12. Does she spontaneously say 'Good morning', 'Please' and 'Thank you' without your having to remind her?
    YES NO
13. Does she often bring friends home?
    YES NO
14. Does she often give presents?
    YES NO
15. Does she often lend her things?
    YES NO
16. In general does your child get on well with her friends?
    YES NO
17. Does she like doing small favours?
    YES NO
18. Is she on good terms with your neighbours?
    YES NO
19. Does she sometimes chat on the phone with someone who has rung you and whom she has never met?
    YES NO
20. Can she be interrupted when she is doing something that interests her without getting irritated?
    YES NO
21. Does she stay calm when she is told off?
    YES NO
22. Is she chatty in general?
    YES NO
23. Does she express herself easily and without getting muddled?
    YES NO
24. Is she incapable of sulking for long?
    YES NO
25. Does she like to tell everything that has happened to her?
    YES NO
26. When she is spoken to does she listen carefully?
    YES NO
27. Does she remember what she is told easily?
    YES NO
28. When she shakes hands does she do it firmly?
    YES NO

29. When she is speaking to someone, are her eyes usually wide open and looking at the other person?
YES NO
30. Does she enjoy dressing up for special occasions?
YES NO

Count the number of YES answers.

RESULTS

24–30 YES answers
Your child has an extraordinary gift of communication. If she puts it to good use she can succeed very well in any job which requires contact with the public. It is up to her which job attracts her.

15–23 YES answers
Your child is quite good at communication. This should be a help to her if she wants to choose a job needing contact with the public. But you should not direct her towards this type of job unless she is very motivated. She will still have to make quite an effort to develop her communication gifts.

Under 15 YES answers
Your child has difficulty in communicating and any job requiring contact with the public would be difficult for her to endure. She is too introverted and solitary to adapt easily to people she does not know.

19

Has your Child got the Gift of Happiness?

You can be gifted at maths, music or tennis. But you can also be gifted at happiness . . . or not. If you have the gift of happiness you make the best of life. Success, money and talent do not necessarily bring happiness.

If your child has the gift of happiness, he will be happy. Isn't this the main thing?

Test for children from three to fifteen

This test is for parents. It is the same test whatever the child's age, because the gift of happiness is the same whether you are three or fifteen.

1. As a baby your child cried at night:

☐ A. A lot.

☐ B. Sometimes.

☐ C. Hardly ever.

2. Your child smiles:

☐ A. Hardly ever.

☐ B. Sometimes.

☐ C. Very often.

3. She laughs:

☐ A. With difficulty.

☐ B. Not much.

☐ C. A lot.

4. If you give her something to eat she particularly likes:

☐ A. She does not say anything but if you ask whether she is enjoying it she says yes.

☐ B. She says she is enjoying it of her own accord.

☐ C. She exuberantly shows her enjoyment.

5. She can sulk:

☐ A. For hours on end.

☐ B. One or two hours.

☐ C. A few minutes.

6. When she hurts herself:

☐ A. She complains loudly.

☐ B. She complains a bit.

☐ C. She mentions it but does not complain.

7. When she gets bad marks and is told off:

☐ A. She gets depressed.

☐ B. She gets in a bad mood.

☐ C. She is casual about it.

8. With siblings and friends:

☐ A. She is often aggressive.

☐ B. Not particularly aggressive.

☐ C. Very friendly.

9. When you take her shopping:

☐ A. She always demands a toy or sweets and makes a fuss if you refuse.

☐ B. She asks for a toy or sweets but says nothing if you refuse.

☐ C. She does not ask for anything.

10. She likes to eat:

☐ A. Very few things, which is a problem.

☐ B. Only dislikes a few things, which is not a problem.

☐ C. Likes practically everything.

11. When she loses in a game:

☐ A. She reacts very badly.

☐ B. She does not like it but gets over it quickly.

☐ C. She does not mind.

12. When she is ill she is:

☐ A. Very difficult to nurse.

☐ B. Not too bad.

☐ C. Very easy to nurse.

13. She lends her toys:

☐ A. Hardly ever.

☐ B. Only to her friends.

☐ C. To all and sundry.

14. If she is offered sweets:

☐ A. She tries to keep them to herself.

☐ B. She offers them round if told to.

☐ C. She offers them round spontaneously.

15. When you ask her to do something for you:

☐ A. She is always grudging.

☐ B. She may or may not be grudging.

☐ C. She is always happy to do it.

16. When she wakes up in the morning:

☐ A. She always takes a long time to wake.

☐ B. She takes a little while to wake.

☐ C. She is fully awake at once.

17. With animals your child is:

☐ A. Totally indifferent or fearful.

☐ B. Not interested in animals in general but may take an interest in a particular animal.

☐ C. Very attracted to animals.

18. If she has to be on her own for a long time:

☐ A. She finds this very difficult.

☐ B. She does not like it but copes well.

☐ C. She accepts it with ease.

19. She gets bored:

☐ A. Very often.

☐ B. Sometimes.

☐ C. Never.

20. Her sleep is:

☐ A. Usually restless.

☐ B. Normal but restless sometimes.

☐ C. Always very calm.

21. She makes friends:

☐ A. With great difficulty and takes a long time.

☐ B. Without difficulty but takes time.

☐ C. Very easily and quickly.

22. She hums for no reason:

☐ A. Never.

☐ B. Sometimes.

☐ C. Often.

Count the number of ticks for each letter.

RESULTS

17–22 As

Your child has a pessimistic and demanding attitude to life, which does not make happiness come easily. Whatever she gets she may still be disappointed and feel she deserves better. She should learn to think more about others, which will help her.

17–22 Bs
Your child does not have a real gift for happiness but can adapt to circumstances. She will not find that happiness comes easily but is not particularly prone to unhappiness either.

17–22 Cs
Your child has a wonderful gift for happiness. She is born to be happy and whatever happens to her will always make the best of it.

10–16 As and 10–16 Bs
Your child has a tendency to want the impossible. She is never satisfied with what she is offered. Teach her to be less demanding and more content with what she has.

10–16 As and 10–16 Cs
Your child is split between two personalities – one demanding, the other easygoing. In other words she has a gift for happiness sometimes.

10–16 Bs and 10–16 Cs
Your child has a gift for happiness with one drawback. She is too inclined to compare what others have and want that. But she gets over it quickly.

Under 10 of any letter
Your child is quite normal – not particularly gifted for happiness but neither is she inclined to make a tragedy of everything. This is the result most children will get.

PART III

20

Ten Rules for Parents

You have now given your child a number of tests or you have answered for him or her. You will have discovered one or more gifts in your child. To give these gifts the best chance to develop you should avoid certain errors:

1. Do not exhaust your child by trying to develop the gift too quickly or intensely.
2. Listen when your child speaks to you.
3. Try to appreciate the child's gift even it is completely unfamiliar to you.
4. Be prepared for possible pauses in the gift's development if the child seems to lose interest.
5. If your child loses interest in a gift allow him to develop another if he wants to.
6. Let your child develop his gift anyhow without necessarily seeking perfection.
7. Do not make your child think he is a little genius because he has a gift.
8. On the other hand do not put down the gift he has.
9. Remember your child's age and do not treat him as either a baby or as a grown-up.
10. Always be encouraging and congratulate him when he does well.

These ten rules apply to all children. But you should also remember that children with very different personalities may have a similar gift. So you should try to find out what your child's personality is like and the environment that suits his development best. The following two tests will help you do this.

21

Test your Child's Personality

Under seven, a child's personality is not yet fixed enough to test. This test is for children between seven and fifteen. Show your child the ten drawings of trees on pages 121 and 122 and ask her to tell you which she likes best. If she hesitates between two trees give her time to decide, but she must choose just one tree.

RESULTS

She chose number 1

Your child has a strong personality and does not like going along with others. She likes to be the leader. Her friends have to accept her leadership. She is not easily discouraged, tenacious, sometimes stubborn and knows what she wants.

If you want her to develop her gift do not antagonize her. For if one day she decides to abandon something in reaction against too heavy a hand, she will never go back on this decision, even if she is secretly sorry for it. The best way to encourage her is to have confidence in her and show her that you will let her do things her way as much as possible. Your child likes responsibility. Let her take responsibility for her own gift and just give her the means to develop it.

She chose number 2

Your child is non-conformist, imaginative, spontaneous and incapable of pretence or rancour. Her sincerity, kindness and sensitivity attract people to her and they forget her need for change and distraction. To develop her gift she needs a solid framework and to avoid distraction. This child needs you a lot, and your understanding and strength. She may be brilliant but finds it difficult to carry things through. She needs protection to succeed.

She chose number 3

Your child wants to show her self-confidence and strength. She needs to impose it and seeks admiration from others. Her problem is that she is much less solid than she appears. To help her you should give her the means to become stronger, while at the same

①

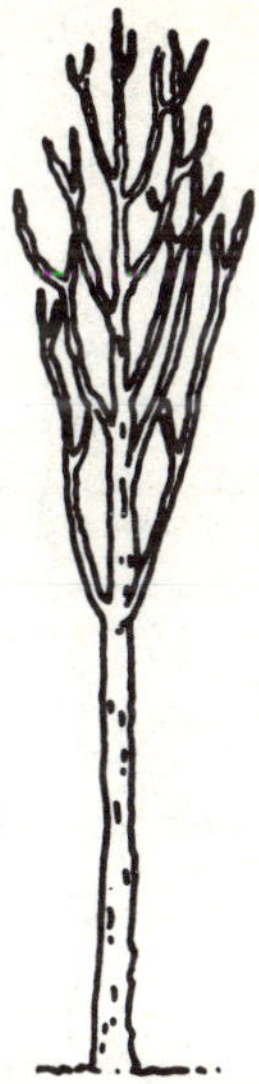

②

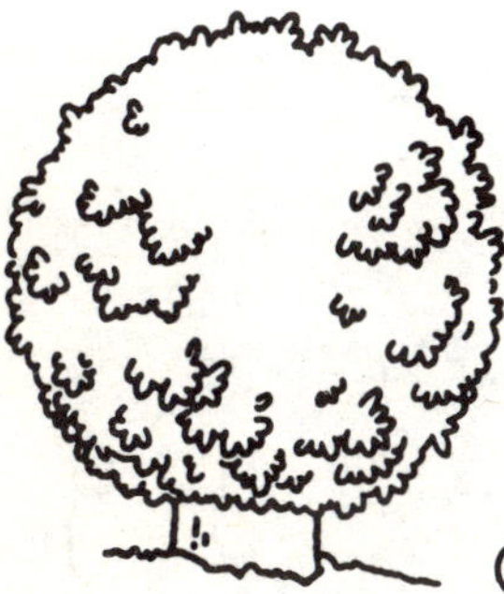

③

④

⑤

⑥

⑦

⑧

⑨

⑩

time discreetly protecting her. Do not let her make decisions on her own, but suggest them adroitly, in such a way that she does not think she has been influenced by anybody. Do not hurt her pride. If one day something goes wrong, be there but do not say 'I told you so. . . '. As soon as she feels better try to behave as if nothing has happened.

She chose number 4
Your child has a very rich personality but her many possibilities may overwhelm her. She would like to do everything, which is not possible, so she finds it hard to choose. She sometimes takes on too much and needs restraining. You must teach her to relax and recover. Her feelings are very intense, which you should take into account. Help her not to try to do everything at once and she should do well.

She chose number 5
Your child has a dreamy romantic temperament. She is sometimes shy and silent. She has a powerful imaginative life, which few people suspect. She may seem unsociable but if others make the first step and are sympathetic she can be wonderful. Above all this child needs love and her whole development depends on it. Negative criticism will make her withdraw and she needs a lot of encouragement.

She chose number 6
Your child needs calm and peace. She cannot stand noise and hassle. Later on she will be good at giving advice to others. But for the moment it is for you to advise her. She needs calm, well-balanced parents with no dramas. Upsets have a bad effect on her development; she will need time to recover.

She chose number 7
Your child is very critical and can even be contemptuous. She only respects people she admires. She is not easily influenced and only trusts her own judgement. It is very difficult to make her change her mind once she has got an idea into her head and she hates pressures being put on her. The development of her gift will depend greatly on the people in charge of her. If she admires them things will go well. If she is critical of them you will have almost insuperable problems. You have to try and make her understand that she will have to take

the responsibility for her own development. This child must either admire or feel responsible for herself.

She chose number 8

Your child is sensitive and vulnerable and needs to please people. Outwardly happy-go-lucky and cheerful she is full of inward self-questioning, but carefully hides this. She likes to add up her good points and needs to be admired. In fact she needs a lot of reassurance and love. You can best help her by being tender and admiring but without treating her as a little genius. Do not forget that she may easily be weak and try to help her be stronger. Being tender does not mean mollycoddling her. She needs to learn to make out on her own but also know that she can turn to you if she needs you.

She chose number 9

Your child likes to appear original and astonish people. She has a strong and surprising nature. But at the same time she may feel anxious and inwardly diffident. She needs to show herself as she is in order to be in harmony with herself. Help her to express herself; the more you talk to her about herself, the better it will be for her. If she learns to cope with her double nature this will be an enrichment for her and she will be able to free herself from her anxieties. This type of child is often misunderstood, which isolates her from her surroundings. You should take care to talk to her and be there for her.

She chose number 10

Your child has strong secret desires and puts up a strong resistance to outside pressure. She needs as much freedom as possible. She can be a fighter and knows what she wants. She is not afraid of being on her own. Do not crowd her with too much attention. She has a strong need to sort things out for herself. Be watchful but do not show it. This child is made for success. You should simply help her find her way and then give her the means to develop.

22

What Environment Suits your Child?

We do not all need the same environment and not many of us get the chance to live in an environment that suits us perfectly. But it is important to find out what would be the optimum environment for a child, so that you can do the best you can for him. The test below is for a child of at least seven. Under that age children are not yet aware of their real needs.

Test for children from seven to fifteen

Show your child the ten drawings of houses on the following pages and ask him which house he would prefer to live in. If he hesitates between two houses let him think it over but he must choose just one.

(1)

2

3

4

5

6

7

8

9

10

RESULTS

He chose house number 1
Your child needs comfort and will make considerable efforts to get it. He is sociable and needs friends round him. But he also needs a room or a corner to himself. So there are two essentials: let him bring friends to the house and give him a place to call his own where he can get away from you.

He chose house number 2
Your child is not ambitious or bossy. He just wants to blossom in the sun. Do not interfere with him too much. Later on he will manage to have a pleasant and cosy life but he can have it now if you create a warm atmosphere for him at home.

He chose house number 3
Your child loves the countryside, the past and traditional things. He does not like to be rushed. He has a strong sense of family, and nothing gives him greater happiness than staying at home. He loves the outdoors and likes to live close to nature.

He chose house number 4
Your child is very ambitious and would like to live 'in the public eye'. He will be capable of making many sacrifices in order to attain this. He is very sensitive to appearances and he likes to feel that where he lives is better than his friends' places. It is important for him to live in a place which impresses others.

He chose house number 5
Your child is brilliant and imaginative and he wants to live in an original way. He hates bourgeois comfort and prefers a weird and futuristic environment. He is not interested in the past. He is fascinated by anything electronic.

He chose house number 6
Your child needs a simple home with no problems, where everything is calm and restful. He likes comfort but does not need luxury. He quickly gets used to having certain things round him and may become deeply attached to them. He does not like change and would hate to move house frequently.

He chose house number 7

Your child wants to succeed but he does not want his success to be ostentatious. He likes a lot of comfort but does not need luxury. He needs a place at home where he can work peacefully and somewhere where he feels he has his private life. He would find it very difficult to cope with poverty.

He chose house number 8

Your child is strongly drawn to the past and he needs an environment full of memories. He is meditative and likes being on his own. He likes to withdraw into his own place like a snail. He wants an ordered secure life and hates being invaded, especially unexpectedly. If you can, give him one or two old things which he likes and which appeal to his imagination. He will become attached to them and they will give him a lot of pleasure.

He chose house number 9

This child's development depends altogether on his family environment. He hates solitude because it makes him depressed. He lacks self-confidence and he needs to feel surrounded by people who care about him. A happy home without dramas or serious problems is essential to him. The framework does not matter to him much.

He chose house number 10

Your child hates crowds or being invaded. He needs peace and solitude, and time to himself to develop well. He can only feel all right when he has things he likes around him. It would be a great mistake to decide on how to decorate his room without consulting him.

23

Is your Child Supergifted?

It is not the purpose of this book to enable you to discover whether your child is supergifted. This can only be done by a specialist. Nevertheless if you really want to know if there is a chance that your child is supergifted you can answer the little test below, which is not infallible but gives some indication. This test was drawn up by an expert on supergifted children, Jean Charles Terrassier, who has written a book on the subject. This test is for children between the ages of six and twelve.

Circle the number of points indicated when the answer is YES.

The child:

1.	Learnt to read before the age of six:	
	On her own or nearly	7 points
	With help	5 points
2.	Reads a lot of books very quickly. (Do not count picture books.)	2 points
3.	Is very interested in encyclopaedias and dictionaries	2 points
4.	Learnt to read quickly but found it difficult learning to write	1 point
5.	Likes being with older children when playing indoors	2 points
6.	Likes talking with adults	2 points
7.	Asks a lot of original questions	2 points
8.	Always wants to know 'why' about everything	1 point
9.	Is bored by routine activities (such as getting dressed)	1 point
10.	Has a sense of humour	2 points
11.	Often has a very large vocabulary but his thoughts are what are the most astonishing	2 points
12.	Likes complicated games (chess, Mastermind, strategic games in general)	2 points
13.	If he is already at college, he was popular with friends at school but is less popular with fellow students.	1 point
14.	Prefers working alone	2 points

15. Is interested in the universe, problems of human origins, prehistory — 2 points
16. Is top of his class with no apparent effort — 2 points
17. Has a highly developed aesthetic sense (music, visual arts, but also his environment), and is sensitive to the harmony of his environment — 2 points
18. Is passionately interested in one or two pastimes and changes these often — 1 point
19. Is very aware of injustice even if he is not the victim — 2 points
20. Makes judgements about people — 1 point
21. When something interests him is capable of making extremely perceptive observations — 2 points

Count the number of points obtained.

RESULTS

If the score was 13 or above

You have more than a one in two chance of your child being supergifted. But if he is not supergifted, there is some consolation. Supergifted children also have disadvantages: they are usually anxious, manually and physically clumsy. They suffer painful feelings of insecurity and isolation. Indeed, their psychological and nervous state is often worrying.

24

What is the Right Job for your Child?

Table 3 What aptitudes are needed for which job?

	1	2	3	4	5	6	7	8	9	10	11	12	13
Actor	*see page 99*												X
Architect			X				X	X					
Press attaché	X					X						X	
Pilot				X			X						X
Lawyer	X					X	X					X	
Singer							X				X		X
Chemist						X	X						
Hairdresser				X					X			X	
Trader	*see page 105*												
Dress designer			X	X	X								
Dancer	*see page 103*												X
Decorator			X					X	X				
Writer			X		X								
Publisher		X					X	X	X				
Mechanic				X			X		X				
Tourist guide	X						X					X	
Businessman/woman						X	X			X			X
Politician	X						X					X	X
Hostess												X	
Journalist	X						X		X			X	
Judge						X	X		X				
Model												X	X
Sailor				X					X				
Doctor	X					X	X		X				
Producer			X		X				X				
Soldier				X		X	X		X				
Musician	*see page 92*												X
Solicitor						X	X			X			
Photographer			X		X								
Painter			X		X								
Policeman/woman						X	X		X				

	1	2	3	4	5	6	7	8	9	10	11	12	13
TV presenter	X											X	
Teacher	X						X		X				X
Advertising	X		X			X	X		X				
Sales person							X			X		X	
Restaurant keeper				X			X					X	
Scholar		X				X	X		X				
Script writer			X		X								
Athlete	*see page 95*												X
Vet	X					X	X						

1. Communication
2. Creativity
3. Artistic creativity
4. Manual dexterity
5. Imagination
6. Logic
7. Memory
8. Visual memory
9. Observation
10. Business sense
11. Musical feeling
12. Sociability
13. Willpower

Note: Of course, we cannot list all possible jobs. But for the most common jobs the above gives the necessary aptitudes. Equally, it is the combination of aptitudes that counts and if your child totally lacks one of them he is probably not cut out for that particular job. And remember, all jobs need motivation. This is not given in Table 3 because it is *always* needed.

[illegible]

~~[illegible]~~

CW01635235

De pequeña, la perrita Blackie pensaba que,
como la nariz humana, ella tampoco pararía de crecer nunca.
Cuando, ya mayor, vio que no iba a crecer más, empezó a preferir
aquello de que «los perros pequeños son más inteligentes».

BLACKIE BOOKS

Crezco

Ben Brooks nació en 1992 en Gloucestershire y ahora vive en Londres. *Crezco* es su quinto libro publicado, (sic), el primero traducido al español y, dicen, punto de inflexión en una carrera más bien experimental. Sus títulos anteriores son *Fences, An Island of Fifty, The Kasahara School of Nihilism* y *Upward Coast & Sadie*. Ben ha sido nominado al Premio Pushcart y su obra ha formado parte de la antología impresa de lo mejor de la web que Dzanc Books publica cada año, y que suele incluir autores que luego se vuelven muy famosos.

BEN BROOKS

Crezco

BLACKIE BOOKS 22

Traducción de Zulema Couso

Título original: *Grow Up*

Diseño de colección e ilustración de cubierta: Setanta
www.setanta.es
© de la ilustración de cubierta: Sergio Ibáñez Narro
© de la foto del autor: Charlotte Adlard

© del texto: Ben Brooks, 2011
Publicado según acuerdo con Canongate Books Ltd,
14 High Street, Edimburgo, EH1 1TE
© de la traducción: Zulema Couso
© de la edición: Blackie Books S.L.U.
Calle Església, 4-10
08024 Barcelona
www.blackiebooks.org
info@blackiebooks.org

Maquetación: David Anglès
Impresión: Liberdúplex
Impreso en España

Primera edición: octubre de 2011
ISBN: 978-84-938745-6-8
Depósito legal: B-37767-2011

Todos los derechos están reservados.
Queda prohibida la reproducción total o parcial
de este libro por cualquier medio o procedimiento,
comprendidos la reprografía y el tratamiento informático,
la fotocopia o la grabación sin el permiso expreso
de los titulares del copyright.

Oh, we kid ourselves there's future in the fucking, but there is no fucking future.

We Are Beautiful, We Are Doomed
Los Campesinos!

Primera parte

Sexo rojo y pequeñas muertes

1

Son las 2:46 y sigo despierto. Hay varias causas para el insomnio, como una glándula tiroides hiperactiva, la diabetes, los espasmos musculares violentos, una comida pesada o el exceso de cafeína. El insomnio también puede ser resultado del estrés. Estoy estresado porque pienso en Keith y en que mató a su ex mujer.

Entro en www.girlsoncam.com, me pongo el usuario POLLADURA y clico en ENTRAR EN LA SALA.

Tú: hola
Sexytai: hola guapo estas cachondo?

Sexytai es pequeñita y muy delgada. Tiene la piel del color de un té flojo y los ojos, color de aceituna, desproporcionadamente grandes. Está tumbada en una *chaise longue* apolillada que tiembla cuando mueve la pelvis.

Tú: claro
Sexytai: vamos a un privado?

Un privado es cuando pagas para ver a la chica «en privado», entonces puedes decirle que se haga un dedo, que grite tu nombre sin parar o que finja ser tu profesora de dibujo. No pago para tener privados con chicas. Si vas con tacto, a veces puedes sacarles un vistazo rápido de los pezones o del clítoris sin pagar nada.

Sexytai: cielo?

Pausa.

Sexytai atrae mi atención a su entrepierna con las manos. Se vende a mí porque, a pesar de la rápida industrialización, Tailandia sigue siendo un país sacudido por la pobreza.

No sé lo que estoy haciendo.

Me aburro.

Soy un silo enorme y vacío.

Tú: eres budista?

Seguro que lo es. El noventa y cinco por ciento de los tailandeses son budistas.

Sexytai: si

Lo sabía.

Tú: theravada?

Pausa.

Sexytai: si privado guapo
Tú: puedo buscarlo en la wikipedia

Pausa.

Sexytai: mira esto

Se saca un pezón nada erecto del sujetador y se aprieta la teta para que apunte hacia mí. Me intimida vagamente, pero me dan ganas de seguir.

Tú: como te llamas?

Pausa.

Sexytai: te quiero dentro de mi guapo
Tú: no digas eso, te cargas el ambiente
Sexytai: vamos al privado
Tú: aqui me gusta, es mas barato

Pausa.

Tú: cuantos baht son una libra?

Se desconecta.

Apunto POLLADURA y SEXYTAI en un trozo de papel porque siento que hemos desarrollado una «conexión especial» y me gustaría volver a hablar con ella otra noche. Quizá la rescate de la pobreza de Tailandia y nos casemos. Marco la categoría «oriental» como favorita. No debería tener favoritos. Papá era mi favorito.

Keith es un asesino.

Papá no.

2

Son las 8:35 de la mañana. Miro el jardín por la ventana, de pie. Keith está ahí, masajeando la tierra. Probablemente se imagina que es el escote de un cadáver. Seguro que restriega la cara contra la tierra.

El cielo está estratificado, como los helados de corte. Salmón. Ámbar. Sepia. Se mezclan y se funden entre sí. Salmoanmbasrepia. Mi habitación huele a cerveza, a tabaco y a papel. El cristal huele a polvo y a luz de sol vieja, atrapada. Los pájaros flirtean entre las nubes.

Enciendo el portátil y me conecto a Facebook. Pone que Georgia Treely está conectada al chat de Facebook. Puede que Georgia Treely no esté conectada al chat de Facebook. El chat de Facebook se está quedando conmigo.

Georgia Treely y yo vamos juntos a clase de Psicología. Quiero tener relaciones sexuales con Georgia Treely, pero no puedo porque cree en Jesucristo y su madre compra en Waitrose. Mi mejor oportunidad sería que Georgia iniciara una rebelión adolescente contra los valores de su entorno familiar. Si eso alguna vez ocurre, me ofreceré como instrumento de la revolución. Cuando le introduzca el pene en la vagina pensará en cuánto odia a su madre y en lo poco razonable que es la hora a la que le pide que vuelva.

No he hablado nunca con Georgia Treely.
Abro una ventana del chat.

Yo: hola
Yo: hola
Yo: hola
Yo: hola
Yo: perdona
Yo: hola
Yo: hola
Yo: no estas
Yo: pero lo leeras
Yo: tal vez no
Yo: no
Yo: hola
Yo: vale
Yo: jo...

Georgia Treely está desconectada.

Cierro el portátil y cojo la ropa del suelo. Keith acaricia la hierba en el jardín. Ya casi es la hora a la que he quedado con Tenaya.

* * *

Estoy seguro de que Keith es un asesino. Si te fijas bien en su historia, verás que su ex mujer desaparece de repente, y eso a él le beneficia. Margaret Clamwell. Que descanse en paz.

Sé que Keith es un asesino porque:

1. Acuerdos de divorcio
   Cuando Keith «dejó» a Margaret Clamwell, no hubo ningún juicio despiadado y el matrimonio acabó sin que Keith perdie-

ra nada: se quedó con todos los activos líquidos y los no líquidos. Es decir, la casa y el Triumph TR 250 de 1968 y también el plan de jubilación y las cuentas de inversiones. (¿Y eso qué es?) Los acuerdos de divorcio no funcionan así. En los matrimonios que no terminan en asesinato, un cónyuge se queda los activos líquidos y el otro los no líquidos. Keith solo podía quedarse con los dos si mataba a Margaret Clamwell. Que es exactamente lo que hizo.

2. Montículo sospechoso
Keith vivía en un barrio de las afueras llamado Sarahdale. La casa que compartía con Margaret Clamwell era el número 7 de Huntington Lane. Si vas a esa casa por la noche con un pasamontañas en la cabeza y una linterna en la mano, encontrarás un montículo extremadamente sospechoso bajo un manzano poco entusiasta. Además, los actuales inquilinos te amenazarán y te echarán de allí. Es el lugar donde Keith enterró a Margaret Clamwell.

3. Complexión
Keith tiene un cuerpo de tipo mesomorfo; es musculoso y fuerte. En la década de los cuarenta, William Sheldon realizó unos estudios que demostraban que el temperamento de los mesomorfos podía inducirles a cometer crímenes. Keith también lleva bigote en forma de U invertida y fácilmente podría encontrar trabajo en un bar gay. Los gays cometen muchos asesinatos, véase el «Doctor Muerte». Keith es un Doctor Muerte. Keith es un asesino.

4. Educación
Keith se crio en un «hogar roto». Su padre le pegaba, su madre se metía heroína y su hermana se fugó para hacer de falsa prostituta en un circo gótico. Lo sé porque Keith disfruta di-

ciéndome lo fácil que es mi vida y hablándome de su niñez en cuanto pasa algo bueno. A veces me da la impresión de que le gustaría romper mi hogar para darme una lección. Keith también es notoriamente poco inteligente. Son dos factores de riesgo para desarrollar tendencias criminales. Eso significa que no hay que culpar a Keith por lo que hizo, pero sí hay que tenerle miedo porque podría matarte. Por eso tengo que mantener a Keith alejado de Mamá.

5. Confesiones
   A Keith le gusta soltar pistas sutiles sobre cómo mató a su mujer. Para ello se vale de frases estereotipadas relacionadas con homicidios. «Eso ya está muerto y enterrado» o «Me dieron ganas de matarla» son cosas que dice al hablar de Margaret Clamwell. Sé que la mataste, Keith. Keith es un asesino.

* * *

Trato de explicarle los hechos a Tenaya una vez más. Es viernes y estamos en Lily's, en los cómodos sofás recosidos junto a la ventana de la galería. Fuera, en la callejuela adoquinada, hay una tienda que vende jabón de lavanda y sales de baño y otra llena de tablas de ouija, incienso y libros de budismo. Una tetera despide vapor entre los dos, no tenemos ningún cigarro porque el gobierno lo ha prohibido. Este año ha sido un mal año para las cosas buenas.

—No puedes estar seguro —dice—. Todavía no. Espera un poco, reúne más pruebas.

—Ya tengo suficientes pruebas —contesto—. Lo hizo él, seguro.

Tenaya es una persona muy práctica. Lo piensa todo con detenimiento. Por ese motivo, o no está del todo convencida de que Keith sea culpable o no está del todo convencida de que la policía estará del todo convencida de la culpabilidad de Keith. Uno de estos dos pensamientos, o ambos, han evitado que se comprometa del todo con mi causa.

—Podríamos exhumar el cuerpo —dice Tenaya.

Me la quedo mirando, entusiasmado, con los ojos abiertos como platos. No entiendo por qué no se me había ocurrido. Es la solución perfecta al problema de cómo incriminar a Keith. Desenterraremos el cuerpo, llamaremos a la policía y entonces Mamá estará a salvo y Keith irá a la cárcel.

—Joder —digo—. Sí. Se me tenía que haber ocurrido a mí. ¿Cuándo?

—Tendrá que ser un sábado o un domingo. No puede ser mañana por lo de tu fiesta ni el fin de semana que viene, por el viaje de Psicología. Solo quedan el 24 o el 25, creo.

Le sonrío. Me emociona que se haga justicia y también la idea de tocar un cadáver. Un cadáver humano de verdad. Un ser humano al que Keith mató, quizá con las manos desnudas o con un cuchillo de cocina o con una recortada o con veneno. Quizá haya un agujero enorme en el cráneo de Margaret Clamwell donde la golpeó con una lámpara o con su trombón y quizá tenga las piernas rotas porque se las rompió para que no pudiera escapar. La policía descubrirá todo esto con la autopsia, pero yo lo sabré antes.

Pagamos el té y vamos a Imran's. Imran's es una tienda de barrio que llevan varios hindúes diferentes que afirman llamarse todos Imran. Vamos ahí a comprar alcohol y tabaco, porque siempre se les olvida pedir el carné o podemos convencerlos de que somos mayores de edad. Tenemos diecisiete. Arma secreta: tetas.

Hoy está el más dejado, el que tiene los ojos saltones y llenos de venillas. Está «leyendo» una revista para hombres detrás del mostrador y se pone a ordenar con prisas cuando entramos.

—Hola —dice Tenaya—. Un paquete de veinticinco gramos de Gold Leaf y un litro de Chekhov, por favor.

El dejado nos mira de arriba abajo. Los ojos se le salen aún más de la cabeza. Me dan ganas de echarme hacia delante, metérselos a la fuerza y decirle que ya es libre de llevar una vida normal.

—¿Tenéis carené? —pregunta.

La voz le suena como el motor de un viejo Citroën.

—¿Cómo?

—¿CARENÉ?

—Vale, sí. Voy a ver. —Tenaya rebusca en los bolsillos el carné de conducir que no tiene—. No lo llevo. Joder. Me lo habré dejado en el coche. No querrás que vuelva hasta allá a cogerlo, ¿verdad?

El hombre está muy nervioso.

Me mira.

—¿CARENÉ? —me grita.

—Lo siento, no creo en eso de llevar documentación. Si lo hiciera, significaría que estoy de acuerdo con un estado totalitario.

El hombre parpadea.

No he conseguido calmar sus nervios.

Vuelve a fijarse en Tenaya. Ella se apoya en el mostrador y junta las tetas apretando con la parte de arriba de los brazos. Se pasa la lengua por el labio superior. Me río, pero transformo la risa en tos. Y la tos me sale convertida en más risas.

El hombre suspira.

—La próxima vez, traer el carené. Prométeselo a Imran. No volveré hacer esto más, ¿oído?

Asentimos. La avaricia vence a la responsabilidad social. Todo el mundo gana.

Mete el vodka en una bolsa de plástico azul y le da el tabaco a Tenaya.

Pagamos y nos marchamos.

Hasta ahora, los planes del día están saliendo bien. Mientras Ping consiga las drogas para mañana y vengan los que tienen que venir, la fiesta estará bien. Que algo vaya bien significa que he follado, me he emborrachado y me he drogado lo suficiente para sentir los efectos que nos describe el señor Gates en la clase de Salud y Desarrollo Personal y Social. Estoy bastante seguro de que se alcanzarán todos estos objetivos. El único que escapa a mi control es el primero, aunque será relativamente fácil de conseguir si vienen suficientes chicas. Si disparas muchas veces, al menos uno de los disparos dará en el blanco, quizá más. Y eso siempre es emocionante.

Después de reunir las provisiones necesarias, cogemos el bus hacia Elsmere, donde Mamá y Keith se están preparando para ir a Cornualles a visitar a los padres de Keith. Van a celebrar su cincuenta aniversario de boda en una fiesta en un pub. Seguramente no querrían que su hijo estuviera allí si supieran que es un asesino. Mamá tampoco tendría que ir, lo que no estaría mal porque seguro que el viaje es una mierda. Keith se emborrachará, le dirá que la quiere, la convencerá para practicar sexo anal y después la matará. Espero que no la mate. Si lo hace, tendré pruebas definitivas de su culpabilidad. Ambivalencia. Tal vez intente escaquearse de los cargos de asesinato alegando que la muerte de Mamá fue el resultado de un experimento sexual que salió mal. La gente a veces hace esas cosas, lo he visto en las noticias.

—Hola, Jasper. Tenaya, ¿cómo estás? —pregunta Mamá.

Se está peleando con la maleta para meterla en nuestro Volvo color mostaza.

—Muy bien, gracias, señora Wolf —responde Tenaya.

Cuando habla con mi madre, Tenaya pone la voz que le ha robado a la chica de una adaptación televisiva de una novela de Dickens.

—Me alegro —dice Mamá—. Jasper, ¿has hecho el programa de mañana?

A Mamá le gusta hacer programas. Tenaya dice que es porque es abogada. No sé si es abogada o no. Lleva un maletín y una BlackBerry. En Psicología, aprendimos que los rasgos obsesivos de carácter son resultado de una satisfacción deficiente durante la fase anal del desarrollo psicosexual. Mamá hace unos programas extremadamente detallados y después le dan ataques de pánico si se retrasa porque tiene que ir al baño o la llaman por teléfono. Cuando se le pasan los ataques de pánico, los programas se han trastocado tanto que siente la necesidad de escribir otros nuevos. La casa está empapelada de programas aburridísimos.

Un ejemplo hipotético:

> 8:00-8:03 Levantarme, salir de la cama, decirle a Keith que se levante.
>
> 8:03-8:10 Lavarme los dientes, ir al baño, hacer un gran esfuerzo por evacuar heces apestosas.
>
> 8:10-8:45 Desayunar. Animar a Jasper a que prepare el programa del día. Preguntar sin parar a Jasper sobre los deberes, las chicas, las drogas y el tabaco. Intentar convencer a Jasper de que no se ponga más de una cucharada de azúcar en el té. Informar a Jasper de que es una decepción constante. Ir a trabajar.

Este es un programa matutino. Mamá escribe tres programas al día: uno para el trabajo, uno para la tarde y otro para la mañana siguiente.

Siempre me insiste en que escriba programas. Me hace escribirlos cuando hay exámenes y cuando ella no va a estar. Ahora pasan las dos cosas, así que escribir el programa es inevitable. Hago dos para que ambos quedemos contentos.

Este es el programa que le enseño a Mamá:

Programa de estudio (para Mamá)

7:00 Despertarme. ¡Buenos días! Desayuno con dos Weetabix (sin azúcar).
7:30 Estudiar. ¡Algún día se lo agradeceré a Mamá!
11:00 Terapia.
12:30 Más estudio.
18:00 Cena de lasaña y judías, colocarme. (¡Es broma, Mamá!)
19:00 + Ver el Canal de Historia | National Geographic | Discovery Channel u otro canal educativo pero divertido para relajarme antes de ir a dormir a las 22:00.
Repetir.

Este es el programa que escribo para mí:

Programa de estudio (para mí)

8:00 Levantarme si tengo ganas. Desayunar té con cuatro azucarillos y fumarme un cigarro.
9:00 Ver *Jeremy Kyle.*
10:00 Baño. Leer *Mi lucha* mientras me baño. ¡Con cuidado de que no se me caiga!
11:00 Terapia.
12:15 Recoger a Ping.
12:30 Hablar de los detalles de la fiesta con Tenaya. Pasar el rato sentado.
16:00 Apartar los objetos rompibles. Dejar ceniceros en varios lugares. Dejar boles de plástico junto a las camas y los sofás.
18:00 Cenar Pot Noodles sabor curry. Colocarme. (¡Lo siento, Mamá!)
20:00 Dar la bienvenida con elegancia a los invitados y aceptar latas gratis de cerveza y tabaco.
21:00 + Diversión descontrolada.
No repetir.

—¿Te vas a quedar, Tenaya? —pregunta Mamá.

—Si le parece bien.

—Claro, pero no olvides decirles a tus padres dónde estás.

—Sí, señora Wolf.

—Y que no venga nadie más.

—Sí, Mamá.

Mamá me da un fuerte beso en la frente y me dice que me quiere.

—Divertíos y portaos bien —nos dice mientras se sube al coche.

—Nos vemos, campeón —dice Keith.

—Sí.

Cuando se dirige a mí, Keith suele utilizar extraños coloquialismos positivos que resultan condescendientes. Cada vez que me habla, mi monólogo interior pone la directa y no para de repetir la palabra ASESINO con la voz de un ama de casa de mediana edad muerta de miedo. Resulta irónico que Keith utilice tantos términos amistosos cuando en realidad es cruel y despiadado.

Mamá me dijo una vez que no entiendo la ironía, lo que resultó irónico, porque me lo dijo mientras sujetaba una caja de palitos de pescado.

Bueno, no, era broma. Solo intentaba relajar un poco el ambiente.

Tenaya y yo observamos cómo el coche se encoge hasta desaparecer. Entonces se lía dos cigarros y entramos en casa.

—¿Viene gente de Layton Hill? —me pregunta.

Me encojo de hombros.

—¿Viene Tom? —pregunto.

Se encoje de hombros.

—Dijo que vendría.

Tom es el novio de Tenaya. Irónicamente, lleva jerséis de punto y unas gafas de plástico negras enormes. A veces, cuando Tom habla, puedo llegar a comprender a Keith y empiezo a creer que quizá tuvo alguna razón de peso para asesinar a Margaret Clamwell con el trombón. A Tenaya solo le gusta Tom porque tiene los pómulos como los ángulos de una escuadra.

—Será mejor que esta vez no te pases, Jasper.

Estoy advertido. La última vez que fuimos a una fiesta con Tom, le puse la droga de los violadores en el vodka y Tenaya tuvo que llevarlo a casa. Luego me tocó confesar bajo coacción porque Tenaya estaba preocupadísima pensando que el vodka iba para ella. Hasta me dijo que temía por su vida.

—Vale —le prometo.

Esta vez, tengo un plan mejor para Tom.

Empezamos a preparar la casa para el sábado. Escondemos los adornos bajo las escaleras y repartimos ceniceros y cubos.

—¿Crees que a la gente le dará por romper cosas? —pregunto.

—Depende.

—Deberíamos pensar en un sistema para controlar a los que se pasen —propongo—. Si destrozamos la casa, Mamá no me dejará ponerme un piercing en el pezón.

—¿Cómo?

—Da igual.

—¿Has dicho un piercing en el pezón, Jasper?

—¿Aún tienes el espray antivioladores?

—¿En el pezón?

—Vale, les echaremos espray antivioladores en los ojos a los que se pasen. Tú haces que se tropiecen y yo me les siento en el pecho y les echo espray en su cara de vándalos estúpidos.

Reparto bolsas de plástico por la habitación. Salvarán el hogar que a mi madre tanto trabajo le ha costado crear para mí.

—Así está bien —dice Tenaya—. ¿Vas a ver a Julia mañana?

—Sí. Puedes quedarte aquí todo el día o venir con Ping y conmigo después al centro, como quieras.

—Ya veré qué hago por la mañana.

A Tenaya le queda ketamina suficiente para hacernos una raya. Leve relajación. Nos dormimos viendo una interpretación de la Royal Philarmonic del *Pájaro de fuego* de Stravinski.

3

Cuando me despierto, hace frío y una densa luz amarilla inunda el salón. El televisor sigue encendido, se ve a una mujer cansada que vende Tupperware. Recoloco el edredón de tal manera que solo queda destapada la cabeza de Tenaya. Preparo té y empiezo a llenar la bañera.

Según mi programa, debería seguir durmiendo porque son las 6:30. Eso significa que si me baño ahora tendré tiempo de trabajar en la novela antes de que empiece *Jeremy Kyle*. Es importante que siga escribiendo cosas, aunque no digan nada coherente. Escribiendo pasajes incoherentes será poco probable que logre una novela fundamental, pero será más probable que si no escribo nada.

El agua de la bañera está caliente y toda la sangre se me concentra en la superficie de la piel, como si intentara descubrir qué está pasando fuera. Como cuando todo el mundo frena para mirar un accidente de coche, a mi sangre le fascina la desgracia de mi piel. Pongo un poco de las sales de baño de Mamá para que el calor huela a lavanda. Los vapores de lavanda me marean y me tranquilizan. Soy una persona relajada y activa. Leo *Mi lucha*.

El señor Glover siempre nos pide que leamos algún capítulo del libro de texto para la clase de Historia. El libro es un desierto. Es un «camino seguro para aprobar el examen», pero no resulta demasiado útil si lo que quieres es entender bien la historia. Por ejemplo, al describir a un racista, el libro de texto diría que «las personas de color parecían no gustarle y solía presentar una actitud violenta hacia ellas», mientras que en su diario, el racista escribiría «sus malditas pieles infernales me ciegan y eclipsan el horizonte». Por eso prefiero leer la literatura original de nuestras personalidades históricas.

Algunos fragmentos que citaría de *Mi lucha* son:

> Lo que hoy se presenta ante nosotros en materia de cultura humana, de resultados obtenidos en el terreno del arte, la ciencia y la técnica, es casi exclusivamente obra de la creación aria.

Creo que Hitler pensaba esto porque nunca tuvo la oportunidad de escuchar Wu-Tang Clan.

> A medio camino entre el hombre y el mono.

Marqué esto. Me pareció gracioso. Se lo enseñé a Kobe durante el descanso y se rio.

> Los pueblos no mueren a consecuencia de las guerras perdidas.

En defensa de Hitler, he sacado el fragmento de su contexto. Le sigue algo sobre que los pueblos solo mueren a consecuencia de la impureza racial. Me hizo gracia, porque Estados Unidos es el candidato favorito a «campeón del mundo» en este momento, y sus ciudadanos son inmigrantes de todo el mundo, dedicados a procrear en una superfructífera orgía de riqueza y poder.

También leí libros escritos por gente del Ku Klux Klan cuando los estábamos estudiando en clase. Tuve que pedirlos en la web del Ku Klux Klan y, como el pedido superaba los 25 dólares, me enviaron una camiseta gratis que decía WHITE KNIGHT WALKING con la foto de un miembro del Klan a caballo. Era de la talla XL, así que me la puse para dormir una noche y Keith me la vio mientras me lavaba los dientes. Al día siguiente, tuvo una conversación secreta con Mamá en la cocina.

—Tranquilízate, Keith. Estoy segura de que es solo una fase, ya se le pasará —le dijo ella.

Algunas de las frases de propaganda del Klan son:

✓ Poned en cuarentena a todos los portadores del sida.
✓ Los falsos maestros de la cristiandad justifican el matrimonio interracial para cegar a la raza aria de modo que no pueda administrar las leyes de Dios.
✓ Somos la niebla.

Cuando tengo la piel de los dedos plegada como cisnes de origami, salgo de la bañera y me visto. Abajo, pongo la tetera al fuego y me siento a la mesa con un cuaderno y un cigarrillo.

Trabajo durante una hora entera en la escena de una violación en la que hay un hombre llamado Martin, con la barba pelirroja y al que le gusta el curry, y una mujer llamada Cindy, que solo tiene siete dedos de los pies y cree que Martin pararía si se los pudiera enseñar. Durante toda la escena, ella intenta quitarse los zapatos mientras él la penetra. También intenta librarse de él repitiendo sin parar: «Solo tengo siete dedos en los pies». A Martin no le importa. Llega un momento en que Cindy hasta parece halagada por la violación. Al sentir que alguien la desea de verdad, se entrega a Martin y la violación deja de serlo para convertirse en sexo.

No sé qué pensar de la escena de la violación, porque es conmovedora pero también inverosímil. Arranco las páginas y las tiro a la basura. «De vuelta a la mesa de dibujo», como diría Keith. Sin embargo, esta hora no ha sido un desperdicio porque he decidido que en la novela debería haber una violación, puede que varias.

Tenaya entra en la cocina. Se sienta enfrente de mí y se lía un cigarro. Cuando se levanta, siempre tiene el pelo como si acabara de follarse apasionadamente a un adicto al crack en una habitación con las paredes de velcro. Personalmente lo prefiero así, pero las chicas suelen tener un sentido distorsionado de su imagen, de modo que no me hace caso cuando se lo digo.

—Te queda bien el pelo así —digo.

—Cállate, Jasper.

—Solo es un piropo.

—¿Cómo va la novela? —me pregunta.

Tenaya siempre apoya mis ambiciones. Le he prometido que cuando gane el Booker nos trasladaremos a Europa del Este y viviremos de té y tostadas.

—Ahí va —le aseguro—. Le voy a añadir la escena de una violación.

—A Sarah DiLeeso la violó un chico de Layton Hill que llevaba una pulsera policial en el tobillo.

—¿En serio? —le pregunto, fascinado—. ¿Crees que me dejaría entrevistarla?

—Va a empezar *Jeremy Kyle* —me dice.

Ha pasado mi pregunta por alto; estaba fuera de tono.

Si alguien intentara violarme haría todo lo posible por hacerle una paja para que se corriera antes de romperme el ano, así no querría seguir con la violación. Sin embargo, si esto no resultara viable, le propondría que yo fuera el que diera y él quien recibiera, porque así sería menos doloroso para mí. Para convencerle le diría cosas como: «Lo has estado pasando muy mal últimamente, deja que haga yo todo el trabajo».

Volvemos al salón y ponemos *Jeremy Kyle*. Es un programa de televisión en el que se arreglan las relaciones de personas especialmente agresivas mediante intensas discusiones circulares y pruebas con el detector de mentiras. Tenaya me pide una camiseta y voy a buscar la del Ku Klux Klan. Frunce el ceño al ponérsela. Le llega hasta las rodillas. Parece una niña de ocho años vestida de Satanás para Halloween.

En el programa de hoy salen un hombre llamado Jay y una mujer llamada Kayler. Los dos sufren de acné severo. Ella tiene sobrepeso y él está flaquísimo. Pero ese no es el problema de su relación. El problema de su relación es que él fumó tanta hierba que se folló al perro y ella lo considera infidelidad. Él lo admite, pero dice que no es infidelidad. Discuten durante un rato, pero ella le hace pasar por el detector de mentiras porque cree que puede ser un «violador de perros en serie».

Antes de que den los resultados de la prueba, subo arriba a cambiarme de ropa para ir a ver a Julia. Suele hablar de lo mucho que he progresado por lo bien que combino la ropa y lo bien planchada que parece. Me decido por unos pitillos azules y una camiseta blanca. Mamá lo calificaría de «presentable».

—Vale, me voy —digo.

—Aquí estaré. Por si te lo estabas preguntando, Jay ha mentido en lo de no ser un «violador de perros en serie».

—Vale, gracias.

* * *

El cielo vuelve a estar gris. El cielo siempre es gris en las afueras. No sé si alguna vez habrá tenido color entre las diez de la mañana y las nueve de la noche.

En la parada del autobús, me encuentro con la anciana esquizofrénica del 26. Mamá me regañó una vez por reírme cuando oí que hablaba de cultivar perros en los árboles durante las fiestas del pueblo.

Las llaman las «fiestas del pueblo» aunque en realidad son las fiestas del barrio.

Esta mujer en particular se llama señora Mulberry, y cree que es posible cultivar personas a partir de semillas hechas de papel de seda y orina. Una vez, el año pasado, Tenaya y yo pegamos la cara contra el cristal de su ventana-mirador y vimos que todo el suelo del salón estaba cubierto de tierra y bolitas de papel.

Hemos estudiado la esquizofrenia en Psicología. Provoca una percepción distorsionada de la realidad. La esquizofrenia de la señora Mulberry es muy original porque la mujer no cree que la persiga ninguna organización gubernamental secreta | horda de alienígenas | culto religioso.

—Buenos días, señora Mulberry —le digo.

—Hola, cariño.

Lleva un bigote postizo y un impermeable azul.

—¿Qué tal va la siembra?

—No demasiado bien. Un virus horrible infectó todas las semillas y me las tuve que comer para que no me crecieran niños con síndrome de Down.

—Lo siento. Quizá la próxima temporada traiga mejor cosecha. ¿Sabía que la gente con síndrome de Down técnicamente pertenece a una especie distinta porque tiene un número diferente de cromosomas?

—Ratas cara chata —dice.

Me siento incómodo con el comentario de la señora Mulberry, pero, siguiendo los deseos de Mamá, asiento y sonrío.

Llega el autobús. El conductor es el de las rastas que parecen kebabs viejos. Subo y me siento en el piso de arriba para que la señora Mulberry no pueda seguirme. Cuando arranca el autobús oigo unos arañazos angustiados que significan que la señora Mulberry intenta seguirme escaleras arriba con la ayuda de su bastón y de sus rodillas de Meccano rotas. Finalmente, suspira y se sienta en el piso de abajo.

He tenido terapeuta desde que nos pillaron a Tenaya y a mí matando un gato. Solo matamos al gato porque me caí accidentalmente encima de él y estaba sufriendo mucho. Lo maté con el pie. Tenaya no va al terapeuta porque su madre no puede permitírselo y también porque insistió en que maltratar a los animales era algo perfectamente normal en chicos de nuestra edad. Alegó que debíamos de estar poniendo a prueba los límites de nuestra relación con el mundo natural. Mi madre dijo que la madre de Tenaya era una «puta hippie gorda» y la madre de Tenaya dijo que mi madre era una «zorra rica».

Mi terapeuta es especialista en arteterapia y se llama Julia. Insiste en que la llame Julia y no «señora Hawthorn» para que la vea como una amiga y me abra a ella, cosa que no hago.

Julia es agradable e ingenua. Se cree todo lo que le digo.

Observo por la pequeña ventana de Julia como el cielo se funde y forma charcos en el asfalto. Ya me ha preguntado por Sebastian (le he confiado a Julia que soy homosexual y que tengo una relación desde hace tiempo), por la *Cunnilingual* (le he confiado a Julia que escribo historias cortas para una revista erótica) y por la meditación (le he confiado a Julia que practico budismo mahayana y que me estoy acercando a la iluminación parcial).

—¿Has tenido más pensamientos oscuros últimamente, Jasper? —me pregunta.

Se le sale el azúcar de la boca. El azúcar solo es aceptable en el té, no cuando se les sale de la boca a mujeres con traje y un sueldo desproporcionado que se piensan que me están dando un champú emocional.

Julia se inclina hacia delante.

La forma de los pliegues de su delgada cara sugiere que era

atractiva pero que no se ha dado cuenta de que ya no lo es. Tiene los ojos verdes y el pelo rubio muy corto, tal como se lo cortan las mujeres de mediana edad que quieren parecerse a Victoria Beckham. Julia no se parece a Victoria Beckham. Julia se parece a Susan Boyle.

—Esta mañana he visto un caracol. Me han dado ganas de aplastarlo con el pie, pero luego he pensado que, si lo hacía, le arrebataría al caracol un futuro de experiencias agradables, así que solo le pasé por encima.

Da unas suaves palmaditas, como un aplauso femenino poco convincente.

—¿Ves, Jasper? Te dije que podíamos progresar. Solo tienes que acordarte de ponerte en el lugar de los demás.

Asiento.

—Empatía —dice.

—Empatía —repito.

Julia coge una hoja de papel de al lado de mi carpeta. Mi carpeta es donde escribe todas las mentiras que le he contado durante el último año.

La hoja de papel tiene tres óvalos. En cada óvalo hay un nombre; Sebastian, Mamá, Keith. Julia me pide que escriba dentro de cada óvalo la expresión que mejor ilustre lo que siento hacia esa persona.

Cuando fui a la clínica por primera vez, me prometieron que la arteterapia era una práctica «curativa» y «enriquecedora» cuya efectividad había sido probada científicamente en estudios realizados con numerosos sujetos. Soy un usuario experto de Google y aún no he encontrado ninguno de esos estudios. En realidad, la arteterapia es paternalista, o lo sería si me la tomara en serio. Julia cree que me está dando un gran apoyo y yo creo que le sigo la corriente, así que las sesiones oscilan como los carruseles y las atracciones de feria, y son fascinantes.

Dibujo una cara con tupé que guiña un ojo en el óvalo de

Sebastian, una cara sonriente con el pelo rizado en el de Mamá y una cara con bigote levantando el pulgar en el de Keith. Julia asiente con un gesto de ánimo. Respuesta correcta.

Después de pasar una hora entera dibujando caras, animales, edificios y «objetos abstractos que representan sentimientos tangibles», me dice que pare.

Julia sonríe.

—Creo que hemos progresado mucho, sin duda. ¿Crees que hemos progresado, Jasper? —me pregunta.

—Sí, Julia. Creo que hemos progresado adecuadamente. Me siento como una persona sana y equilibrada, gracias por tus cuidados y tu atención.

Se sonroja. Sus mejillas son campos de amapolas vacíos.

—¿Qué tal el Klan? —me pregunta.

Hace un mes, decidí sacarle provecho a la camiseta del Ku Klux Klan poniéndomela para una sesión de terapia y diciéndole a Julia que me había unido a ellos. Le expliqué que organizaba reuniones bimensuales en mi habitación con otros miembros del Klan de los alrededores de Ivythorne.

—¿Hay muchos miembros del Klan en Ivythorne? —me preguntó.

—Sí, muchos. ¿Se acuerda de aquel destacado artista afrocaribeño que murió el año pasado?

—Sí, John Ducell. Murió de cáncer.

—Sí, claro.

Julia se quedó con la boca y los ojos muy abiertos cuando se lo dije. Después, cambió de tema.

—Va bien, gracias —le digo—. La semana que viene vamos a pintar unos grafitis en el club social caribeño.

Cada vez que Julia se traga mis mentiras o no consigue disuadirme de participar en crímenes de odio, siento una profunda decepción por el año 2010. No me gusta cómo actúa la gente hoy. El señor Hutchinson lo llama «la plaga de la era posmoderna». La plaga es la tolerancia. La plaga ha hecho que se tolere incluso a los intolerantes. Por eso puedes entrar en www.kkk.com y comprar camisetas con eslóganes del White Power.

Internet está bien porque se puede ver porno gratis, pero mal porque se puede comprar ropa racista.

Julia pasa dos hojas de papel de un lado de su mesa al otro.

—Uy, mira, se ha acabado el tiempo —dice, sonriente—. Que pases un buen fin de semana, Jasper.

—Gracias.

Enfrente del Oaktree Centre me lío un cigarrillo y llamo a Ping. Me dice de quedar en McDonald's. Un chico asiático me adelanta y cruza las puertas de cristal automáticas con dibujos de árboles negros. Lleva unos pantalones cortos y unas deportivas plateadas, se va rascando las manos. Unas costras largas como la cola de una cometa le suben por los brazos. Parece doloroso.

Cuando llego a McDonald's, encuentro a Ping recostado contra un páramo distópico de envoltorios de hamburguesa y sobrecitos flácidos de kétchup. Está mandando un mensaje. Me pregunto a quién. No me ve entrar, así que me pongo detrás de él y le anuncio mi presencia dándole un fuerte golpe en la cabeza al tiempo que digo:

—¡Coco bongo!

—Que te den, maricón —me suelta al mirarme.

Sonrío.

—Vamos —digo.

4

—Hola, tío —dice Jonah. Acaba de llegar a Elsmere.

Estamos en la parada del 38 recogiendo a gente para la fiesta. Parece que hay unos veintiún chicos y tres chicas.

—Va a ser un puto festival de la salchicha —dice Ping.

—No pasa nada —le digo—. Vendrán más chicas después. Tantas que la fiesta se convertirá en una orgía.

Jonah se ríe.

—Sí, tío, montones de rajas.

Jonah lleva unos vaqueros ajustados de chica y los lóbulos de las orejas con dilataciones de catorce milímetros de diámetro, según él. Tenaya dice que son asquerosas y que por eso dejará de follar a partir de los treinta. Él dice que está celosa.

—Hay una fiesta en el valle —dice Ben McKay—. Un montón de gente se ha ido para allá.

—Qué de puta madre —dice Ping.

Jonah nos pasa una lata de cerveza a cada uno y dice que seguro que todo saldrá bien.

Son las ocho, más o menos. No sé la hora exacta porque me he dejado el teléfono en casa. Me pongo nervioso cuando no sé la hora exacta. El cielo está totalmente oscuro y las farolas de tungsteno proyectan charcos de luz naranja en la acera. Las cervezas están heladas, mala suerte, porque la noche no es cálida.

Vemos a dos chicos en chándal bajo una de las farolas cerca del final de Ivythorne Road. Tienen un aspecto desproporcionadamente intimidante para su edad, unos catorce años.

—Mierda —suelta Ping.

Jonah le dice que no sea tan cagado.

Pasamos por delante de los chicos.

—Bonitas orejas, tío —le grita uno de ellos a Jonah—. Podría meter la polla por uno de esos agujeros.

Se echan a reír.

—Me alegro por ti, minipolla —le responde Jonah.

Dejan de reír.

Chándal Blanco se acerca con la bici.

—¿Qué coño has dicho?

—Minipolla —repite Jonah, sonriendo.

Ping deja escapar un gemido.

Chándal Blanco rodea el cuello de Jonah con el brazo y lo tumba con una llave mientras Chándal Azul Marino se acerca. Empiezo a preguntarme qué les pasa por la cabeza. Somos más de veinte y ellos solo dos. Depredadores estúpidos.

—Quema a este gilipollas —dice Chándal Blanco.

Chándal Azul enciende un mechero y acerca la llama al pelo oxigenado de Jonah. ¿Qué están haciendo?

—¿Qué? ¡NO! ¡Haced algo! —Jonah grita y forcejea—. ¡Ping! ¡Ben! Ayudadme, joder.

Somos veinte, pero nos quedamos ahí plantados. De repente, alguien grita «¡Corred!» y todo el mundo se larga, todos menos Tenaya y yo. Ella sonríe, con un cigarrillo en la mano, como si tuviera un plan infalible. Observamos cómo Jonah se va quedando sin flequillo. No debe de ser su mejor momento. Me siento mal por él, pero también me alegro de no ser yo.

—¿Por qué cojones no hacéis nada? —grita.

Tenaya se acerca a Chándal Blanco y le apaga el cigarrillo dentro de la oreja.

La veo iluminarse con una luz roja.

El chico grita.

Suelta a Jonah.

Corremos de vuelta a casa, entramos de golpe y nos desplomamos en el sofá. Mi pecho es un tren de vapor sin carbón. Estoy mareado. Jonah se toca el pelo, se estremece y empieza a liarse un porro.

—Joder —dice.

—Ya —responde Tenaya.

—Gracias.

Nos fumamos el porro. Nos lo pasamos cada tres caladas para compartirlo equitativamente. Relajación.

—No está tan mal, ¿no? —pregunta Jonah con el flequillo entre los dedos.

—Casi ni se nota —dice Tenaya.

Creo que sí se nota, pero no digo nada. A veces soy extremadamente delicado.

—Joder, menos mal.

Llaman a la puerta. Cuando abro, me encuentro a los desertores, borrachos y sonrientes. Llegan tres coches pequeños y por un momento me preocupo, pero dentro van Sarah DiLeeso y algunos más del curso superior. Seguro que todo el mundo tratará la casa de mi familia con el respeto que se merece. No son de los que robarían la cubertería o se mearían en la bañera.

Entramos.

Una hora después, cuatro chicas están mezclando vodka en la alfombra. Alguien ha puesto hip hop con el *surround* conectado. Hay dos chicos besándose en el sofá. La música que suena es Wu-Tang Clan. La canción, «Shame on a Nigga».

Oigo a Sarah DiLeeso y a Jonah cantando.

Ping y yo vamos a la cocina a cocer ketamina. Como está borracho trata de mantener una conversación filosófica, pero no se le da muy bien.

—... seguro que tenemos alma porque, eh, todos esos rasgos humanos que no se pueden explicar, ya sabes, tío, genéticamente o...

Ping hace esto muchas veces. Es un poco idiota.

Asiento con la cabeza mientras deja resbalar el líquido transparente del envoltorio de celofán a la olla. Abro una cerveza. Nos sentamos en la encimera de mármol y enciendo un cigarro.

—Creo que Abby Hall tiene algo para ti —dice Ping.

Cambio de tema radical.

Abby Hall es una rubia regordeta con claras huellas de acné en los pómulos que se empeña en llevar leggings a pesar de la anchura de sus pantorrillas. Cree en los ángeles y no bebe. En las fiestas se hincha de Red Bull y habla sin respirar.

—Estás de coña.

—No, no es coña.

Me imagino una alineación compuesta por las chicas de la fiesta, desnudas. Abby Hall sonríe y hace malabares con sus tetas llenas de acné. Las chicas judías me dicen que no mire. Emma Howes está tremenda. Ana Korsakov no está mal. Tiene un polvo, sí. Dejo fuera a las que tienen novio.

—No lo intentes con Ana —dice Ping—. Eso ya está hecho.

Guiña un ojo. Lo hace para dejarme claro que está hablando de sexo.

Ana Korsakov es pobre. Sus regalos de Navidad son del Ejército de Salvación.

Me prometo que me masturbaré si no aparecen más chicas. Así me aseguro de no tener que tragar (lo siento) con una chica gorda para luego arrepentirme.

—Yo le entraría a Abby —dice Ping.

—Sí —digo—. Solo que no lo harías.

Se ríe.

—Lo haría si me pareciera a ti.

—Ya —contesto—. De puta madre. De todas formas, me ligaré a Georgia Treely en Devon. Está más buena que Ana.

Ping se ríe.

—Vale.

Ahora oigo a Die Antwoord sonando en el salón. Die Antwoord es un grupo de rap de Sudáfrica. Dicen cosas como «mierda de otro nivel». En Orientación Profesional, quería escribir eso en la hoja de «Expectativas de futuro». Tenaya me dijo que, si lo hacía, el de Orientación Profesional pensaría que había tomado LSD y llamaría a Mamá. Asentí con la cabeza y escribí «presentador de programa de televisión para niños».

Vuelvo al salón. Uno de los chicos gays del sofá le está haciendo una paja al otro. Ana Korsakov y su amiga regordeta los observan y se ríen. La habitación está llena de parejas abrazadas que creen ser felices. Mi vejiga es un globo de aire caliente. Voy arriba al baño y paso junto a Tenaya, que se está peleando con Tom; experimento una secreta sensación de optimismo, pero soy demasiado considerado para decir nada. Hoy estoy muy compasivo. Decido no darle la Viagra.

Ben McKay está durmiendo en la bañera rodeado de un halo de vómito fluorescente. Me doy el gusto de mear sentado, le cojo el tabaco y vuelvo abajo. No me cae bien Ben McKay. A Ben McKay le gusta Coldplay.

—Ya está, tío —dice Ping.

Ponemos la droga de la olla en un montoncito blanco sobre el mármol turquesa. Saca la tarjeta de crédito, corta dos rayas y las aspiramos con billetes de cinco libras enrollados. No noto ningún efecto después de la primera raya. Ping se está riendo. Empiezo a notar algo después de ocho rayas.

* * *

Soy un lobo. Jasper James Wolf. Mírame. Soy precioso. Tan elegante y esbelto. Tengo un pelo estupendo. Soy bastante fuerte. Pero me hundo. Quizá estoy caminando sobre el océano. Las baldosas de la cocina son de hielo. Puedo vencerlas con mi ingenio. Un ingenio que supera al de Stephen Fry. Vamos, chicas, mirad qué ojos tengo. Podéis acariciarme si queréis. La música es limonada en mis venas. Tal vez debería teñirme el pelo de anaranjado. El pelaje. No sé cuánta fuerza tengo. Si puedo, debería evitar tocar a la gente. Eso es, sube las escaleras. Esto me gusta. Me lo estoy pasando bien. También tengo náuseas y sueño. Mucho sueño. Ocho en una escala de somnolencia del uno al diez. Yo puedo con él, pues tengo toda esa fuerza de la que he sido dotado. Gracias, sol. Mira, un baño. Hola, Abby Hall. Chsss, no deberíamos hablar. Sí, soy guapísimo. Puedes decírmelo con las manos. Vamos a tumbarnos aquí. En la bañera. Anda, Ben McKay está ahí. ¿Tienes vómito en los leggings? Quítatelos. Todo irá bien. Te lo prometo. Te prometeré muchas cosas. Sé que mis garras son salvajes. Tu boca es mía. Risitas. Dentro de tus ojos. Mis garras te hacen cantar. Tu canto es sugerente. ¿No brilla todo? Esto está muy bien. Hola, Abby Hall. Sí, alrededor de tus pies. Tíraselos a Ben McKay. ¡A los leones! Soy un lobo, ¿sabes? Esto debe de hacerte muy feliz. Sí, así es. Tus gemidos son un sí. Princesa. Eres mi princesa. Yo soy tu lobo. Estamos en el suelo del baño. Deberíamos dejar las garras ya, aunque le das muy bien. Vamos a correr por campos de piel. ¿Qué? No pasa nada. Soy un lobo, puedo soportar un poco de sangre. Yo tengo sangre, tú tienes sangre. Tu sangre sobre mí. Yo dentro de... Oh, esto es... Vámonos de aquí. Vamos a la cama. A la cama de mis padres. Cama de tamaño extra, extra grande. Sí, estamos sobre terciopelo. Unión. Dueto. La flauta y la trompa. Oh. Sí. Así. Gracias. Tus muslos son toboganes de agua. Un parque temático peludo. Dale al conejo. Oh. Sí. Tu sangre en las sábanas.

Date la vuelta. Estoy en tu nuca. Esto es la luz. Estamos vivos. Hola, Abby Hall.

* * *

Son las 5:16. Mi garganta es un desierto lleno de pesticida y mi cabeza una autopista. Estoy tumbado junto a Abby Hall. Por lo que se ve, me he quedado con todo el edredón en algún momento de las últimas horas. Las tetas le cuelgan del pecho como las bolsas de plástico con peces de colores de una feria. Tiene la nariz taponada, de modo que su respiración suena como un gato ronroneando.

La noche de ayer me perseguirá durante semanas. Como un pedófilo, o Keith, acosando a sus víctimas.

Me levanto. Tengo sangre en y alrededor del pene. Nunca nada me había dado tanto asco. El futuro inmediato será apenas soportable, y eso si Abby Hall sigue durmiendo. La rechoncha Abby Hall y sus tetas y su acné repugnantes.

Joder.

La has cagado, Jasper. Georgia Treely es la única mujer del mundo.

Abajo me encuentro a Tenaya. Tiene los ojos hinchados e inyectados en sangre. Está sentada entre dos montones de kleenex usados, hay un viejo volumen de una recopilación de ensayos de Sartre sobre la mesa.

—Buenos días —digo. La voz me suena lastrada por el sangriento fantasma de mi pasado.

—Buenos días —responde.

Me lanza un par de vaqueros del suelo. Les quito un condón lleno que llevaban pegado y me los pongo. Tienen pinta de ser de chica. Nada importa ya. No hay futuro.

—Voy a hacer café y cigarros. Luego podemos sentarnos fuera, y así me cuentas —le digo.

Asiente con un movimiento muy ligero de la cabeza.

Lío los cigarros mientras el agua hierve. Alguien me ha instalado una vía de tren en la cabeza. Yo me instalé la vía de tren en la cabeza. Lo hice con vino barato y sexo horrible. Sexo horrible, horrible. Veo el fantasma de la droga de ayer en el mármol de la encimera. Hay varias personas durmiendo en el suelo de la cocina, imagino que debe de ser bastante incómodo, pero no parece importarles. Ana Korsakov y Ping están acurrucados en la toalla amarilla de Keith, bajo la mesa de la cocina. Hay un charco de sangre y un cuchillo de carne en el fregadero. Qué raro.

Ping entreabre los ojos cuando el agua hirviendo alcanza el clímax.

No me importa que Ping se reservara a Ana Korsakov para él porque de todas formas a ella yo no le gusto. No le gusto porque, en una fiesta que hizo el año pasado, le di un puñetazo a su pitbull y le puse un ojo morado. Fue divertido. Me llamó *suka*. Me dijo que era un «cabrón» en ruso.

—Buenos días —me dice mientras se levanta.

—Eh.

—Tengo ganas de vomitar.

—¿Ana y tú?

Ping se restriega los ojos. Miramos a la chica pequeña y despeinada dormida sobre sus piernas.

—No lo sé —susurra—. A ver, me gusta y eso, pero no se la deja meter. Aunque es buena tía y eso.

—¿No lo habéis hecho?

—Rusa ortodoxa.

—Cederá antes o después.

—Joder, eso espero. Tocamos en Twelve Cats la semana que viene. O la otra.

Ping tiene un grupo de ska que canta canciones sobre la marihuana.

—Puede.

Preparo tres tés, dejo uno para Ping y voy hacia la parte de atrás cruzando el salón.

—Toma —digo al pasarle a Tenaya su té y su cigarrillo—. Es el tabaco bueno.

Salimos fuera y nos sentamos en el suelo de madera, pero nos cambiamos a la cama elástica porque Tenaya dice que está incómoda. Nos tumbamos de espaldas y encendemos los cigarros.

La mañana hace promesas tempranas desde el borde del mundo y encima de nuestras cabezas el cielo tiene el color azul del perro de Slush Puppy. Hace frío, pero es un frío estimulante, no matador. Mi cabeza va catalogando todas esas cosas, aunque no acaba de asimilarlas.

—Este té sabe a culo, Jasper.

—Lo siento —digo—. Cuéntame qué ha pasado con Tom.

—Ya sé que no te caía bien, Jasper —empieza Tenaya—, pero yo creía que era un tío de puta madre.

—Sé que pensabas que era un tío de puta madre, Tenaya —comento—, pero la verdad es que es un pedazo de gilipollas.

Se incorpora un poco y me da un puñetazo en el hombro.

—Ha cortado conmigo.

—¿Y ahora qué hago con tanta Viagra?

Me da otro puñetazo.

—¿Por qué? —pregunto.

Vuelve a tumbarse.

—¿Nos oíste ayer peleándonos?

—Sí.

—Pues fue porque Rajid me dijo que Tom se lo había comido a Alice Jennings y yo se lo pregunté a la cara. No estaba muy segura de si era verdad o no porque Rajid tampoco estaba seguro del todo. —Alice Jennings es una de las judías ricas.

Lleva botas Ugg y se peina hacia atrás—. Cuando estábamos discutiendo, pasa Jonah y dice: «¿Ya se ha enterado?».

Tenaya da una buena calada al cigarrillo.

—Pero has dicho que él ha cortado contigo —comento.

—Bueno... Es que pensaba perdonarle.

No sé muy bien cómo suena una burla pero suelto un fuerte bufido por la nariz tratando de reproducir un sonido que se parezca lo máximo posible a como creo que sonaría. Se me escapan algunos mocos, que aterrizan en mi pecho desnudo. Los limpio con la parte de debajo de la taza de té.

—No le di mucha importancia, y además me gusta mucho. Da igual, porque un rato después me dijo: «Sé que quizá estás pensando en perdonarme, pero yo jamás podría perdonarme a mí mismo, así que se acabó».

Esto me hace partirme de risa.

Tenaya se echa a llorar.

Sus lágrimas le declaran la guerra a mi risa.

Gana ella.

Es una victoria de la culpa.

La cojo de la mano y dejamos de hacer ruidos emocionales. Dios ha diluido el cielo azul Slush Puppy y ahora cae sobre nosotros una luz brillante.

—¿Por qué hay sangre y un cuchillo carnicero en el fregadero? —pregunto.

Tenaya sonríe.

—Vinieron unas chicas de la fiesta del valle porque les cerraron la suya y una intentó apuñalar a Jonah porque decía que había intentado violarla, pero se resbaló con un poco de Irn-Bru que se le había caído a Jonah y se cortó el dedo.

—Joder —digo—. Claro. —Es divertidísimo y desconcertante a la vez—. Había guardado la Viagra disuelta en una botella de Irn-Bru.

Tenaya se echa a reír.

—¿En serio tenías Viagra? Te dije que no te pasaras.

—Ya da igual. ¿Qué pasó después?

Tarda un poco en recuperar la compostura.

—Emma Howes metió el dedo en una caja de Fosters de la nevera y llevó a la chica al hospital, pero no consiguieron llegar porque estaba borracha y derrapó con el coche y se metió en la cuneta. Llamó a Jonah hace media hora o así y él se fue a sacarlas.

Nos sentamos de cara al fondo del jardín. Los conejos se están despertando y empiezan a patrullar el perímetro de la conejera. Se llaman como las Tortugas Ninja: Raphael, Donatello, Michelangelo y Leonardo. Quería llamarlos como los Motorratones de Marte, pero esos solo son tres.

—¿Dónde te metiste? —me pregunta.

—En ninguna parte. Ping y yo nos metimos la ketamina, me dio sueño y me fui a dormir.

Cuando no me cree, Tenaya levanta las cejas y mueve las aletas de la nariz. Es lo que está haciendo ahora.

—Vale, no es eso lo que pasó. Estaba puestísimo de keta y me tiré a Abby Hall a pesar de que está gorda y de que tenía la regla.

Me llevo las manos a la cabeza justo cuando Tenaya estalla en carcajadas. Esperaba que lo hiciera, por eso me he tapado los oídos con las manos.

Dos brazos gruesos y peludos me rodean desde atrás y unos labios cálidos me besan en el cuello.

—Buenos días, mi niño —oigo que dice Abby Hall.

Tenaya vuelve a partirse. Jonah sale de casa y también se echa a reír. Intento convencer a mi corazón para que deje de latir.

5

Cuando conseguimos que todo el mundo se marche, Tenaya me dice que me vaya a dormir. Estoy cansado para discutir. Pongo Radio 4 muy baja y me duermo con la voz de un hombre que habla de la velocidad de Internet en las zonas rurales de Irak.

Tenaya recoge mientras yo duermo para que cuando Mamá y Keith vuelvan se lleven una grata sorpresa.

Keith está en bata tomando café cuando bajo por la noche. Lee *El código Da Vinci*. Keith es analfabeto.

—Hola —digo.

(Asesino.)

—Hola —responde Keith.

(Asesino.)

—¿Lo habéis pasado bien en Cornualles?

(¿Has matado a alguien en Cornualles?)

—Sí, gracias, ha estado muy bien.

(He asesinado y violado a varias pensionistas inocentes.)

—Genial.

(Voy a delatarte a la policía y te encerrarán el resto de tu vida, aunque, bueno, al final serán quince años, o solo siete si consigues no violar a nadie en la cárcel.)

—La fiesta fue de muerte.

(Demasiado fácil.)

—¿Sí?

—Sí, creo que tu madre se lo pasó bien.

(La asesinaste con tu sable y después con una espada de verdad, y después te la comiste en una lasaña.)

—¿Dónde está?

(¿Qué has hecho con ella?)

—Está arriba, dándose un baño.

(Un baño en su propia sangre.)

—Vale —digo—. Nos vemos mañana.

Como mi cabeza aún da saltos mortales vuelvo a mi habitación y me tumbo. Enciendo el portátil y entro repetidamente en varias redes sociales en busca de señales que indiquen que alguien se acuerda de que sigo vivo.

Nadie se acuerda.

Pienso en trabajar en mi novela pero, en cambio, juego al solitario desnudo en el ordenador durante una hora y me quedo dormido.

* * *

Me levanto pronto, me visto para ir a clase y bajo a desayunar. Mamá me ha preparado un té sin azúcar. Me da las gracias por haber cuidado la casa y se va a trabajar. Keith ya se ha marchado. Antes de emprender los seis minutos de camino hasta el instituto, voy al cobertizo para coger el tabaco, el mechero y, con suerte, lo que quede de marihuana. Encuentro a uno de los chicos de Layton Hill tirado en un rincón bajo mi abrigo viejo. Parece que acaba de recuperar el conocimiento y no para de repetir que tiene «hambre, muchísima hambre». Qué interesante: le han cortado la parte de la entrepierna de los vaqueros y de los bóxers. Lo acompaño por el jardín, le hago coger un trozo de pan y lo guío hasta la puerta principal; camina delante de mí, pero lo dejo avanzando en la dirección opuesta.

El St. Mary's es un instituto respetado, galardonado con varios premios y con un estatus envidiable que exige pasar un examen para entrar. Layton Hill es un instituto con un sistema penal sorprendentemente laxo y un gran mercado de drogas ilegales. Mamá dijo que antes de mandarme allí me pondría un profesor particular en casa. Lo mismo me da. Los dos institutos parecen cárceles de plástico y huelen a plastilina.

A primera hora tenemos Religión con la señora Norton. Es una mujer arrugada que lleva ropa de cáñamo con cuentas de madera y a la que le da miedo el futuro de nuestras almas malditas. Nos lo repite regularmente. Más o menos una vez a la semana. Ping la llama «Candidata a follarse a un estudiante para después confesarse en busca de una penitencia indulgente alegando que fue un "acto de Amor ordenado por Dios"».

La señora Norton parece haberse olvidado de dar los buenos días y está al frente de la clase sosteniendo uno de los viejos proyectores. Lo sujeta con tanta fuerza que la piel de las manos se le ha quedado sin sangre y empieza a parecerse a los testículos de un cadáver. Jonah tiene la mano levantada, pero ella no le hace caso.

—¡INFIELES! —grita—. Somos corderos perdidos. Tenemos frío y estamos solos.

La señora Norton tiene una enfermedad mental. Es un secreto muy mal guardado.

Ping y Jonah ya se están riendo.

—Nuestros cielos son de carbón. Nuestros pies son espinas. ¡Buscad al Señor mientras aún pueda ser hallado!

Tenaya saca la novela de Ha Jin que lleva a medio leer.

Me interesa poco adónde quiere llegar la señora Norton hoy con todo esto. Es famosa por liarla en clase de mil maneras diferentes.

—Miradme todos. Miradme y creed. Invoco al poder de Dios para canalizarlo en este proyector.

Oh.

—Tenéis que creer, tenéis que abrazar la fe con todas vuestras fuerzas.

Ping se ha dado la vuelta y está hablando con Sarah Fields.

Jonah está toqueteando el móvil.

—Necesitáis creer, invocad ahora a Dios para que camine entre los hombres.

La señora Norton se llama Acacia, que es un tipo de arbusto con espinas.

—Marcos, 9, 23: para el que cree, todo es posible.

Parece increíble, ¿no?

—Debéis levantar este proyector en el aire con vuestra fe.

Me estremezco.

Pasó de verdad.

Cuando el proyector cae, el brazo se hace pedazos y el cuerpo aplasta el pie de la señora Norton.

—¡Sois una clase de malditos! —empieza a gritar.

Tenaya y yo nos levantamos y nos vamos.

Salimos por la puerta principal y vamos a fumar a la parada del autobús 61.

Una vez la señora Norton tiró todos los estuches por la ventana, uno a uno, diciendo que con el poder de Dios podíamos salvarlos de su astillado futuro. La abuela de Ana presentó una queja formal contra ella y el instituto envió al señor Golding para que supervisara sus clases. Aquello supuso que, durante una semana, tuviéramos clase de verdad y nos tocara interpretar pasajes bíblicos y aplicarlos a serias cuestiones éticas. Cuando el señor Golding se marchó, tras haber cumplido su misión, la señora Norton tiró la mochila de Ana por la ventana y Ana se cambió de Religión a Sociología.

—¿Por qué no la han despedido? —le pregunto a Tenaya.

—Porque puede dar clase.

—Pero no lo hace.

—Pero puede. Además, todo el mundo aprueba estudiándose el libro de texto.

Ping sale del instituto con su paquete aplastado de Marlboro Light.

—¿Qué te ha parecido, guaperas? —dice.

—¿Qué ha pasado?

—Se ha roto el pie. Puede que los dos. Jonah va a llevarla al hospital.

—¿Qué? ¿Por qué la va a llevar Jonah?

—Todos los profesores han dicho que están ocupados. Por cierto, ¿has visto a Abby?

—No. ¿Por qué?

—La has puesto a tope, follagordas. Le va contando a todo el mundo lo que pasó. —Sonríe—. El Barón Rojo —me dice.

Mueve los dedos como hace la gente para imitar a un fantasma, aunque la verdad es que los fantasmas no tienen dedos.

Resoplo.

Si Abby no me deja en paz, tendré que pensar en un plan para defenderme. Si viene al viaje de Psicología y al viaje a Devon después de los exámenes, está claro que me los estropeará con sus besos en el cuello y sus enormes brazos como troncos cubiertos de musgo abrazándome. Se cargará el Plan Georgia. Ver a Abby Hall sobándome no pone mucho.

A veces, la mejor defensa es un buen ataque. Deberé tenerlo en cuenta.

—Ha sido un poco raro —dice Tenaya.

No respondo.

Abby Hall sale por la puerta del instituto. Corre hacia mí sacudiendo sus piernas de giganta, me roba el cigarro y lo tira al suelo.

—Es una costumbre asquerosa, Jasper. Si no quieres perderme, tendrás que dejarlo.

Debido a una cobardía extrema heredada de mi padre, me

da un miedo espantoso herir emocionalmente a la gente. Por eso, durante los seis minutos en que Abby Hall me abraza y pone sus labios en mis mejillas, no digo absolutamente nada. Me pellizca el culo y se muerde el labio. Tenaya y Ping se sonríen. Suena el timbre de la segunda clase y volvemos adentro.

La segunda clase es Psicología. Eso significa que no aprendo nada porque me siento detrás de Georgia Treely. Observo cómo su pelo refleja la luz de los fluorescentes baratos. Levanta la mano más a menudo que el resto. Lleva pulseras de cuentas de plástico en las muñecas. Las muñecas son zonas erógenas. Georgia Treely es católica devota, vegetariana obstinada y filántropa generosa. Tenaya dice que le extraña que me parezca atractiva con esta forma de ser; sin embargo, esto no es lo que me atrae de ella. Lo que encuentro atractivo de ella son: los arcos de los pómulos, las pestañas, la esbelta figura en forma de guitarra, los tobillos, los pies pequeños, los pechos, el pelo, el cuello y la boca. Es un collage hecho con las mejores partes de los cuerpos que salen en el *Vogue*.

No soy superficial; cuerpo sano, mente sana.

Cuando termina Psicología, he aprendido dos cosas: Georgia Treely tiene una nueva pluma de Winnie the Pooh y que Georgia Treely tiene una nueva pulsera de plástico amarilla.

Me marcho al acabar Psicología porque después de comer solo queda Educación Física. No hay nadie en casa. Subo a mi habitación a conspirar.

6

Son las 20:02 y estoy en casa de Tenaya, que se está duchando. La madre de Tenaya se ha quedado dormida a mi lado en el sofá con las plantas de los pies descalzos pegadas a mi muslo derecho. Tiene las piernas moteadas de pelos negros que empiezan a crecer. Parece un niño grande y cansado.

En la televisión dan la primera película de Harry Potter. Un montón de barcos brillantes se mueven sobre el agua negra. He visto esta película más veces de las que he follado. Es una estadística que tengo que invertir. Empezaré por no verla otra vez.

Me levanto con cuidado para no darle un golpe a la madre de Tenaya al ponerme de pie. Seguramente tampoco lo notaría. No se despertaría ni aunque le tirara del pelo y le lamiera las orejas. El alcohol no es nada sano porque, cuando te emborrachas y te duermes, no te acuerdas de lo que hiciste en sueños.

A veces me siento muy culpable de las cosas que pasan en mis sueños. Le he hecho daño a gente mientras duermo, y no importa si lo saben o no.

Cuando subo, Tenaya está sentada en la cama, en su habitación que está en el tercer piso. Lleva una toalla enrollada que le presiona las tetas contra el pecho. Asoman por el borde como las frentes de dos niños curiosos. El pelo mojado le abraza la forma de la cabeza. Grita mi nombre y me dice que salga.

Demasiado lenta.

Al otro lado de la puerta, me dejo caer sobre la moqueta. Me miro las líneas de las manos. Ha ocurrido algo muy deprisa. No sé qué hacer. Ha sido demasiado lenta y lo he visto. Tiene columnas de largas marcas en la parte de arriba del brazo. ¿Qué significa eso? En la radio, he oído hablar de personas que se cortan a sí mismas. No le encontré ningún sentido.

Llamo a la puerta de la habitación. No dice nada. Llamo otra vez.

—Tenaya —digo.

—Sí.

—¿Puedo entrar ahora?

—Vale.

Cuando entro, se ha cambiado y se ha puesto un vestido y una chaqueta. Me siento en el borde de la cama. La autolesión es una fase por la que pasan muchos adolescentes, según dijeron en la radio. Suele ser un grito para pedir ayuda.

—¿Necesitas ayuda? —le pregunto.

—¿Para qué?

En la radio no lo dijeron.

—Para tus brazos.

—¿Que si quiero ayuda para mis brazos?

—Bueno, no sé.

—¿Podemos dejar el tema?

—Vale.

Me levanto y enciendo la televisión. Está en el mismo canal que la de abajo. Harry Potter. Tenaya se ataca a sí misma. El Gran Salón está lleno de niños radiantes que se comen unos filetes enormes. Nos acomodamos. Yo me echo sobre las almohadas y Tenaya se tumba boca abajo, con las pantorrillas levantadas. A veces es mejor esconderse en lugares en los que nunca has estado.

* * *

Cuando me despierto son las 23:14. Sacudo a Tenaya hasta que abre los ojos. Se da un golpe en el ojo intentando quitarse las legañas. Se arregla la falda y se sienta.

—Tengo hambre —digo.

—Ya.

—Iré a preparar té.

—Bajo en un momento.

Bajo los cuatro pisos hasta la cocina del sótano. Es un búnker silencioso y oscuro. Una única bombilla desnuda proyecta su tenue luz amarilla contra las paredes. Es una de las de bajo consumo. Los padres de Tenaya creen que una bombilla salvará el planeta. Yo creo que es demasiado tarde para salvarlo.

La tetera hierve con fuerza, enfadada porque la he despertado. Le dejo la taza de Harry Potter a Tenaya y yo cojo una marrón y torcida que su madre me hizo en un taller de cerámica; lío dos cigarros y pongo la mesa. Estoy siendo atento. Conseguiré que Tenaya se sienta segura y cómoda para poder averiguar por qué está pidiendo ayuda.

Baja las escaleras, sonríe levemente y se sienta delante de mí. Da un sorbo al té para probar cómo está. Meto un dedo en el mío.

—¿Podemos hablar ahora de tus brazos? —pregunto.

Tenaya enciende uno de los cigarros y apoya la cabeza en una mano.

—No.

—¿Por qué tienes cortes en los brazos?

—Jasper.

—Oí hablar de las autolesiones en la radio. Dijeron que era

una manera habitual de pedir ayuda. —Intento sonreír con todas mis fuerzas—. ¿Puedo ayudarte?

—No lo hice por ningún motivo.

—Entonces, ¿por qué?

—No lo sé.

Enciendo mi cigarro y le doy un trago al té. Las manos de Tenaya parecen más pequeñas que nunca, y tiemblan. Los huesos se destacan como removedores de cóctel debajo de la piel.

—¿Es por Tom?

—No todo tiene un motivo, Jasper.

—¿Tom es el motivo?

—Puede.

La miro fijamente a los ojos, como hacen los policías de la televisión cuando saben que un testigo oculta algo.

—¿Estás bien?

No dice nada. Baja la mirada a la taza. Intento imaginar qué haría el hombre de una película. En una película el hombre se inclinaría hacia delante, le levantaría la cara y vería algo en sus ojos que lo explicaría todo. Si lo hiciera, creo que Tenaya me pegaría.

Aplasta el cigarro y levanta la mirada.

—Hay días que me pasa —dice—. No sé por qué. A veces simplemente no estoy bien. No sé. No es por Tom. No es por nada. Ese es el tema. Quizá sea Tom. No lo sé, Jasper. Lo siento.

—Ah. —No sé qué decir. Me enfrento a emociones humanas reales. Debería hacer algo. Quiero hacer algo—. ¿Hay algo que te ayude? —pregunto.

—La gente —responde—. Tener gente cerca.

—Vale. Pues mándame un mensaje la próxima vez que te sientas así, por favor.

—Gracias, Jasper.

—Acabamos de tener una conversación seria.

Tenaya se ríe. Se termina lo que le queda del té y se levanta.

—¿Aún tienes hambre?

—Un poco.

—¿Una tostada con judías?

—Gracias.

Lío más cigarros mientras ella prepara las tostadas y calienta las judías en el microondas. Veo su sombra en los azulejos de la cocina. Será una buena esposa. Una buena esposa y una buena madre y una buena adulta. Mejorará. Intentaré estar siempre cerca de ella hasta que lo consiga.

Comemos en silencio escuchando Radio 4. Cuando termino, decido enterarme de si voy a ser padre.

—Tenaya —digo—. Por curiosidad, ¿las chicas se pueden quedar embarazadas cuando tienen la regla?

Intenta no reírse.

—No —responde—. Bueno, es básicamente imposible.

No voy a ser padre. Me ha tocado la lotería.

—¿Por qué? —pregunta.

—¿No es obvio?

—¿Abby?

—Sí.

Tenaya se muerde el labio.

—¿No te lo han dicho?

—¿Decirme el qué?

—Abby no tenía la regla. Fue su primera vez.

—¿Qué?

—El himen, Jasper. Le rompiste la flor.

Me cago en la puta. Puede que aún vaya a ser padre.

No.

No, voy a serlo, no.

Eso no puede pasar.

De todas maneras, se me acaba de ocurrir una idea para alejar a Abby Hall de Devon y asegurar el éxito del Plan Georgia.

—¿Hay vino?

Puto machacaflores.

—En la nevera.

—¿Podemos ir arriba?

—Vale.

Una vez arriba, Tenaya se queda dormida a mitad de un episodio de *Las chicas Gilmore*. Intento decidirme: Loralai o Rory. No puedo. Enciendo el portátil de Tenaya y juego al buscaminas. Consigo el mejor tiempo en el nivel intermedio, pero eso no quiere decir nada porque Tenaya es malísima en el buscaminas.

7

Es martes por la tarde. Hemos acabado las clases y Tenaya y yo estamos en Lily's con una tetera entre los dos. Lleva manga larga. Intentó irse directamente a casa después de clase pero le dije que no.

Le enseño mi plan para mantener a Abby Hall lejos de los próximos acontecimientos. Mi plan tiene forma de carta.

> Estimada Abby Hall:
>
> Le escribimos para informarle de que, a pesar de su abundante consumo de drogas ilegales durante la primera etapa del embarazo, el examen prenatal no muestra signos de defectos genéticos ni de anormalidades cromosómicas en el feto.
>
> También puede interesarle saber que gracias a la elasticidad relativa de sus labios, causada por las relaciones frecuentes, el parto será prácticamente indoloro.
>
> ¡Le deseamos mucha suerte con su gestación y esperamos verla en marzo!
>
> RAMAD CHANKRIH
> Director de Bebés, Drogas y Otras Cosas
> del hospital de London Road.

Tenaya se ríe y se le sale un poco de té por la nariz.

—Nadie creerá que eso lo han escrito en un hospital —dice—. El abuso de las drogas no provoca defectos genéticos ni anormalidades cromosómicas.

—Sus padres no lo saben.

—Claro que sí. Yo lo sé.

—¿Y?

—Los médicos no utilizan exclamaciones.

—Los médicos entusiastas, sí.

—Has escrito «la elasticidad de sus labios», Jasper. —Arquea las cejas—. Nadie se creerá que un médico haya dicho eso.

—Sí se lo creerán. Es vocabulario científico.

Tenaya coge la carta y se pone a leerla, riéndose.

—«Ramad Chankrih, Director de Bebés, Drogas y Otras Cosas del hospital de London Road.» ¿Y eso?

—Son términos comunes. Si pongo «Director de Pediatría y de Abuso de Sustancias» puede que sus padres no lo entiendan. Quiero que tengan muy claro a qué se refiere la carta.

Tenaya repasa con un boli el logo de su paquete de Benson and Hedges. Lo presiona sobre la esquina derecha de la carta y deja la marca del emblema. Asegura que eso le da autenticidad a la carta. Pagamos el té y nos vamos.

En casa, Mamá y Keith están sentados a la mesa de la cocina tomando un café. Preparo una taza de té y Keith empieza a hablar justo cuando me iba para arriba.

—Hola, campeón —dice. Creo que ha aprendido esa palabra viendo programas estadounidenses—. Tu madre y yo estábamos pensando en ir todos juntos de vacaciones. ¿Qué te parece?

—Suena bien.

(Nos matará a los dos en algún país del tercer mundo donde haya policías corruptos y pueda sobornarlos para que «hagan la vista gorda».)

—¿Qué te parece Lanzarote?

(Jesús dijo que «pusiéramos la otra mejilla». Jesús es el cómplice de Keith.)

—Ping fue hace dos años y me dijo que estaba bien.

(«Grandes extensiones de terreno desierto», me dijo. Perfecto para enterrar cuerpos.)

—Tienes el viaje de Psicología esta semana, ¿verdad? —me pregunta Mamá.

—Sí, el viernes y el sábado. Vamos a ver asesinos en Plymouth.

—Qué emocionante —comenta Keith.

Ya conozco a Keith, que es un asesino, y lo que puedo decir de ellos según lo que he observado en él es que saben integrarse. Los asesinos pueden ser camaleones sociales. Se necesitan muchas pruebas empíricas para conseguir una condena. Eso significa que ir a ver asesinos no será particularmente emocionante porque intentarán parecer ciudadanos normales integrados en la sociedad.

—Sí —digo—. Muy emocionante.

Pongo a descargar una película de cine negro en el ordenador y meto la carta para Abby en un sobre color sepia. Saqué su dirección de la guía telefónica porque sé que el nombre de su padre es Amadeus. Cuando la llevo a la oficina de correos me pregunto durante un segundo qué pasa cuando a los trabajadores de la oficina les dan cartas para ellos. Seguramente la política de Royal Mail es que, aun así, las metan en el sistema, pero sospecho que se las llevan a casa a escondidas. No lo pienso demasiado porque tengo ganas de volver a casa y masturbarme.

En mi habitación, la película ha terminado de descargarse. No la veo porque, ahora mismo, mi pene es un volcán reprimido, o una vieja presa, o una nube negra, o una chocolatina Bounty derritiéndose.

Entro en www.girlsoncam.com, me pongo DRPOLLA7 de apodo y empiezo a chatear con ChochitoJvn.

ChochitoJvn: hola
Tú: hola
ChochitoJvn: no quiero dinero

Me siento ofendido y flácido. La chica parece joven y lleva un jersey de Mickey Mouse. Tiene las piernas al aire.

Tú: vale
ChochitoJvn: a que te dedicas?
Tú: voy al instituto

Me sorprende mi honestidad.

ChochitoJvn: yo tambien iba al instituto. tuve que dejarlo
Tú: por que?
ChochitoJvn: dinero. necesitabamos dinero. se puede ganar dinero metiendote cosas por el culo en Internet
Tú: hummm... entonces no deberias intentar sacarme dinero?
ChochitoJvn: no importa. me toca pasarme todos los dias delante del ordenador me pagues o no me pagues

Enciende un cigarro. Tiene los ojos como los de un gato viejo.

ChochitoJvn: que quieres que haga?
Tú: me da igual, lo que tu quieras

ChochitoJvn se quita el tanga bermellón. Es una primera vez sin precedentes. Las chicas nunca se quitan la ropa interior en los chats públicos. Después, se queda ahí sentada, fumándose el cigarro, con los muslos abiertos como el mar Rojo. Soy Moisés.

Me pongo un calcetín de Keith en la polla. Le he cogido el gusto a utilizarlos como venganza. Estoy vengando en secreto la muerte de Margaret Clamwell a través de la masturbación de guerrilla.

Cuatro minutos después, el calcetín está lleno y yo vacío.

ChochitoJvn: has terminado?
Tú: si gracias
ChochitoJvn: de nada. me prometes una cosa?
Tú: vale
ChochitoJvn: por favor estudia mucho en el instituto

Se desconecta.

Eso resulta desconcertante. Para orientarme, escribo el borrador de un e-mail que enviaré cuando esté seguro de que Amadeus Hall ha leído mi carta.

<para:rainbowsandfireflies@hotmail.co.uk>

Re: desgracia

Querida Abby:

Te escribo para felicitarte por tu nueva adquisición, ¡un feto!

Kiera me lo contó ayer. Siento que tus padres te hayan castigado y que no puedas ir al viaje de Psicología el día 12 ni a la fiesta en la casa de campo el 22. Estoy seguro de que habrá otras fiestas cuando ya no estés embarazada, ¡y serán igual de divertidas!

También quería confirmarte que el bebé no es mío porque no follamos. Sí te metí los dedos, pero estoy seguro al noventa y cinco por cien de que no tenían semen, así que el bebé no puede ser mío. Por favor, ¡no le digas a nadie que soy el padre de tu hijo! Si lo haces, iremos al programa de Jeremy Kyle, haremos una prueba de ADN y todo el mundo se enterará de que eres una mentirosa. Ya sabes lo que piensa Jeremy de los mentirosos. Sería una experiencia humillante para los dos (pero sobre todo para ti).

¡Ah! Y además tienes ladillas, Abby. ¡Me las has pegado! Lo sé porque te vi rascarte la ingle cuando estábamos bebiendo con el embudo de cerveza, por eso se te cayó y te la echaste toda por la camiseta. Intenté afeitarme el pelo púbico y limpiar la zona infectada con lejía y un estropajo de aluminio, pero no ha funcionado. Después de una breve visita, la doctora Sarah Mathers me recetó la loción Permethrin 1%. ¡Te la recomiendo!

Abby, aunque me pegaste las ladillas e indirectamente me has dejado sin vello público y es muy probable que les cuentes a tus amigos que te he dejado embarazada, espero que pases un buen verano y tengas una buena gestación.

Atentamente,

JASPER J. WOLF

El e-mail tiene tres propósitos: con suerte, convencerá a Abby de que soy inocente de haber escrito la carta; me eximirá de la paternidad si al final resulta que sí la dejé embarazada y le hará creer que no sufre la maldición de las ladillas sola. Aunque no sea cierto.

Me parece que Abby es sugestionable, así que, como Julia, se creerá las cosas que le cuento.

Decido no enseñarle el e-mail a Tenaya porque probablemente pondrá objeciones éticas.

8

Son las 7:09 y Mamá intenta despertarme con la mano. Me la ha puesto en el hombro. Me enfado porque es martes, el primer día real de las vacaciones que nos dan para estudiar, así que no tengo que levantarme a las 7:09.

—No, Mamá, estoy de vacaciones, no tengo que levantarme —le explico.

Por un instante pienso en utilizar técnicas de disuasión más agresivas (insultos).

—Sí, Jasper, tienes que levantarte.

—Que no, Mamá. Déjame.

—Han llamado del instituto. Venga, siéntate.

Me siento. Aún tengo legañas en el ojo izquierdo. Solo me salen legañas en el ojo izquierdo. Papá las llamaba migajas de luna. A veces acumulaba tantas mientras dormía que por las mañanas iba ciego.

—¿Conocías a una chica que se llama Tabitha Mowai, Jasper? —me pregunta Mamá.

—No, Mamá. No conozco a ninguna Tabitha Mowai. ¿Puedo volver a dormirme ya?

—Han llamado del instituto porque quieren que vayáis esta mañana. Van a organizarle un funeral. Se ahorcó anoche.

A veces Mamá me deja decir cosas insensibles sin que me dé cuenta de que son insensibles. Espera hasta que he terminado de hablar para dejar claro por qué son insensibles. Creo que lo disfruta en secreto. Una vez me dejó hablar durante tres minutos sobre que el sobrino de Keith no sabía nada de las calles, ni de bandas ni de drogas (no es que yo sepa mucho), de modo que no debería abrir la boca para hablar de esos temas. Entonces me dijo que el sobrino de Keith había perdido a su hermano en una pelea de bandas y que a él le habían disparado varias veces, como a 50 Cent o Eminem.

Ojalá Mamá se casara con Eminem. Rapearía sobre cuánto me quiere. Mi pistola y yo siempre estaremos aquí para ti, hijo. Qué bonito.

Sale de la habitación sin decir nada más. Me quedo, solo y en silencio, atormentándome por mi insensibilidad.

Decido llamar a Tenaya para que me dé más detalles sobre el incidente.

—Hola —digo.

—Hola. ¿Te han llamado del instituto?

La voz le suena húmeda.

—Sí. ¿Por qué lloras? ¿La conocías?

—No, pero es triste.

—Muere gente todos los días. Lo ves en la televisión y no lloras siempre.

—Esto es diferente. Iba a nuestro instituto.

—Pero no la conocías. Ni siquiera sabías qué pinta tenía.

Tenaya suspira.

—¿Por qué lo hizo? —pregunto.

—¡Ya sabes por qué lo hizo! —Empieza a preocuparme que tal vez yo tenga algo que ver—. Era la chica del bate de béisbol.

Qué alivio, no tengo nada que ver con la chica del bate de béisbol. Scott Jeppersen es el responsable de su reciente y humillante ascenso a la fama hace dos semanas. No sé cómo la convencieron para darle un uso más interesante a un bate de béisbol, en directo y ante una webcam. Por supuesto, Scott Jeppersen, el único miembro del público, decidió utilizar la grabadora de su teléfono. Vi el vídeo porque Jonah lo tenía en su móvil. No era más que un vídeo porno borroso en el que salía una chica anormalmente joven, todavía sin tetas de verdad. Bueno, no es que las tetas del porno sean de verdad.

—De eso hace siglos.

—Pero se sigue hablando del tema. Alguien le llenó la taquilla de bates de béisbol.

—¿En serio? Se habrá gastado un pastón. —Tenaya no responde—. ¿Cómo lo hizo?

—Se colgó con la media de rugby de Scott, en el garaje.

—Interesante. ¿Una media de rugby es lo bastante larga para rodear el cuello y una viga?

—Nos vemos luego, Jasper. Adiós.

Cuelga.

Me pongo los pantalones del instituto y me siento en la cama.

Es extraño pensar en lo fácil que resulta ponerle fin a tu vida. Es posiblemente la decisión más importante que puedes tomar y, aun así, requiere muy poco esfuerzo. No hay que rellenar formularios ni ahorrar dinero ni estudiar en la universidad. Para cruzar las líneas imaginarias trazadas en el mundo se necesita mucho más. Pasaportes, visados, dinero. En cambio, si quieres morir, solo tienes que atarte una media de rugby alrededor del cuello y desapareces para siempre. Llevarán tu cuerpo al crematorio, y allí el tío Eb se pondrá a gritar, Mamá se desmayará y pondrán a Leonard Cohen mientras te conviertes en cenizas.

Scott Jeppersen debe de estar muriéndose de la culpa. En cierto modo es un asesino, pero para él seguramente es peor que para Keith porque no tenía intención de hacerlo. Scott Jeppersen no planeó matar a Tabitha Mowai, por eso no podrá integrarse como Keith. No habrá leído ningún libro sobre cómo cometer un asesinato y después actuar como si no lo hubieras hecho. Además, todo el mundo sabrá que es un asesino, mientras que nadie sabe que Keith asesinó a Margaret Clamwell. Excepto yo, y Tenaya. Aunque Tenaya solo cuenta la mitad porque no está del todo convencida.

Puede que Scott sea el asesino, pero toda la gente que vio el vídeo y pensó que era divertido aunque bastante desagradable es cómplice del asesinato. Si nadie hubiera visto el vídeo ni lo hubiera pasado, Tabitha Mowai probablemente seguiría viva, yo seguiría durmiendo y Tenaya no estaría llorando. Sin embargo, Tabitha también tuvo su parte de culpa. La perdición le llegó a causa de su trágico defecto: la falta de modestia. Shakespeare lo llama *hamartia*. Para que se cumpliera el destino de Tabitha se necesitaba su *hamartia*, pero por sí sola esta no habría sido suficiente.

Me quito los pantalones y los calzoncillos y cruzo el rellano para darme una ducha. Keith me ve.

—Joder, macho, ponte algo.

Le sonrío.

—Lo siento, Keith.

Me devuelve la sonrisa. Tal vez sea pedófilo además de asesino.

En la ducha siento el agua bailando sobre mi piel, sé que estoy vivo. Tabitha Mowai no lo está, aunque podría estarlo. Sus padres dirán que debería estarlo, pero el debería no existe. A pesar de que estoy triste por su familia, al mismo tiempo ella me da envidia. No me da envidia que haya muerto, sino que haya satisfecho su curiosidad por la muerte. Porque será así, ¿no? La verdad es que no lo sé. Creo que, cuando la gente se suicida, no es solamente para escapar de una presión emocional abrumadora. Solo se trata de dejar crecer la curiosidad por la muerte hasta que es más grande que la presión emocional abrumadora. Probablemente sientan una pequeña excitación en el momento justo antes de morir. Como antes de abrir los regalos de Navidad o justo antes de follar con alguien con quien nunca has follado.

Me enrollo una toalla a la cintura para salir del baño por si acaso Keith se ha escondido tras alguna puerta con su cámara. Me lío un cigarro y voy al instituto.

A menudo salgo sin comer nada por la mañana. El desayuno es la comida menos importante del día para la gente que fuma.

El instituto tiene un aspecto particularmente poco interesante antes del funeral, como si lamentara la pérdida, igual que los alumnos que ahora lloran cuando unas semanas antes se habían reído al ver el vídeo. Las cristaleras sin limpiar parecen haberse vestido con más polvo aún para presentar sus respetos, y los suelos de madera plástica brillan como unos ojos tristes. Todo el mundo guarda silencio, en todas partes. Silencio absoluto, con las cabezas agachadas y las manos sobre el regazo. No creo que nadie llegue a entenderlo.

Los profesores dicen que la gente (sobre todo las chicas y los homosexuales) se emociona especialmente cuando alguien muere porque eso les recuerda a los seres queridos que han «perdido». Yo creo que la gente se emociona porque se da cuenta de que un día también morirá, algo que se suele olvidar con facilidad. Al final, esto provoca que la gente recurra a la filosofía un tanto arrogante de vivir cada día como si fuera el último. Luego, un par de días después, vuelven a olvidarlo. En Occidente se cree que emborracharse es lo más divertido que se puede hacer, por eso se bebe tanto en los velatorios. A mí me parece más divertido el sexo, así que, si alguna vez voy a un velatorio, probablemente intente pillar. No resultará difícil porque las chicas se sentirán vulnerables. Solo tendré un ligero sentimiento de culpa cuando me corra en sus caras borrachas y llorosas.

Estoy sentado al lado de Tenaya en el vestíbulo, en una de las incómodas sillas de plástico azul unidas en filas como si las obligaran a darse la mano contra su voluntad. No se nota que no se ha maquillado, aunque yo sí me doy cuenta. Sigue siendo bastante guapa. Mantiene su 8,5. Yo soy un 7.

Llega Scott Jeppersen. Llora con la cara prácticamente tapada por un pañuelo. Como asesino, tendrá que acostumbrarse a ocultar su identidad.

—Pobre Scott —dice Tenaya.

—¿Qué? La semana pasada dijiste que era un gilipollas.

—Es un gilipollas, pero ahora tendrá que cargar con la muerte de una chica.

—Si compartes vídeos de una chica que se masturba con objetos deportivos —Ana Korsakov me mira, enfadada—, no puedes pensar que a la chica le va a hacer gracia ser el centro de atención.

—Sí, pero no creo que él quisiera que ella se matara.

—Homicidio involuntario, entonces. Cinco años. Ella seguirá muerta y él seguirá teniendo parte de la culpa.

Alguien tose. El director ha subido a la tarima con su traje de rayas y su típica corbata roja (el señor Hutchinson es del Partido Laborista, algunos profesores hacen bromas sobre el tema). Lleva un taco de cartulinas amarillas llenas de notas. Me pregunto qué pondrá. Probablemente, solo los datos principales, que son:

- ✓ Tabitha Mowai, de origen afrocaribeño, comedor del instituto gratuito.
- ✓ Masturbación con bate de béisbol, YouTube.
- ✓ Scott Jeppersen, asesino (no de los que van a la cárcel).

Tal vez haya también algún consejo para el discurso:

- ✓ Evitar palabras que puedan parecer referencias al béisbol (por ejemplo, base).
- ✓ Referirse a Jeppersen como «el novio» y no como «el asesino».
- ✓ No culpar a los estudiantes, aunque son culpables.
- ✓ Intentar parecer sincero, como si conocieras bien a la chica. Tomar como referencia la relación entre el profesor Dumbledore y Harry Potter. Hablar de ella como «un miembro activo de la comunidad estudiantil».

Mucha gente llora o deja que se le llenen los ojos de lágrimas. Estadísticamente, es muy probable que esa gente no conociera a la chica, o que la conociera solo de haber visto el vídeo, no de verdad. Todo esto me resulta extraño. No entiendo los acontecimientos. Creo que soy un ser humano roto. Soy parapléjico emocionalmente y todo el instituto está jugando al fútbol.

Como estoy preocupado por mi discapacidad, solo pillo algunas de las palabras trilladas que el señor Hutchinson utiliza en el discurso, como «querida», «preciosa», «inteligente» y «llena de vida». En retrospectiva, parece que fuera candidata a delegada de primera clase, solo que no fue delegada porque el señor Hutchinson se lo está inventando todo. Seguramente, sus notas dirían que era «mediocre».

Tras la reunión, algunos van al pub. Tenaya y yo no queremos ir al pub. Tenaya y yo vamos a su casa. Es una enorme casa victoriana, con hiedra trepando por la fachada delantera como los asquerosos dedos de un pedófilo. Sus padres pidieron una hipoteca impresionante para poder comprarla, y por eso han tenido que reformarla ellos mismos y pasarse del tabaco normal al de liar. Su padre es rechoncho y rosado y su madre padece un trastorno, lo que significa que es muy rara. Los dos llevan zapatos Crocs y huelen a romero.

A veces su madre pone vino en la tetera. Otras veces se mea en el césped y comenta que lo hace para animar a la hierba.

Estamos sentados en su sótano con una tetera entre los dos. El vapor sale del pitorro con indecisión, como si el aire fuera un castillo enemigo. Tenaya ha dejado de llorar, pero tiene la mirada fija en su té. Pienso en tocarle los párpados para notar que siguen húmedos.

—No puedo creerme que ya no esté —comenta.

No digo nada. Yo sí que me lo creo porque suicidarse es muy fácil. Hasta un perro podría hacerlo.

Una vez, Mamá me dio una charla sobre el suicidio. Creo que fue porque Mamá a veces pasa por periodos depresivos y le preocupa que yo los padezca por herencia genética. El único rasgo que he heredado de ella es el cinismo.

—No te suicides nunca, es un acto muy egoísta —me dijo.

Yo le contesté que la egoísta era ella por prohibirme suicidarme porque, en algún momento de mi vida, puede que sufra un dolor físico o emocional insoportable. Parecía disgustada así que le puse la mano en el hombro y le dije que por el momento no sufría ningún dolor físico o emocional insoportable. Mamá aseguró que ella tampoco.

Le digo a Tenaya que no quiero hablar de la muerte porque es aburrido. Le pregunto si le apetece jugar al Scrabble y me dice que sí, así que voy a buscar el tablero que está debajo de su cama.

Su estado de ánimo no le deja formar palabras que no sean macabras, como *sangre*, *ataúd* o *podrido*, aunque no le den la máxima puntuación. Yo pongo PESTAÑA, ella pone ADIÓS; yo pongo JUEZ, ella pone JASPER. Le digo que no puede poner eso. Ella me pregunta que quién soy y le respondo que no lo sé. Gano yo.

Puntuación final:
Jasper: 315
Tenaya: 185

Empieza a llover y le digo a Tenaya que me marcho. Fuera, el cielo es cemento, las gotas resuenan al caer en la acera y se esconden en mis zapatos. La lluvia huele a bosque y se come la familiaridad de las calles. Cuanto más me mojo, más consciente soy. Consciente de que estoy vivo. Tabitha Mowai, no. Margaret Clamwell, no. Tengo las mejillas entumecidas y sonrosadas. Las de Tabitha estarán pálidas y acartonadas. Me pregunto si a los muertos les saldrán moratones si les das un puñetazo. Me muerdo el brazo alrededor de la muñeca y me dejo una marca a modo de reloj. Duele porque estoy vivo, todo esto resulta muy desconcertante, pero sé que aún me esperan muchas cosas, toda una vida. A Tabitha Mowai, no. Eso es aún más triste que los fetiches de la anorexia o que la pedofilia o que la gente que llora porque se siente culpable por ver vídeos porno de alguien que se ha suicidado.

9

Me levanto a las 10:20. El sol ya se ha despertado y se ha instalado en mi habitación. Todo es luminoso y cálido, como en un invernadero. Abro las ventanas e inspiro, el aire siempre huele a tierra porque nuestra vecina es una señora mayor que tiene un huerto en el patio trasero. A veces le da tomates a Mamá. Mamá dice que admira a nuestra vecina por mantener una actitud proactiva aunque haya perdido a su marido. Dice que las mujeres pueden arreglárselas solas tras la muerte de sus maridos, pero que los hombres no pueden seguir adelante solos tras la muerte de sus esposas. Eso le pasó al padre de Mamá. Cuando murió la abuela se le llenaban las uñas de mugre y se le olvidaba ducharse o afeitarse. A veces se pasaba días sin comer para ahorrar lo suficiente para visitar a una prostituta vietnamita que le recordaba a una chica que conoció durante la guerra.

Mamá está trabajando y Keith sigue durmiendo porque ha hecho el turno de noche. Preparo té y me saco un cigarro y el periódico al porche. En portada hablan detalladamente del secuestro y asesinato de una chica. El mundo se ha olvidado de Tabitha porque el mundo sigue adelante pase lo que pase. El mundo es un asesino cruel. No se detiene. Los padres de Tabitha seguramente sí se han detenido. Se sentirán tremendamente culpables por todo durante mucho tiempo. Cada vez que la señora Mowai vaya a coger su Conejito Rampante verá la cara de su hija y se ahogará en olas de culpa y tristeza.

En el periódico sale una foto de la chica, de antes de ser asesinada. Tiene los ojos grandes, de color roble. Pienso que probablemente la haya asesinado Keith porque no hay muchos asesinos en esta ciudad. Me apunto su nombre en el brazo. Me será útil después.

Vuelvo arriba y enciendo el ordenador. La sensación de la moqueta entre los dedos de los pies es reconfortante. Abby no estuvo en el funeral, sus padres deben de haber recibido mi carta y estará castigada. Eso significa que ha llegado el momento de enviar el e-mail.

Le doy a ENVIAR y me reclino en la silla. Abby Hall es un gran danés al que no me apetece dar de comer o adiestrar. Tengo los «remordimientos del comprador».

Aunque vi a Abby rascándose la ingle, no puedo estar seguro de que tenga ladillas. Abby no me pegó las ladillas ni me afeité el pelo púbico ni fui al médico. Me sentía culpable de que Abby sufriera tal desgracia y supuse que le vendría bien saber que otros sufrían como ella.

Es hora de tomar más té. El té contiene teína, que te mantiene alerta pero relajado. Lo acabo de leer en la caja de bolsitas de té.

El timbre de la puerta emite su zumbido melancólico justo cuando el agua hierve. Como ni Mamá ni Keith pueden responder, la responsabilidad de contestar al teléfono o de abrir la puerta recae sobre mí. A veces, cuando nado en mares de soledad, esta tarea me resulta terapéutica.

—Buenos días. ¿Ha aceptado a Dios en su vida?

Parpadeo y me quedo mirando al hombre.

—Eso suena serio —respondo—. Será mejor que entres.

El hombre tiene poco más de treinta años. Lleva el pelo rubio muy corto, bien repeinado sobre el contorno de su cráneo. Mi voz interior favorece una actitud confiada al ver el par de ojos azul turquesa y el traje entallado.

Acepta un té sin azúcar y nos acomodamos en dos sillones adyacentes.

—Actualmente, ¿mantiene alguna relación con Dios? —me pregunta el hombre.

Tiene una voz agradable y aflautada. Siento que puedo confiar en él. Espero que no abuse de mi confianza.

—Sufro trastornos de ansiedad, así que mantener relaciones estables resulta difícil.

—Jehová nos quiere, seamos como seamos.

Da un sorbo al té en mi taza de Harry Potter y me pasa un ejemplar de *La Atalaya*.

Los testigos de Jehová creen que, tras la batalla cataclísmica del final de los tiempos, 144.000 personas subirán al cielo. A esta burguesía espiritual la denominan «el pequeño rebaño». Tampoco creen en el infierno. Estos son los únicos datos de los testigos de Jehová que me interesan.

Keith los llama «los que incordian a Dios».

—¿Cuánta gente crees que irá al cielo? —le pregunto.

Me mira, mira el té y vuelve a mirarme.

—Unos cuantos elegidos.

—Pero ¿cuántos exactamente?

No estoy siendo pedante, solo sondeo.

—Ciento cuarenta y cuatro mil —responde.

Creo que está avergonzado. Nos observamos mutuamente.

—Hay seis mil setecientos millones de personas en el mundo —le digo. Asiente—. Eso me entristece. ¿Quieres un cigarro?

—No fumamos.

Los cultos son muy opresivos. Excepto el de la familia Manson. Ellos probaron muchas cosas interesantes.

Le digo que espere un momento y saco el teléfono. Esta es la cuenta que hago con la calculadora del móvil:

144.000 / 6.700.000.000 = 0,000021492537313432835

0,000021 × 100 = 0,0021

—Un cero coma cero cero cero cero veintiuno por ciento de la gente que vive ahora irá al cielo —le comento mientras le pongo una mano en la pierna, pero me siento incómodo y la retiro.

—Creo que debería marcharme —responde.

—Lo entiendo.

Observo su encantadora cabeza rubia desaparecer en la distancia. Qué hombre tan valiente. Debe resultar difícil lidiar con el conocimiento de que existe el paraíso pero que lo más probable es que no va a ir.

En dos días me habré olvidado de él, como todo el mundo se ha olvidado de Tabitha Mowai, como todo el mundo al final se olvida de todo.

10

Cuando nos reunimos delante del instituto esta mañana, Abby Hall no estaba. Me sentí liberado, un triunfador.

Una adivina me dijo el año pasado en Brighton que lograría todo lo que me propusiera. Quizá esté empezando a cumplirse. Quizá saque cuatro sobresalientes y escriba un premio Booker y me tire a Georgia Treely. Solo que todo esto no pasará porque me faltan motivación, talento y encanto.

Vamos en el autobús. Huele a señora mayor y a mareo. Tenaya está leyendo a Sylvia Plath y permanece en silencio, incansable. El aire es chocolate. Todo el mundo tiene la boca ocupada con cotilleos sexuales o comiendo patatas de vinagre y sal. Estamos parados, pero ya se me empieza a revolver el estómago.

El conductor del autobús se presenta, se llama Ben; intenta ganarse nuestro favor con humor («¿Qué hizo el autobús cuando chocó con la panadería? Pan») y arranca. El ruido del motor, unido al movimiento ebrio del autobús, crea un suave veneno que convierte mis tripas en un dolor punzante.

Vamos a Plymouth en una excursión de Psicología. Es un viaje optativo «divertido», como premio por el duro trabajo que supondrán los exámenes. Nos quedaremos en un hostal y nos llevarán a una charla con varios asesinos y violadores. Seguramente intentarán darle a la charla algún giro interesante para sorprendernos o divertirnos. Creo que me aburriré y me pondré en plan cínico porque estaremos escuchando a gente mala que ha hecho cosas malas cuando preferiría escuchar a gente buena que ha hecho cosas buenas, aunque eso es menos útil en Psicología. O, al menos, para el tipo de psicología que damos en el instituto. Debería haber optativas, Psicología Positiva y Negativa, porque nuestra Psicología consiste básicamente en estudiar a asesinos en serie y esquizofrénicos, mientras que yo preferiría estudiar a gente enamorada y niños que han superado el cáncer.

Algunas chicas quizá encuentren atractivos a los asesinos. Ana Korsakov dijo una vez que Jeffrey Dahmer «estaba muy bueno» y que tenía «un aire misterioso». Es un estadounidense que mató a diecisiete personas e intentó convertirlas en zombies sexuales. También puede que alguna de las chicas encuentre atractivos a los violadores porque sé al menos de tres que fantasean con ser violadas. Por ejemplo, cuando me tiré a Sarah Ivor, intentó que la asfixiara.

El segundo día también visitaremos un museo del crimen.

La señora Norton está leyendo la lista con una voz que parece un lloriqueo acolchado. Aunque no es profesora de Psicología, viene porque uno de los profesores está en la boda civil de su hermana. El profesor de Psicología que no está en una boda gay se llama señor Mandalay y hoy se le ve particularmente nervioso. Al señor Mandalay le gusta la música folk, divagar y las noches junto al fuego. Me enteré de todo esto una noche que Tenaya y yo estábamos borrachos y nos pusimos a buscar a los profesores solteros en webs de citas.

—¿Kimberley Acheman? —lee la señora Norton.

—Sí.

—¿Sarah Asti?

—Sí.

—¿Imran Balki?

—Sí, señor.

Hay una pequeña explosión de risas. La señora Norton está sorda.

—¿James Falk?

—Sí.

—¿Abby Hall? —Pausa embarazosa—. ¿Abby?

A las chicas de la fila de atrás les da un ataque de risa.

—Tiene un permiso de maternidad, señor.

La señora Norton murmura «¡Infieles!», y sigue leyendo la lista. Me siento un poco culpable, pero tampoco me agobia el tema.

—¿Ha funcionado? —pregunta Tenaya.

—Parece que sí.

—¿Sabe que lo hiciste tú?

—Le envié un mail para desmarcarme de la carta. No me ha contestado. Imagino que sus padres le han prohibido utilizar el ordenador.

—Se enterará.

Tenaya vuelve a sumergirse en el fino libro con un sutil giro de la cabeza.

Abby Hall no se enterará y, aunque se entere, no importa. Ahora mismo solo me interesan las consecuencias a corto plazo, es decir, un viaje sin Abby y una casa de campo sin Abby. Libertad para llevar a cabo el Plan Georgia. Me encargaré de las consecuencias del tema Abby cuando se presenten. Este tipo de pensamiento a corto plazo se llama miopía. Es peligroso.

—¿Sabes qué? —pregunta Ping con la cara metida entre los dos asientos que tenemos delante.

—¿Qué? —le pregunto.

En respuesta, saca una enorme bolsa con autocierre llena de marihuana. Sonrío.

—El viaje estará genial —me dice antes de darse la vuelta.

La emoción indirectamente derivada de las drogas disminuye durante las siguientes dos horas. Tenaya termina el libro y se queda dormida apoyada en mi hombro. Lío una lata entera de tabaco y una de las chicas de detrás amenaza con contárselo a la señora Norton hasta que Ping se levanta y dice:

—¿Qué es eso, Susie? ¿Exceso de equipaje?

(Ping se lo comió a Susie Smith en una fiesta el año pasado y después lo describió como un «cuello de pavo».) Cuando Ping se duerme, envío mensajes de «me pones cachondo» desde su móvil a sus primas. Me como una barrita de cereales Nutri-Grain y me quedo dormido de aburrimiento.

* * *

Urgh. Plymouth es una blitzkrieg de cemento horrible. Si fuera una persona, sería de las que comen lo mismo todos los días y se masturban con fotos de trenes de vapor. Todos los edificios parecen haber sido diseñados por un urbanista maníaco-depresivo.

—Todos en fila —dice la señora Norton—. La universidad queda cerca.

Son las 11:47. Aquí todo es del color del aburrimiento y de la rendición. Me recuerda a Mamá y a Keith porque son una pareja extremadamente resignada. No intentan elevarse espiritualmente ni ellos ni a su primogénito (las dos hijas de Keith trabajan de bailarinas eróticas en Birmingham), y se les ve particularmente satisfechos viviendo en las casas más pequeñas del barrio menos verde de las afueras y viendo repeticiones de capítulos granulados de *Holby City* cada noche. Corren sobre una cinta que no les pone en forma. Por suerte, mi madre no me carga a mí su fracaso, así que seguiré intentando mejorar hasta que pueda permitirme beber zumo sin diluir. Eso es lo que distingue a un hombre hecho y derecho.

Cuando bajamos del autobús, Tenaya dice «perfecto» mientras observa el paisaje. La señora Norton sonríe, pero Ping suelta un «la hostia» que le borra la sonrisa.

Las únicas personas que veo mientras caminamos tienen la cara del color de la arcilla seca. No levantan la vista del suelo. La acera. Nuestro avance en doble fila es una marcha fúnebre.

Cuando llegamos a la universidad, un hombre bajito y débil con ojos amables nos lleva a una sala larga con una pantalla de proyecciones. Sonríe mucho, no solo a las chicas. Nos sentamos en las sillas verdes de plástico a la espera de nuevas instrucciones.

—¿Nos vamos ya? —pregunta Ping.

—Quiero ver al violador —le digo.

—¿Por qué?

—El comportamiento pervertido es interesante.

—Eres muy raro, tío.

El violador resulta ser un hombre alto y delgado, con la piel como el Blu-Tack y las manos inquietas. Cuando habla, las palabras le hacen daño. Me hace sentir un individuo fuerte, completo. Creo que eso es parte del propósito del viaje.

—Ho-ho-hola, me llamo John. Hice algo muy malo y hoy os voy a hablar de eso y podréis aprender de mí y ayudar a otra gente cuando crezcáis.

Tenaya toma apuntes. Ha escrito NO VIOLAR en su cuaderno.

—¿A-alguien sabe qué hice?

Sacude la cabeza. Varias chicas de otros institutos levantan la mano. Ping también la levanta.

Parece que el violador no sabe que teníamos programas en la silla.

—¿S-s-sí? —le dice el violador a Ping.

—Pedofa.

Todos nos reímos. Las chicas del internado nos miran con

rechazo. La señora Norton aprieta la mandíbula y se le salen los ojos. El violador mira al suelo.

—Pu-pues no. Vi-vi-violé a... Era...

—¿Violaste a una niña? Si violaste a una niña, sigues siendo un pedofa —afirma Ping.

La señora Norton le coge por la capucha y lo saca de la sala. Todo el mundo se ríe. John el Violador fuerza una sonrisa. Todo esto hasta me divierte un poco.

—¡Eso es asqueroso! —grita alguien.

—N-n-no violé a una niña.

Una de las chicas del internado, que está sentada a nuestra izquierda, levanta la mano. Todas llevan americanas rojo fuego con pequeños árboles estampados en los bolsillos del pecho. Un porcentaje sorprendentemente alto de ellas luce coletas rubias que se rizan como chorros de lejía.

—¿S-s-sí? —le dice al brazo incandescente.

—¿Por qué lo hiciste? —pregunta la chica—. Es horrible.

—No te preocupes, nadie se molestaría en hacértelo a ti —grita Jonah.

Más risas. Risas como piedras escondidas que solo aparecen para que los violadores que hablan en público tropiecen. La señora Norton hace gestos como una loca para que Jonah salga, así que Tenaya y yo nos levantamos también y nos quedamos todos fuera junto al bordillo, sin expresión alguna.

—¿Adónde vamos? —pregunta Ping.

—No lo sé. Ese tío era asqueroso —dice Jonah.

—No hemos visto al asesino —comento con tristeza. Aunque ya conozco a Keith, pensé que sería útil compararlo con otros asesinos—. Quería ver al asesino.

Antes del viaje, el señor Mandalay nos repartió unos folletos titulados «Asesinos en serie: Guía de estudio». En ellos se explicaba una teoría llamada «La tríada de la sociopatía», según la cual las características comunes de la niñez de los asesinos son la crueldad animal, una obsesión por el fuego y mojar la cama persistentemente después de los cinco años. He probado varias formas de obtener información sobre la actitud de Keith respecto a estos temas.

Crueldad animal
En una reunión familiar el año pasado le di una patada a Missy, la perra de la abuela, y le susurré a Keith: «Menuda bola de mierda asquerosa, ¿verdad, Keith?». Me sonrió. Porque le gustó. Porque es un asesino.

Obsesión por el fuego
Cuando Mamá enciende fuego en el salón, Keith se enfada porque dice que debería dejar que lo hiciera él. Intenta esconder su afición a encender fuegos diciendo que «a las mujeres se les da como el culo».

Mojar la cama
Esta fue difícil. Al final, tuve que tragarme el orgullo por el bien de la investigación. Me supo a sucio, a vómito rancio. Cuando Keith bajó una mañana, lo llevé aparte para tener una conversación de hombre a semihombre. Le encantan. Le confesé que había mojado la cama y le pregunté si era normal en un chico de mi edad. Me aseguró que no pasaba nada. Porque él mojaba la cama continuamente durante la adolescencia. Porque es un asesino.

Encendemos un cigarro y vamos a un bar enfrente de la universidad. Se llama Ezee. Las notas de jazz se intercalan con el silencio. Jonah pide las cervezas porque es el único que tiene dieciocho. Nos sentamos para tomárnoslas.

—¿Qué queréis hacer esta noche? —pregunta Ping.

—Podemos quedarnos y salir mañana.

—Pero ¿por qué no quieres salir hoy, sangre de mi sangre?

—A Jonah le ha dado por llamarme «sangre de mi sangre» porque, casualmente, le sirve tanto para referirse a nuestra amistad como para reírse de mi polvo de borrachera—. Abby no ha venido.

—Eso, ¿por qué no ha venido? —pregunta Tenaya en plan burlón, mirándome con su cara redonda.

—¿Va a Psicología? —pregunta Ping.

—Se sienta a tu lado —le digo.

—Lo siento, sangre de mi sangre. No me había dado cuenta porque estaba ocupado estudiando mientras tú jugabas con su chocho a ver quién aguantaba más tiempo sin apartar la vista.

Todos se ríen. Ping no es de los que atienden. Empiezo a acostumbrarme a que se partan a mi costa. No me puedo creer que hiciera sexo rojo con Abby Hall. Hice sexo rojo con Abby Hall. Abby Hall. Sexo rojo.

Cuando nos terminamos las cervezas caras, Jonah va a comprar una caja de cerveza barata y vodka a una tienda y esperamos fuera de la universidad. Cuando sale, la señora Norton tiene un aspecto sorprendentemente equilibrado y sereno a pesar de la terrible experiencia que había sufrido antes. Ella y el señor Mandalay nos llevan a donde vamos a dormir, el albergue Hope House Hotel.

—Buenos días —saluda la señora Norton a la recepcionista—. Tenemos una reserva para dieciocho, a nombre de St. Mary.

La recepcionista teclea y revuelve algunos papeles antes de llegar a una conclusión.

—Lo siento, no me aparece nada.

—¡Pero si hemos reservado!

—Lo siento, señora, no puedo ayudarla.

La señora Norton y la joven recepcionista se quedan mirándose un rato.

—Peter, haz algo —dice la señora Norton. Se le están hinchando las manos.

—Creo que hicimos una reserva —susurra el señor Mandalay.

En la cara de la recepcionista aparece una enorme sonrisa.

—¡Era broma! —dice. La señora Norton y el sentido del humor no se llevan muy bien—. Bienvenidos al Hope House Hotel.

* * *

Estamos sentados en la moqueta de la habitación de ocho. Ana tiene la cabeza apoyada sobre el regazo vaquero de Ping y Jonah está liando cigarros en calzoncillos. Tiene los músculos de las pantorrillas delgados pero bien definidos. Eso ha sonado gay.

Algo sorprendente de Jonah es que es un católico devoto, a pesar de su promiscuidad. Cada vez que Jonah folla, después se ducha con agua fría para «limpiarse». Dice que esa es la única razón por la que no ha follado al aire libre. Como prueba de su fe, Jonah dejó que uno de los chicos del curso siguiente le tatuara la Virgen María en la espalda con una máquina que compró en eBay por un billete de cinco. El chico solo tenía tinta negra así que le hizo el contorno nada más. A veces, cuando liga, Jonah deja que la chica le pinte el tatuaje con rotuladores de colores.

—¿Cuál es el plan? —pregunta Jonah.

—No quiero salir —le digo.

—¿Alguien tiene vasos?

—Sí, he comprado un huevo de vasos.

Jonah saca la botella de vodka de la bolsa de plástico. Echamos unos tragos. Ana no quiere. Es como un fuego que me abrasa la garganta al bajar.

—No me gusta el vodka —dice Ping.

—A nadie le gusta el vodka, imbécil —le responde Jonah—. Ese es el tema.

Abrimos las cervezas para aliviar el ardor. Los dedos de Ana juguetean sobre la mano de Ping. Jonah ha puesto música en su iPhone.

Tenaya me dice que quiere salir a buscar tabaco, así que bajamos las escaleras de cemento y salimos por las puertas de contrachapado del albergue. La simpática recepcionista está fuera, fumándose un Richmond tranquilamente. Ping dice que el Richmond es el peor tabaco. Dice que son potentes para dejar a los hombres impotentes.

Fuma de forma muy sombría. Es el único aspecto sombrío que tiene, algo que solo se manifiesta mientras fuma. Resulta extraño ver cómo los pequeños gestos dejan ver una parte tan grande de la personalidad, como cuando Keith repite clichés sobre asesinatos o cuando Mamá les guiña el ojo a mis amigos. No se puede esconder toda la vergüenza.

—Hola —dice la recepcionista—. ¿Vais con el instituto?

—No —le contesto.

Nos alejamos y nos terminamos los cigarros con un rubor incómodo, hablar con gente que sonríe mucho cansa más que un triatlón.

11

Son las 8:45. En mi cabeza está tocando un grupo de mierda. Jonah acaba de intentar despertar a Ping quitándole el edredón y ha destapado a Ana, desnuda, enroscada alrededor del culo color café de Ping como una sanguijuela medio sexy. Ping se ha cagado en todo y Jonah se ha reído.

—Hora de desayunar —le dice Jonah.

Hoy lleva una camiseta blanca sin mangas y unos vaqueros negros muy ajustados. Su pelo es un nido de cera de ayer acosada por el fantasma de la almohada.

Bajamos al comedor, que es como la cafetería del instituto pero llena de gente con pinta de vagabundos y mochileros. Bufet de desayuno continental. Tenaya coge un cruasán y yo tostadas con mermelada. Algunos de los viejos se enfadan con Jonah porque se ha bebido toda la botella de leche que era para el café y lo está negando, a pesar de que las manchas blancas alrededor de la boca le delatan.

Nos sentamos a una de las largas mesas. Hombres sin afeitar matan a Jonah con la mirada. Igual nos toca pelearnos para salir. Ana sigue intentando coger la mano de Ping mientras él intenta comer. Es una especie de guerra no declarada. Aunque se están peleando, los dos actúan como si no, como cuando una chica te da besos en el cuello y tú le empujas sutilmente la cabeza hacia abajo para que te la chupe.

—He tenido un sueño rarísimo —dice Ana.

Dejo de escuchar.

* * *

Estamos en el museo del crimen. Ya llevamos aquí dos horas. He visto infinitos aparatos de tortura, porras antiguas, pistolas y objetos para esclavizar. Hace un rato, Jonah ha cogido una de las capuchas del Ku Klux Klan de una estantería, se la ha puesto y ha corrido hacia Imran gritando: «¡Se acerca tu fin!». Imran le ha dado un puñetazo y la señora Norton casi se desmaya. Ahora Jonah tiene un círculo de moho hinchado alrededor del ojo izquierdo.

Tenaya y yo observamos una vieja silla eléctrica de Estados Unidos. Tiene el apodo de «Chula amarilla». La placa informativa dice:

> **Primera Silla Eléctrica**
> Inventada por Alfred P. Southwick en 1887 como método de ejecución para sustituir la horca. Se le ocurrió cuando vio morir a un borracho por tocar unos cables que estaban al descubierto. Aún se utiliza en Estados Unidos.

—No puedo creer que aún la utilicen —dice Tenaya.

Me encojo de hombros.

—Yo sí —comento.

Junto a la silla hay una maqueta chapucera de Auschwitz dentro de una urna de cristal en forma de cubo. Ninguno de los objetos expuestos está ordenado de forma lógica. Al lado de Auschwitz exponen una de las exageradas pistolas de Bugsy Malone. El edificio huele a gato y a papel mojado.

—Auschwitz —dice Tenaya. En voz muy baja.

Sé que está pensando lo mismo que yo. Piensa en la excursión de Historia, cuando visitamos el campo. Cuando nos sentamos en un semicírculo de sillas de plástico y escuchamos cómo un superviviente nos narraba su experiencia, despacio. Se le veía tan frágil como una jaula de algodón de azúcar, con el fantasma borroso de un número en el brazo izquierdo. El señor Glover lloró. Tenaya me apretó la mano hasta que dejé de sentirla. Jonah experimentó algo no muy diferente a lo contrario de una experiencia religiosa.

La mayoría de la gente deambula por el museo tocando cosas con las manos y la nariz. Es algo que suele pasar en la vida. El año pasado, fuimos a la Tate y todo el mundo quería aparentar que le interesaba el arte pero lo único que querían de verdad era tocarlo. Se pasaron horas sobando las esculturas de mármol. Si algo he aprendido tras llevar vivo diecisiete años es que a la gente le encanta tocar cosas.

Cosas que a la gente le gusta tocar:

Coños
Cosas caras en las tiendas
Gelatina que aún no está lista
Mecheros
Cuellos
Cosas muertas
Perros
Cristal
Cicatrices
Piercings
Cosas que están en el suelo pero que no deberían estar ahí
Mofletes de niños
Nieve
Las rodillas de otros

Botones
Culos

A la gente también le gusta tocar la muerte. Lo hacen practicando rappel o viendo reportajes sobre Israel en las noticias. Tocar tiene que ver con la curiosidad. La curiosidad tiene que ver con la muerte.

Después de verlo todo, Jonah insiste en que vayamos a la tienda de regalos. Ahí venden gomas amarillas, sacapuntas y piedras enormes y brillantes. En todo pone MUSEO DEL CRIMEN DE PLYMOUTH. En un rincón de la sala hay una señora mayor sentada detrás de una caja registradora de plástico gris leyendo una novela rosa de Maeve Binchy y masajeándose las sienes en un movimiento orbital de los dedos, lento pero constante.

—Menuda mierda —dice Jonah.

Tira un abrecartas de plástico al montón.

La señora mayor hace una mueca. No levanta la vista.

—¿Podemos irnos ya? —pregunto.

Jonah no contesta. Se acerca a una estantería de reja de metal llena de artículos de broma. Polvos picapica, jabón negro, caramelos con sabor a meado. Los artículos de broma son los peores. A Jonah le encantan los artículos de broma. Se siente como si compartiera un chiste privado con el resto del mundo.

—Mira esto —me dice Jonah poniéndome un pequeño paquete en la mano.

Se ríe a carcajadas. Le doy la vuelta. Hay una foto de un crucifijo y pone: CONDÓN CATÓLICO. Jonah se está partiendo. Se ríe aún más.

—Es un... —Más risas—. Es un... —Carcajadas—. Es un condón con la punta cortada. —Le parece graciosísimo.

—A mí no me parece tan gracioso —digo—. Creo que es irresponsable.

Volvemos a la sala principal, donde la señora Norton agita los brazos mientras intenta contar cabezas.

—¡Chicos! —grita la señora Norton. Está junto a un antiguo uniforme de policía—. El señor Mandalay y yo nos vamos. Podéis quedaros todo el tiempo que queráis, o volver al albergue, o visitar la ciudad. Pero os ADVIERTO que tenéis que volver a las SEIS EN PUNTO y que quien no esté a esa hora RECIBIRÁ UN SEVERO CASTIGO.

Todos asienten y se dispersan. Ping y Ana desaparecen juntos con los brazos entrelazados como los aros olímpicos.

—¿Y ahora qué? —pregunta Jonah sacándose un paquete de tabaco del bolsillo de atrás.

—Creo que me vuelvo al albergue —responde Tenaya.

Aún carga con el fantasma de Tom. El tiempo es el único exorcista adecuado.

Asentimos con la cabeza y Tenaya me da un golpecito en el brazo y se marcha.

—Tú no te vas a ninguna parte —me dice Jonah.

—Vale —le digo.

De todas formas, yo también quería hacer algo.

—¿Qué hora es?

Saco el teléfono.

—Las cinco.

—Genial —dice—. Vamos a tomar un café. Luego tengo una sorpresa, y después de la sorpresa compraremos cervezas y ya veremos qué pasa esta noche.

—¿Cómo que ya veremos qué pasa esta noche?

—La sorpresa hará los planes por nosotros.

—La sorpresa no será una puta, ¿no?

—Y una mierda te voy a pagar una puta.

Salimos a las monótonas y grises entrañas de Plymouth.

12

—¿Mefedrona?

—Sí.

Jonah sonríe.

Mefedrona. La sorpresa era mefedrona. La mefedrona es una droga legal que se puede comprar por Internet. Se vende como «fertilizante para plantas». Ofrece el amor del Dalai Lama y el carisma de Hitler y lo único que pide a cambio es que, después, pases un ratito en el agujero negro de la depresión.

—No sé —digo—. ¿En serio?

Ahora mismo no estoy preparado emocionalmente para enfrentarme a graves cambios de humor.

—No seas tan nenaza. —Jonah señala la puerta del baño con la cabeza.

Estamos en la típica cafetería de mesas de formica frecuentada por albañiles y gente en paro. Todas las camareras son polacas o de por ahí. Nadie levanta la vista cuando entramos al baño.

Casi no hay espacio en el cubículo. Hay charcos de meado en el suelo con rollos de cartón arrugados flotando como fetos abortados.

Jonah despliega el polvo escondido en un envoltorio hecho

con un flyer de «Una noche de dubstep delirante». Con el carné de la biblioteca hace cuatro rayas sobre la tapa del váter y nos las metemos. Nos dejamos caer al suelo. Con la espalda apoyada en la pared, miramos las baldosas de enfrente durante unos minutos. Me quema la nariz y siento una cascada de aguas fecales en la garganta antes de notar cómo se extiende por mi cabeza.

Mi cabeza está a punto de explotar.

—¿Estás bien? —pregunto.

—Sí. ¿Más?

—Palabra.

—¿Palabra?

—¿Qué pasa? Lo escuché en un rap.

Jonah sonríe y niega con la cabeza. Rasca otras dos rayas del papel y lame un lado del carné de la biblioteca. Nos las metemos y nos sentamos. Me siento tremendo.

—Gracias —digo.

—De nada.

—Gracias, en serio. Te quiero, tío. Pero no de forma gay ni nada. Tienes unos gemelos de puta madre.

—Lo sé. No nos lo decimos lo suficiente. Yo también te quiero, tío. Somos muy jóvenes. Todo va de puta madre —dice Jonah.

Tiene la mano sobre mi brazo.

Le pongo la mano en el hombro.

—Sí. SÍ. La gente no se quiere lo suficiente. Les encanta la guerra y el dinero. Yo no quiero guerra ni dinero, te quiero a ti.

—Sí, a la mierda la guerra y el dinero.

—La guerra y el dinero me pueden chupar la polla.

—Os quiero a ti y a Tenaya y a Ping y a Ana.

—¡A Ping y a Ana! Son felices juntos. Son la leche. Como pequeñas estrellas.

—Se casarán y todos iremos a la boda.

—Sí, y les diremos lo guays que son.

—Todos existiendo felices.

—¡A la mierda la guerra y el dinero!

—Bodas, eso es lo que tendríamos que hacer.

—Deberíamos casarnos todos.

—¡Pues sí, joder!

Las piernas se nos doblan como briznas de hierba en un huracán.

Empujamos la puerta y salimos otra vez al café. Les sonreímos a las camareras extranjeras y vamos hacia la puerta. Jonah la empuja.

—¡Perdona, perdona! —grita la camarera—. ¡No paga!

Es preciosa. Como una estrella del porno o una modelo del *Vogue* o algo. Tiene unos pómulos y unos ojos enormes y yo me alegro mucho de que exista.

—Lo sentimos MUCHO —dice Jonah—. Por favor, por favor, perdónanos.

Saca un billete de veinte del bolsillo y se lo pone en la mano. Yo saco uno de diez y hago lo mismo. Treinta libras por dos cafés.

—Muy generosos —dice, y corresponde a nuestras sonrisas desechas.

—Eres guapísima —le digo.

Jonah y yo nos abalanzamos sobre ella arrastrando su pequeño cuerpo a un intenso abrazo triple.

—Por favor, sé feliz —le digo—. Te mereces ser feliz.

Fuera, el aire es maravilloso. Huele a popurrí. Nos lo bebemos como hombres que se ahogan. Nos llena de luz.

—Vamos a buscar alguna discoteca, a repartir amor.

—Vale —digo—. La gente debe saber que los queremos.

—Sí, tenemos que gritarlo y abrazarles.

Son las 20:00. Probablemente, no habrá ninguna discoteca abierta. Da igual, caminamos. Seguimos las calles.

Jonah enciende un cigarro.

—Precioso, joder —dice.

Me pasa uno.

—Ah —digo.

Pasamos un Tesco Express, una zapatería sin nombre, una tienda de jabones, un Starbucks y un Debenhams. Todos son preciosos. Un callejón se abre a nuestra izquierda. Las paredes están cubiertas de salpicaduras escabrosas de pintura de neón.

—Allí —dice Jonah.

Recorremos el callejón a saltitos. Aparece un cartel clavado al edificio de ladrillo rojo de enfrente.

FUNKYTOWN: EL CENTRO DE LA MÚSICA DISCO

—¡Hostia! —grita Jonah—. Me flipa la música disco.

—Joder, música disco, sí.

Dicho eso, entramos. No hay porteros porque una discoteca setentera no es el sitio al que suelen ir los menores. Es el sitio al que van las mujeres de mediana edad y los hombres un poco por encima de esa edad.

Funkytown es precioso. La música, tan agradecida como los himnos del instituto, rebota contra la bola de espejos. La bola de espejos es preciosa. Así es como debe de ser uno de los ojos de Dios. El papel pintado es un collage de colores brillantes y el suelo, un espejo de madera. La gente baila en parejas y sonríe. Son felices. Soy feliz por ellos. Hay grupos de gente en la barra y parejas en la sala. Beben, son personas. Tengo ganas de decirles: «¡Enhorabuena!».

—¡Enhorabuena! —digo.

Jonah me abraza.

—Vamos a la barra —dice—. Vamos a invitar a algo a esas MUJERES TAN GUAPAS.

Lo dice muy alto para que le oigan. Tienen que oírlo porque son preciosas. Hay que decírselo. Vamos a decírselo. A decírselo y a invitarlas a algo y a asegurarnos de que sean tan felices como monjes en un bar de striptease. ¡Todos somos personas!

Hay dos mujeres. Las dos de poco menos de cuarenta, digo yo. Son preciosos rayos de sol. Una es rubia, con el pelo tan tieso como mi polla cuando la miro. Lleva un vestido estrecho de lunares y un cinturón rojo brillante ajustado a la cintura. Seguro que ve el programa de Gok Wan. Lleva los ojos perfilados, como enmarcados. Es preciosa. La otra tiene el pelo corto, castaño, y lleva un vestido veraniego blanco. Es preciosa.

—¿Qué bebéis, preciosas? —pregunta Jonah. Le dicen lo que están bebiendo y él les pide otra copa. Yo estoy ocupado sintiéndome brillante y lleno de amor, así que no me doy cuenta. Me pone una cerveza en la mano y me alborota el pelo—. ¿Cómo está yendo la noche, chicas?

La rubia sonríe.

—Muy bien, gracias. ¿Qué tal vosotros, chicos?

—No estaba mal, pero acaba de mejorar muchísimo —dice Jonah.

La morena se ríe.

—¿Quieres bailar, encanto? —pregunta mientras le tiende la mano.

Él la coge y pasean tranquilamente hasta la pista. Me alegro mucho por ellos.

Ahora solo quedamos la rubia y yo. Es preciosa. En una película, podría hacer de Cleopatra, Helena de Troya, Keira Knightly o Reese Witherspoon. Huele a flores y nubes concentradas. Su cabeza es un busto de mármol del sol.

—¿No te gusta bailar? —me pregunta.

—¿Qué? ¿Yo? No, podemos bailar si quieres. Podemos hacer lo que quieras. ¿Qué te haría feliz? Vamos a hacer lo que te haga feliz.

—Oooh —exclama como si estuviera viendo fotos de bebés—. Eres un encanto.

—Gracias —le digo—. La gente no es lo bastante amable. A la gente solo le importa el dinero y, mmm, los barcos, los castillos y cosas así. A mí no me importa nada de eso. ¿Eres feliz?

—Sí. —Asiente con la cabeza.

—¿Quieres bailar?

—Estoy feliz aquí, pero bailamos si quieres.

—Ni hablar —le digo—. Acábate la copa, iré a buscar otra.

Le pido más bebida al camarero. Lleva una camisa de cowboy y tiene un ligero aspecto mexicano. Estoy encantado de conocerle. Le doy cinco libras de propina. Al dárselas, le digo: «Comparte la riqueza», y él se ríe.

—Bueno —dice la rubia—, ¿a qué te dedicas?

Animado por el «fertilizante para plantas» como estoy, me doy cuenta de que en esta situación la sinceridad solo me llevaría a un callejón sin salida en el que no me follo a nadie.

—Soy policía —le digo—. Y Jonah es un magnate del porno. —Creo que eso le gustaría—. Los dos tenemos veintidós, pero yo soy mucho más maduro.

La rubia se ríe. Tiene los dientes como pastillas de chicle bien colocadas en el paquete. Sus labios son del color de la sandía.

—¿A qué te dedicas tú? —le pregunto.

—Soy recepcionista en una compañía de seguros, y Susie es camarera. Ni se te ocurra preguntarme la edad.

Me guiña un ojo.

Parecemos personajes de una película feliz. Estoy en un bar ligando con una mujer preciosa que se enamorará de mí y nuestro amor florecerá como un girasol en un verano eterno. Gracias, Jesús.

Jonah vuelve cuando se le cansan las piernas y me da con el codo para que le acompañe al baño.

—¿Por qué tenéis que ir juntos al baño? —pregunta la morena.

—Necesito un acompañante —responde Jonah—. Nunca cago solo.

En realidad, vamos al baño para poder llenarnos la nariz | garganta | cabeza de más mefedrona. Queda un montón. Aún no hay peligro de bajones.

—Tío, esta noche nos las vamos a calzar —dice Jonah—. Joder, son increíbles. Es perfecto.

—Preciosas.

Salimos del baño.

En la barra, nuestras presas han reconstruido la Muralla China con chupitos de sambuca negra. La sambuca negra es preciosa.

Jonah rodea a la morena con los brazos por detrás y le da un beso en la mejilla. Ella sonríe. Yo le sonrío a la rubia.

—¿Listos? —pregunta.

—Cuatro cada uno —dice la morena—. El último se enrolla con el barman.

Todos reímos. Soy feliz. La rubia es la última en acabar. Todos tenemos manchas negras alrededor de los labios, en el cuello y en el pecho. Todos sonreímos. Yo sonrío. La rubia me lame las manchas de sambuca del cuello. Su lengua se siente como la cara de Abby Hall.

—Oye —dice la morena—. Tenías que enrollarte con el barman, tonta.

La rubia se ríe. Jonah une las puntas del índice y del pulgar, se los mete en la boca y silba dos veces. ¿Se llama silbido de lobo? Se le da bien. Soy feliz.

El barman se acerca porque ha oído el silbido de Jonah. La rubia lo coge por la camisa vaquera con su manita, tira de él y le acerca la cara. Todos nos reímos. Están sonando los Jackson 5. Escucho a la gente cantando. Jonah canta. Vamos todos a bailar.

* * *

Funkytown cierra.

He llegado a la segunda base con la rubia y tengo buenas razones para creer que Jonah ha llegado a la tercera con la morena. Las buenas razones son que me puso los dedos debajo de la nariz y me dijo: «Huélelos, tío». Nos abrazamos. Soy feliz.

Salimos fuera, hace frío y el viento está entusiasmado. Una chica con unos shorts de lentejuelas está vomitando en un cubo de basura, mientras un chico con el pelo lleno de gel le aparta las extensiones de la cara. Jonah se ríe. Le doy mi abrigo a la rubia y me besa.

—Qué encanto —me dice cuando se lo doy.

—Entonces, ¿vamos a nuestra casa? —pregunta la morena.

Decimos que sí y echamos a andar.

Su casa resulta ser un adosado de las afueras. ¿Se nos están pasando los efectos de la mefedrona? Se lo digo a Jonah. Asiente. Cuando entramos, intentamos ir al baño, pero la morena nos interrumpe.

—Sea lo que sea, podéis hacerlo en la cocina.

—Pero dejadnos un poco —añade la rubia.

Les damos un poco. Jonah rasca ocho rayas y nos las metemos todas. Una de las chicas pone música. No la conozco.

—Es Etta James —dice la morena.

Nos abrazamos todos.

—Esto es precioso —digo.

—Muy precioso —dice Jonah—. Sois increíbles.

—No, vosotros sois increíbles —dice la morena.

Nos abrazamos todos.

La rubia me lleva a un sofá que huele a vino barato. Detrás hay un piano vertical. Un perro holgazanea por la habitación como un niño que hubiera llegado de repente al escenario de un teatro.

—Se llama Peter —dice la rubia.

—Hola, Peter.

Jonah y la morena desaparecen. La rubia me está besando en el sofá. Se recuesta y tira de mí hasta que quedo tumbado sobre ella. Nunca había estado tumbado encima de unas tetas con tanta experiencia. Guía mi mano por su muslo, hacia arriba. Yo la guío por el borde de sus bragas de encaje. El tacto de su coño es como el de un estropajo.

—Vamos arriba —me dice.

Me coge de la mano y tira de mí escaleras arriba. No aparto la mirada de su precioso culo y pienso en lo feliz que soy.

Voy a follármela. Será una buena práctica. Quiero ser lo más bueno posible para Georgia en Devon. Tengo que trabajar mi resistencia.

Su habitación es... No me fijo. Nos tiramos debajo del edredón. Mi camiseta vuela pronto, y mis pantalones, y mis calcetines. Unimos fuerzas para intentar quitarle el vestido, pero ninguno de los dos quiere desenredar los labios así que resulta difícil. Difícil pero no imposible. Me considero un experto quitando sujetadores, eso no supone ningún problema. Los dos estamos casi desnudos. Me tumbo entre sus piernas como un punto en la boca de Pacman. Nos besamos. Da palmadas a ciegas con la mano izquierda sobre la mesita en busca de un condón. Lo encuentra. Me lo pone. Entro. Suspiros. Gemidos. Soy un yoyó. Le doy la vuelta. Palmada en el culo y movimiento hacia delante y hacia atrás. Suspiros. Gemidos. Dormir.

13

La bajada de la mefedrona es el tipo de esquí que menos me gusta. Empiezas odiando a todos los que te rodean. Como un pedófilo en una residencia de ancianos. Quieres estar solo. Entonces te das cuenta de que en realidad no quieres estar solo sino dejar de existir. Quieres doblarte sobre ti mismo una y otra vez hasta que ya no existas. Así es como me siento ahora.

No encuentro la hora por ninguna parte. Aún está oscuro. No sé dónde está mi teléfono. Me pongo nervioso cuando no sé qué hora es. Mi garganta es como una autopista de Arizona. Estoy tumbado junto a la mujer mirando la parte de atrás de su pelo teñido con tinte barato, sintiendo crecer el arrepentimiento. Desprecio profundamente a esta mujer, y esta casa. También desprecio a Jonah, pero debería encontrarle.

Joder, seguro que hasta tiene hijos.

Estoy totalmente desnudo. No consigo encontrar mis calzoncillos, pero sí los pantalones. El vaquero es como un rallador de queso contra mis testículos. Joder. Dios, mi cabeza. Vale, Jasper J. Wolf, cálmate. No es el momento de un 11-S existencial. Tienes que actuar. Encuentra tu ropa. Encuentra a Jonah. Lárgate.

Me molesta la moqueta en los dedos de los pies. Salgo de la habitación, cruzo el rellano y me meto en el baño. Jonah está ahí, en la bañera, con el agua lloviendo sobre su cabeza. El tatuaje de la Virgen María me mira como un discapacitado. Jonah murmura una oración.

—¿Puedes dejar esa mierda para que nos larguemos? —le digo.

Se da la vuelta.

—Vete a la mierda. ¿Qué sabrás tú de ningún Dios? Vas a ir al infierno.

Aún siento los residuos de la mefedrona como un mar de tinta china en la cabeza. Odio a Jonah. Quiero desaparecer. ¿Por qué andamos, hablamos o nos movemos?

—Vámonos de aquí de una puta vez, por favor —le digo.

Cierra el agua y sale.

—La cabeza me está matando.

Que no se me olvide darle una patada a Peter en las costillas al salir.

Cuando llegamos al albergue, los demás están más felices que nosotros. O menos hechos polvo. Ping y Ana están enredados el uno en el otro, susurrando, y Tenaya lee en la cama.

—¿Dónde coño os habíais metido? —pregunta Ping.

Jonah se tira en la cama.

—Jasper y yo hemos hecho un pacto de no hablar nunca sobre lo que pasó ayer por la noche. Como mis amigos que sois, confío en que respetéis el pacto y no intentéis sacarnos ningún tipo de información.

Tenaya se ríe.

—¿Chicas feas?

—Peor —contesto.

—¡Cállate! —Jonah se enrolla la almohada en la cabeza y suelta un gruñido.

En el autobús de vuelta a casa me quedo dormido sobre el hombro de Tenaya mientras la lluvia besa las ventanas y la señora Norton lee su Biblia en voz alta.

Segunda parte

Exhumación y fuego

14

Mamá y Keith están montando una estantería de Ikea en el salón. De momento, parece un barco. Keith no para de soltar tacos. Mamá suspira. En el caso de que llegara el apocalipsis, los dos estarían jodidos porque les faltan las habilidades prácticas necesarias para sobrevivir en nuestro futuro distópico. Un hombre capaz de matar leones con las manos probablemente les dispararía y los despellejaría. Se haría un impermeable con sus pieles.

Estoy en la cocina con un libro de texto de alemán, sin estudiar. Es más divertido observarles. Un salón diáfano es como un cine barato.

—Keith, ¿dónde está el A4? —pregunta Mamá.

—No hay ningún A4, cariño.

—Pero, mira.

Le pone las instrucciones a Keith en la cara. A mi madre no le gustan las instrucciones. Las llama destrucciones. Es un chiste. La gente cuenta chistes cuando no sabe qué otra cosa hacer. En los hospitales se cuentan muchos. No suelen ser demasiado buenos.

—Están mal —dice Keith—. Las instrucciones están mal.

Mamá está horrorizada.

—Voy a llamar a Ikea —dice—. Me pienso quejar de que no sale el A4.

Keith sonríe.

—A cuatro patas te pondré yo luego.

Se ríen. A Keith ni siquiera se le dan bien los juegos de palabras. No tengo ni idea de qué le ve Mamá. Igual la tiene como la trompa de un elefante.

—Perdonad —digo—. Hola. Soy Jasper, tu único hijo, y estoy intentando estudiar.

—Ah —exclama Mamá.

—Nos tendremos que poner de cara a la pared, cariño.

Se besan. Asqueroso. Subo a mi habitación.

Mi móvil está encima de la cama. Vibra. Da vueltas sobre la almohada como un molinillo. Es Tenaya.

—¿Jasper? —dice.

—Mis padres están intentando montar muebles —le comento—. Keith ha hecho una broma y se han besado. Es asqueroso.

—Estoy pensando en Tom.

—¿Aún?

—Compartimos cosas importantes durante mucho tiempo, Jasper. Es normal que piense en él.

Suspiro profundamente junto al teléfono.

—No era un buen novio. Es una persona irritante.

—Jasper, no me estás ayudando.

—¿Con qué tengo que ayudarte?

—No sé qué hacer.

—Me queda medio gramo. Si quieres, te lo puedo llevar.

—Arg.

Cuelga.

No sé qué he dicho. He hecho lo que he podido. Lo intento. Tienes que intentar entender a los demás, Jasper. Imagínate que eres la otra persona.

Tom era mi novio y ya no lo es. Quería mucho a Tom. Tom me engañó. Tom me dejó. Tom tiene unos pómulos geniales. Tom seguramente será un rico vendedor de arte. No sé qué hacer ahora. Tom. No sé qué hacer ahora. Le quería.

Julia: empatía.

Tenaya: heridas en los brazos.

Radio: el estado mental de los adolescentes que se autolesionan puede deteriorarse si no reciben la ayuda que tan claramente están pidiendo al hacerse daño

Oh.

OH.

Bajo corriendo y me lanzo a la calle por la puerta principal. Le grito adiós a Mamá. Corro a toda velocidad. Soy un anuncio de zapatillas Nike.

Subo por nuestra calle, giro a la izquierda en el Hungry Horse, paso el instituto, paso a una mujer con un piercing monroe y un cochecito vacío, paso a dos hombres que beben cerveza barata sentados en una tapia, paso la iglesia baptista y el Happy Shopper y la casa de Ben McKay.

La casa de Tenaya.

Me lanzo hacia la valla del jardín. Sus padres crían gallinas por si llega el apocalipsis. Veo a Tenaya de espaldas a mí detrás de las puertas acristaladas de la cocina. Probablemente tendrá la mano llena de paracetamol. Tengo que detenerla.

Cosas que veo cerca de las puertas acristaladas:

Pala
Planta de marihuana
Banco
Cubo de plástico

El cubo de plástico es la única opción. Ni unas mancuernas, ni una pluma. Lo cojo y abro las puertas acristaladas. Le pongo el cubo en la cabeza y hago toda la fuerza que puedo hacia abajo. Grita. Se da la vuelta para ponerse de cara a mí. No ha funcionado. ¿Lo intento otra vez?

—JASPER, ¿QUÉ COÑO HACES?

—Mmm.

—¿Qué coño estás haciendo?

La cojo de las muñecas y se las aprieto. Sus manos se abren como flores. No lleva paracetamol.

—Dijiste que te ibas a suicidar —exclamo.

Tenaya se sonroja.

—No dije eso.

—Lo estabas pensando.

—No.

—Sé que lo pensabas. He aprendido a empatizar.

—Cállate, Jasper.

Se sienta en uno de los taburetes de la cocina. Me quedo de pie.

—No sé nada —dice.

—Tenía miedo —le confieso—. Jonah es asqueroso y Ping tiene a Ana.

—A veces... —dice—. No lo sé.

—Yo tampoco. Pero te dije que me mandaras un mensaje cuando te pasara. Compraré el vino ese de dos por cinco libras de Imran y podemos ver *Dentro del laberinto* en tu cama y te dejaré que me depiles las cejas.

—Te he llamado.

—No me había quedado muy claro.

—Vale.

—Voy a poner un poco de agua a hervir.

Esto es lo que la gente dice cuando quiere que alguien sepa que todo va a salir bien pero no saben cómo.

En la pared de la cocina de Tenaya hay una mancha con forma de cabeza de conejo. Apareció cuando la madre de Tenaya le tiró una taza de café al padre de Tenaya. Nadie lo limpió. Han dejado los trabajos de renovación de la casa.

—Has dicho que ibas a poner agua a hervir —dice Tenaya.

—Solo lo he dicho porque... —Ella no lo entendía—. Vale.

Subimos el té a su habitación y vemos capítulos viejos de *Sexo en Nueva York* desde debajo del edredón. Big no se merece a Carrie.

—¿Iremos mañana al Twelve Cats? —pregunto.

—Supongo.

—Están mejorando.

—¿Vendrás conmigo al Asda después?

—¿Por qué?

—Tengo que comprar comida. Mi madre no compra nada. Solo se emborracha y pide comida para llevar.

—Vale.

—Gracias.

—Ping dice que antes podríamos pasar por su casa.

—Mmm.

Tenaya asiente con la cabeza y se queda dormida. Cojo un libro al azar de la estantería y me siento en la ventana a leer. El libro se titula *Mujeres arriba*. Habla de las diferentes formas en las que la gente folla en su imaginación.

15

19:38. El grupo de Ping toca en el Twelve Cats esta noche. Me pondré mi camiseta del lobo. En los conciertos, puedes moverte y rozarte contra las chicas sin que te digan nada porque todo el mundo se lo está pasando bien.

El grupo de Ping se llama Deep Emotional Skaing. Los juegos de palabras le parecen divertidos. Los juegos de palabras son para los viejos y los poemas malos. El año pasado ganaron un concurso local; pusieron algunas de sus canciones en iTunes y les grabaron un CD. El CD se llamaba *Fuck the Free World, Mary Jane*. No significa nada.

Después de vestirme, bajo y meto la cabeza en la nevera. La fría luz amarilla me lame la cara. Hay una botella sin abrir de leche entera. Desenrosco el tapón y despego la cosa blanca. Me pongo derecho y me la bebo de un trago.

Mamá aparece detrás de mí.

—Jasper —me dice—, no hagas eso. Otras personas tienen que beber de ahí también.

—Pero, Mamá, da buena suerte beber directamente de una botella de leche recién abierta.

—No me importa, Jasper. Coge un vaso.

Dejo la botella de leche en la nevera.

—Mamá —digo—. Voy a ver al grupo de Ping esta noche. ¿Me das dinero?

Mamá frunce el ceño.

—¿Cuánto?

—Diez de los grandes.

—No digas de los grandes, Jasper.

—¿Por qué?

—Porque es lo que dice la mafia.

—Vale. ¿Me das diez libras, por favor?

Mamá suspira y me pasa un billete del monedero. Resoplo para que sepa cuánto se lo agradezco. Salgo para coger el autobús.

* * *

La madre de Ping me abre la puerta. Va en albornoz. Tiene el pelo mojado. La polla me grita en los pantalones. Está enfadada conmigo porque no la dejo meterse en el coño de la madre de Ping. Probablemente tiene un coño precioso. Un abismo perfectamente afeitado.

—Hola, Jasper —dice—. Están arriba. Sube.

—Gracias, señora Lin.

Paso a su lado y subo corriendo las escaleras. Ping, Ana y Tenaya están sentados en la cama, riéndose. Ping y Ana se cogen de la mano. Me pregunto quién se rendirá antes, la polla de Ping o la virginidad de Ana. Las chicas creen que la virginidad es como una muñeca de cristal de valor inestimable. En realidad solo son tres minutos de vergüenza seguidos de decepción seguidos de la pregunta: «¿En qué piensas?».

—¿Qué estáis haciendo? —pregunto.

—Tengo un móvil nuevo —dice Ping.

Me lo enseña. Parece una BlackBerry falsa. No es divertido.

—No le veo la gracia.

—Jonah me contó lo del viaje de Psicología.

Trago saliva.

—¿Qué?

—Ya sabes.

—Gilipollas.

Ana se ríe. Zorra frígida. Miro a Tenaya. Ella mira el dibujo del edredón.

—Está a punto de enterarse de que hay un pequeño en camino.

Me río.

—Ya, ya.

—¿Quién va a hablar? —dice Tenaya.

—Yo —dice Ana.

—Tú no puedes.

—¿Por qué no?

—Por tu estúpido acento —respondo.

—Déjala en paz.

Ping se cruza de brazos.

—No seas tan nenaza.

—No —dice Tenaya—. Es que ya conoce tu voz.

—Mi hermana ha vuelto de la universidad —dice Ping—. Le diré que hable ella.

—¿Lo hará?

—Sí. Yo siempre llamaba al instituto haciéndome pasar por mi padre cuando ella no quería ir.

Ping sale de la habitación y vuelve unos minutos después con su hermana. Es una chica enorme con las tetas planas y una sola ceja. Lleva una camiseta de Oxford Brooks. Resulta difícil creer que salió de la madre de Ping. Creo que no quería ir a clase porque seguramente la llamaban Frida Kahlo y le clavaban bolis.

Le decimos hola y Ping le explica lo que tiene que decir. Asiente con la cabeza. No dice mucho más, pero cuando Jonah le coge el teléfono se convierte en una actriz merecedora de un Oscar.

Esto es lo que escuchamos:

¿Jonah?
Soy Susan, de Plymouth.
Estoy embarazada.
(Nos reímos tapándonos la boca.)
Sí, estoy segura.
Me he hecho una prueba de embarazo.
Sí, aciertan prácticamente siempre.
No sé, un noventa y nueve coma siete por ciento o algo así.
Sí, pero no es muy probable, ¿no crees?
Madura, vas a ser padre.
(Ana se ahoga de la risa.)
Sí, voy a tenerlo.
Sí, tendrás que pasarme dinero hasta que cumpla dieciocho.

Ping le quita el teléfono a su hermana de la mano.

—¡Feliz día del padre! —grita, y cuelga inmediatamente para no oír la tormenta de gilipollas, cabrones y joderes de Jonah. Nos partimos de risa.

* * *

00:15. Un montón de gente sudada nos empuja de un lado para otro a Tenaya, a Jonah, a Ana y a mí. Los Deep Emotional Skaing tocan en un escenario bajo. Jonah ha comprado pastillas. Me dio una en el baño. Me dijo que no sabía qué eran. Me siento diferente. Me siento bien. Tengo calor. Suena como si el grupo estuviera tocando una nota alta sin parar. La nota ha crecido y se ha tragado la sala. Todos estamos dentro de la nota. Es nuestro castillo. La espalda de un tío sin camiseta se estrella contra mi cara. Sabe salada. ¿Quién se supone que soy? Tenaya mueve la cabeza. El pelo le vuela sobre la cara. Ping pone caras raras. Tiene los dedos clavados en el bajo. Ryan Samuels es el cantante. Ryan Samuels grita, la cara se le ha puesto del color de las Biblias de Gedeón, está a punto de explotar y bañarnos con trocitos sanguinolentos de mejilla. Se lanza desde el escenario. Levantamos las manos. Le sujeto la entrepierna. Aprieto. No soy gay. Lo pasamos hacia atrás. Salta al suelo, le quita la cerveza a alguien y vuelve a subir al escenario. Ryan Samuels tira la cerveza al público. La gente grita. Quieren más cerveza. Empiezan otra canción. Ping está de rodillas. Ping cree que es muy bueno. Solo toca una nota. Estoy dentro de la nota. Esta nota es nuestra nueva casa, por el momento, que es para siempre.

* * *

Cuando el grupo termina de tocar, salimos a fumar. Tenaya y yo nos sentamos a una mesa de picnic mojada. El efecto de la pastilla se nos está pasando. Ahora solo vibro ligeramente. La gente está en pequeños corros, hablan en voz alta sobre la música. Ping sigue en el backstage recogiendo sus cosas. Ana sale corriendo del pub con un ron con cola y se sienta a nuestra mesa.

—¿No ha sido increíble? —dice.

—Genial —comento.

—Es brutal —dice Ana.

—Es Ping —respondo.

El amor es una secta.

Tenaya me lanza una mirada que significa que estoy siendo un gilipollas.

—¿Volverás a Moscú el año que viene?

Ana sonríe. Está enamorada de Charles Manson. Asesinará

porque él se lo habrá dicho. Nadie entenderá por qué. La policía se la llevará y no gritará, pero sus ojos serán los ojos del último tigre de Bengala que queda en Bután.

—No —dice—. Me quedo aquí. Buscaré trabajo en una cafetería o algo así. Ping y yo vamos a vivir juntos. Va a intentar que el grupo llegue hasta el final.

—Hasta el final —comento—. Vaya.

—Jasper —susurra Tenaya.

Me da un golpe en la pierna por debajo de la mesa.

—Le quiero —dice Ana.

Las chicas pueden ser muy gays. Incluso a Tenaya le cuesta aguantarse la risa.

Ping sale por la puerta de atrás. Tiene la cara roja y lleva una corona de sudor. Ana corre hacia él y hunde la cara en su camiseta empapada en salmuera. Él le da un beso en la cabeza. Tenaya y yo le decimos que el grupo ha estado genial, que están mejorando mucho y que la nueva canción sonaba como si fuera un éxito de la radio. Me aseguro de utilizar las palabras «hasta el final».

Unos minutos después, nos despedimos y vamos a coger el 96 hasta la zona comercial donde está el Big Asda. Es un trayecto corto en autobús. Tenaya se queda dormida en mi hombro. Cuando llegamos a la parada, le doy despacio con el codo para despertarla. Parpadea como si no supiera dónde está y luego sonríe.

El Big Asda está abierto veinticuatro horas al día, siete días a la semana. La 01:21. Es la única luz que queda encendida en la gran zona comercial. Por las ventanas se desbordan enormes charcos de luz que se extienden sobre la noche asfaltada como cuerpos de ángeles desnudos.

Tenaya saca un carrito de la fila y entramos por las puertas automáticas. Mi temperatura corporal aumenta de repente. Un guardia de seguridad que está rellenando un sudoku levanta la vista. Hace una pequeña reverencia cuando entramos. Parece un hombre amable y educado. Ojalá Mamá se hubiera casado con él.

—¿Por dónde empezamos? —pregunto.

Tenaya se encoge de hombros.

Atravesamos el pasillo de los refrigerados. Está vacío. Tenaya mete una botella grande de leche semidesnatada en el carrito. Yo cojo un batido de chocolate. Ella lo saca y me pregunta si tengo ocho años. Me sugiere que mejor compre Actimel. Le digo que preferiría darle el dinero a un heroinómano.

En el pasillo de los alimentos deshidratados, mete un saco enorme de lentejas en el carro. La miro con asco. Mete también pasas, ciruelas y anacardos. Es demasiado. Me tumbo delante del carrito, abatido.

—¿Qué haces? —grito.

—¿Qué haces tú? —repite.

Me pongo de pie.

—Somos dos niños de diecisiete años solos en un supermercado y vas y compras unas putas ciruelas. Deberías comprar bolsas gigantes de nuggets de pollo, y cerveza polaca y cigarros.

—Jasper —dice—. Desde que mis padres compraron esa puta casa no hacen más que emborracharse y pedir comida barata para llevar. Comemos eso al mediodía y para cenar y, lo que sobra, para desayunar. No quiero más comida de mierda.

Tiene sentido.

—Vale.

—Pero ve a por nuggets de pollo.

—Vale.

Corro a la sección de congelados y cojo la bolsa más grande de nuggets de pollo que veo. Tenaya está en las verduras cuando la encuentro. Ha cogido una lechuga iceberg, tres puerros, cuatro tomates y una cebolla roja.

—¿Ya? —pregunto.
—Sí, solo me faltan cigarros.
—¿Vas a hacer los nuggets cuando volvamos?
—Sí.
—¿Y podemos ver *Las chicas Gilmore*?
—Vale.

16

Me aburro. Me he pasado el día fingiendo estudiar. En realidad, estaba jugando al 3D Pinball Space Cadet en el ordenador. Llegaré al nivel de «almirante de la flota». Mi perseverancia será recompensada.

18:30. Me he zampado una cena abundante a base de salchichas, puré de patata y salsa de cebolla. He llamado a Jonah para ver qué hacía. Me ha dicho que no hacía nada y que fuera para allá. Salgo de casa ahora.

—Voy a casa de Jonah, Mamá —digo—. Adiós.

Lo digo gritando hacia el salón vacío.

Mamá aparece de la nada.

—Ten mucho cuidado —me dice—. No vuelvas tarde.

—Sí, Mamá.

—A las diez, como mucho.

—¿A las diez? Qué tontería, Mamá.

—Ah, ¿sí?

—Sí, no vendré más tarde de las once.

Cierro la puerta al salir.

He tenido la última palabra.

El autobús 38 va a casa de Jonah. Solo se tardan siete minutos. Me siento en uno de los asientos vacíos y observo cómo el cielo se desconcha como la pintura vieja. Hay una mujer de pie junto a mi asiento. Tiene la mano enroscada fuertemente en la barra. Aprieta. El color se le ha desvanecido de los dedos y se le ha subido a los pechos modestos y a las mejillas de aspecto triste. Se ha mordido las uñas hasta la mitad y se le han llenado de manchitas rojas.

No entiendo bien a la gente.

No me comeré mis propios dedos.

No me ahorcaré con una media de rubgy.

No asesinaré a mi ex mujer metiéndole el hueso de la nariz hasta el cerebro de un puñetazo.

* * *

Jonah no abre la puerta hasta que llamo al timbre seis veces. Entramos en el salón y nos tiramos en el sofá. Está viendo la versión de dibujos de Disney de Robin Hood, esa en la que Robin Hood es un zorro.

—Esta parte es muy buena —dice Jonah.

Un pequeño conejo blanco con un gorro enorme acaba de lanzar una flecha por encima de un muro, en mitad de un partido de bádminton entre una gallina y una zorra.

—Sí.

Por razones que no entiendo, siempre lloro cuando veo a otra gente llorar en televisión. Por eso no veo *Secret Millionaire*. Solo espero que el futuro dome los caballos salvajes de mis ojos. Aún creo que la razón por la que Samantha Black no quiso hacerlo conmigo el año pasado fue porque lloré viendo *Juno* y pensó que era gay.

Espero que nadie llore.

El pequeño conejo no parece demasiado contento.

—Jonah —grita la madre de Jonah desde la cocina—. Jonah, sal del salón, quiero ver las noticias.

La madre de Jonah ve las noticias todos los días desde que

su marido murió en Afganistán. Solo busca a alguien con quien enfadarse. Lanza tacos indiscriminadamente. Lo he visto muchas veces. Insulta a Trevor McDonald, a Hannah Montana y a Gok Wan. A todos los llama cabrones.

—Vamos arriba a jugar a la Xbox —dice Jonah.

—¿En serio?

—Sí. Podemos jugar al Halo en la Xbox Live.

Jonah sabe que me gusta escuchar a gente enfadada gritar en la Xbox Live.

—Vale —digo.

No me suelen gustar los juegos de ordenador porque son aburridos y malos para el desarrollo del carácter. Sin embargo, jugar al Halo en la Xbox Live está bien porque puedes charlar con gente extranjera agresiva y después dispararles. Normalmente, este tipo de comportamiento no está permitido.

En la primera partida que jugamos, un tal BurgerThing424, que tiene acento del norte y una escopeta, llama novato a Jonah y después se ríe de él. Jonah lo llama puto paki. Le pregunto cómo sabe que es un paki y Jonah me dice que lo sabe porque el BurgerThing424 este no para de dispararle en la nuca. No entiendo el chiste.

Jonah se sube al depósito de agua. Dice que va a disparar a la gente desde allí. Me manda que me esconda, que vaya por ahí con el jeep o que haga algo, que si intento meterme en el juego, nuestro equipo perderá seguro. Asiento. Solo quiero escuchar lo que dicen. Me paseo por el búnker recogiendo armas inútiles y corazas.

—Te tengo, paki cabrón —dice Jonah, sonriendo.

—No seas tan racista —le digo.

—No seas tan marica.

—Ni tan homófobo.

—No me das miedo.

Para demostrarlo, Jonah lanza un enorme explosivo desde

lo alto del depósito. A pesar de estar seguro en el búnker, mi mitad de la pantalla dividida tiembla. Jonah se parte.

—Menuda mierda —comento.

—¿Qué? ¿Has visto eso?

—¿El qué? —pregunto—. ¿Esos píxeles que se han movido por tu pantalla mientras la voz de un tío de Manchester en paro gritando «que te jodan» ha invadido tu habitación?

—No seas gilipollas.

—No soy gilipollas, esto es una mierda.

—Vale, acabamos esta y salimos a fumarnos un porro.

—Vale.

Nuestro equipo acumula puntos poco a poco. Jonah permanece en su sitio cargándose a varios miembros del otro equipo, que no paran de reproducirse y correr por el entorno virtual.

Al final me aburro y me pongo a correr como un loco por las zonas más expuestas.

Muero muchas veces.

—¿Qué coño haces? —me pregunta Jonah.

—Estoy cogiendo la vida por los cuernos —respondo.

Tira el mando y suspira.

—Vamos fuera.

Fuera, nuestro aliento forma medusas fantasmales en el aire. El humo de marihuana clava sus garras dentro de mí. Me relajo. Nos sentamos en el borde del porche y nos mojamos los pies con el césped húmedo.

—Jonah —digo—. ¿Has pensado en qué vas a hacer cuando acabemos el instituto?

Se encoge de hombros.

—Aún me queda otro año para pensarlo.

—Pero tendrás alguna idea.

Apaga el porro chafándolo en la hierba junto a su pie. Enciende un cigarro y me pasa otro.

—El ejército —dice—. Supongo que el ejército.

Enciendo mi cigarro. Me siento tenso. Intento no sonar chillón ni insensible.

—El ejército —repito.

—Ya sé lo que piensas, no te molestes.

—Vale.

—¿Y tú qué?

Intento modificar mi lenguaje corporal para parecer menos negativo.

—Voy a ser un escritor premiado —digo—. Me compraré una casa en la costa del Sol, dormiré todo el día y follaré toda la noche.

Jonah se ríe.

—¿Podré ir a visitarte?

—Sí —contesto—. Claro que sí.

Volvemos a entrar y vemos *Factor X* desde la cama de Jonah. No digo nada. Jonah interrumpe a menudo con comentarios.

Cosas que Jonah dice mientras vemos *Factor X*:

Tío, debería ganar, está muy buena.
En serio, tío, me la follaría.
¿Es marica o qué?
Es marica.
Todo el mundo vota a los gays.
Seguro que mi madre le vota.
¿Crees que podría participar?
Creo que podría ganar.

Entonces canta la canción de *El rey León*.

Le digo que me marcho.

—Vale —me dice—. Nos vemos, tío.

Jonah me cae muy bien. Espero que no vaya al ejército. Podría ser un joven Russell Brand.

En la calle, no se ve ninguna estrella. Las únicas luces que hay en la oscuridad son las que hemos puesto nosotros: farolas, luces de las casas, aviones que parpadean. Me siento como un intruso en una enorme obra de arte conceptual. Dejo pequeñas huellas de barro. Mientras espero el autobús, dos chicos se paran delante de mí con sus bicis. Solo usan el freno de delante, así que se paran después de un largo y arqueado derrape. Llevan bufandas subidas hasta los ojos y la capucha puesta, una azul y una negra. Tengo mucho miedo.

—Muy bien, tío —dice Capucha Azul.

—Sí, tío —respondo.

En estas situaciones es importante hablar de la misma forma en que te hablan.

—El teléfono, tío —dice Capucha Negra.

Huele a fluidos corporales y a perro mojado.

No me muevo.

Estoy en estado de shock.

—El puto teléfono —repite.

No me preocupa que me peguen. Me preocupa mearme en los pantalones.

—Sueltaelputoteléfonoya —dice. Una única y larga palabra compuesta. No es muy pegadiza.

Rebusco en el bolsillo. Le quito la tapa al teléfono y saco la tarjeta sim. En casa se la pondré a mi viejo Nokia 3210 y todo seguirá igual. Así aprenderán.

Les doy el teléfono.

—Ylacartera —dice Capucha Azul.

Pienso en sacármela y mearles encima.

—No tengo cartera.

Un meado amarillo neón ácido que les dejará ciegos para siempre.

—¿Loqué?

Gilipollas.

—Eh.

Capucha Negra me empuja.

—Pírate, gilipollas.

Vencido, me pongo a andar hacia la noche. Mi corazón es como un tambor.

Uno de los chicos me tira una piedra que me da en la cabeza. Me toco y la mano se mancha de rojo. Me pregunto si voy a morir lapidado.

Otra.

Esta vez, en el cuello.

Son talibanes y yo una mujer falsamente acusada de adulterio.

Corro.

En casa, bajo la cálida luz de mi habitación, me siento delante del ordenador. Giro la cabeza. Me duele el cuello.

No sé qué hacer. Decido no contárselo a Mamá. Si lo hago, se preocupará mucho por mi seguridad y no me dejará salir de casa sin un guardia armado o un enorme y feroz mastín.

Sé qué tengo que hacer.

A veces, cuando estoy enfermo o triste, me pongo el CD antiguo de Avril Lavigne y pienso en lo feliz que era en 2003, cuando besar a una chica que sabía a Panda Pops en una fiesta del instituto era suficiente para pensar que no había nada mejor.

Escucho el disco de Avril Lavigne y canto las letras en silencio, mirando al techo. Si Mamá me viera, le preocuparía que fuera gay. No soy gay. Soy joven y estoy un poco asustado.

17

Estoy sentado a la mesa de la cocina, enfrente de Mamá. Los dos tenemos una taza de té, la suya con dos cucharadas de edulcorante artificial sin azúcar, la mía con cuatro. Es domingo. Lleva sus pantalones de licra y huele a sudor porque se ha pasado la mañana en el gimnasio. No le he contado nada de la brutal agresión que sufrí anoche. Me acabo de levantar y mi pelo es un montón de paja. Son las 11:15.

—Jasper —dice Mamá—. Espero que sepas que los exámenes son muy importantes.

—Sí, Mamá.

—Y que también es muy importante que aproveches estas vacaciones para estudiar.

—Muy importante —repito asintiendo.

—Quizá lo bastante importante para pensar en despertarte antes del mediodía.

—Solo son las once, Mamá.

—Da igual, Jasper. Cuando yo estudiaba para el examen de secundaria, me levantaba todos los días a las siete para poder estudiar lo suficiente.

—No quiero ser un... Eso que tú eres.

Mamá suspira.

—Eres demasiado joven para saber lo que quieres.

Keith baja en bata por las escaleras, frotándose un ojo y rascándose los genitales. Tiene el pelo gris pegado en ángulos curiosos y las uñas amarillas de los pies avanzan pesadamente. Asesino, sin duda.

—Buenos días, chaval.

A veces me pregunto cómo es capaz de inventarse un apodo nuevo cada vez que me ve. Debe de ponerse *Friends* todos los días y coger apuntes. Me imagino el interior de su armario lleno de post-its con sugerencias de apelativos cariñosos diferentes para cada día. Algún día lo seguiré a todas partes durante un buen rato para comprobar si se le agotan las opciones.

—¿Ves? —digo—. Keith también se acaba de despertar.

—Keith no tiene que hacer unos exámenes importantes pronto.

—Deja tranquilo al chico, cariño. No es un asunto de vida o muerte —dice Keith.

No sé por qué la gente hace eso. Me revuelve el pelo. Tiene las manos manchadas de sangre, metafóricamente. Pongo las manos sobre la mesa. Mamá las mira y después me mira a mí. Arruga la cara en una expresión poco atractiva. Sabe que voy a pedirle algo.

—Mamá —digo inclinando la cabeza ligeramente hacia un lado para recordarle que soy un hijo adorable y encantador—. Si en los exámenes saco unas notas que superen la media nacional, ¿puedo ponerme un piercing en la nariz?

El pezón probablemente sería demasiado, la nariz es razonable.

Mamá baja la cabeza. No cree que sea un tema serio.

—No, Jasper —dice—. No puedes.

—La clave de una buena relación madre-hijo es el compromiso —le digo—. Me esforzaré en el instituto si me prometes las libertades personales que me merezco.

Mamá tuerce la boca. No sé qué le pasa por la cabeza. La mente de Mamá funciona de forma sencilla, no puede manejar demasiados pensamientos.

Mira a Keith.

Él sonríe.

Vuelve a mirarme.

—Vale —dice—. Este es el trato. Puedes hacerte un piercing en la oreja si sacas mejores notas que la media del instituto.

¡Mamá ha excavado un túnel por debajo de mi plan! Sabe que la media del instituto es superior a la nacional.

—En las orejas queda gay —contesto—. ¿Ceja?

—Oreja.

—¿Labio?

—Oreja.

—¿Un implante subdérmico en el hombro izquierdo?

—Oreja.

—¿Ombligo?

—El trato es en la oreja o nada, Jasper.

Respiro profundamente. Ojalá dejara de decir «trato». Mamá se cree que es Noel Edmonds.

—¿En el pene, entonces?

—No seas asqueroso —replica Mamá—. Algún día me agradecerás que no te haya dejado mutilarte el cuerpo.

—No es asqueroso, Mamá. En realidad, es muy sensual. Aumenta la estimulación sexual para los dos. Tienes la mente muy cerrada.

Keith le da con el codo a Mamá y hace un sonido sexual. Mamá le ignora. Se me acerca más. Es Julia.

—Jasper —dice en voz baja apartando la taza de té a un lado como si le diera miedo que me fuera a esconder detrás—, ¿eres sexualmente activo?

—Ups —exclamo—. Me parece que se nos ha acabado el tiempo. Lo siento, Mamá.

Subo.

Me tumbo en la cama e intento no pensar en la madre rubia. Es difícil porque mi imaginación llena la habitación con un montón de gente gritando: «¿Que has hecho qué?», y no tengo respuesta que darles. Pongo Los Campesinos! en el portátil. Borro mi cabeza con una almohada.

Suena el teléfono.

—¿Jasper? Soy Tenaya.

—Ya.

—¿Qué haces esta noche?

Me levanto, miro a mi alrededor y me rasco la ingle.

—Nada, supongo. ¿Por qué?

—¿Puedo ir a tu casa?

—Claro.

Debe de estar cansada de pasar el rato junto al fantasma de Tom. Se habrá dado cuenta de que la compañía de verdad es mejor que unas manchas horribles en los recuerdos felices.

—Gracias. ¿A las seis?

—Claro.

—Te veo luego.

—Adiós.

Me siento en mi silla giratoria (Keith la robó de la basura de su oficina) y me acerco hasta el escritorio de madera falsa. El libro de Psicología ya está abierto, extendido como una mujer desnuda delante de mí. En realidad, no, nada que ver con una mujer desnuda, es mil veces menos seductor. Si fuera una mujer desnuda, estaría aprendiéndome su cuerpo con los ojos y estrujándome la polla como si fuera un tubo de pasta de dientes casi vacío. Pero no lo es. Va de algo sobre el autismo y cómo detectarlo. No quiero ser un detective de autismo. Quiero irme a dormir.

* * *

Tenaya llega a las 17:30. Lleva un vestido blanco de verano y unas botas viejas. Vuelve a estar guapa, y sonríe. En la cocina, se sienta sobre la encimera con las piernas colgando mientras hiervo agua.

—¿Qué tal va lo de Tom? —pregunto.

—Creo que lo he superado.

—¿En serio?

—Sí. Creo que superar algo no significa olvidarlo sino aprender a vivir con el recuerdo.

—Ah.

Se ríe.

—Como tú conseguiste vivir sin Abby.

—Perder a Abby fue duro —comento—. Pasé muchas noches sin dormir y muchas horas llorando y tapándome la cara con las manos.

—¿Se enteró de que fuiste tú?

—No estoy seguro.

—Supongo que algo sospecharía.

Llevamos las tazas de té arriba y nos tumbamos en la cama. Pongo a Feist en el portátil.

—Exhumaremos a Margaret Clamwell mañana —dice Tenaya.

—De puta madre —contesto. Lo había olvidado—. Creo que Keith tiene unos pasamontañas en algún sitio, podemos usarlos.

—¿En serio quieres ponerte un pasamontañas?

—Sí, ¿por qué no?

—¿No es un poco de criminales?

—No sé, quizá. Pero, en cuanto tengamos el cuerpo, todo el mundo sabrá que Keith es el criminal, no nosotros. Seremos héroes.

—¿Y qué pasa si no hay cuerpo?

—Hay un cuerpo.

—Si estás seguro...

—Estoy seguro.

* * *

Cuando me despierto, la única luz en la habitación es la que proyecta la pantalla del reproductor de DVD. El televisor se ha puesto en modo *stand by*. Tenaya se ha quedado dormida, doblada como una herradura, en la parte derecha de la cama, con el vestido puesto y enrollado por la espalda.

Bajo y me como cuatro Weetabix con cuatro cucharadas de azúcar y un vaso de leche. El reloj de la cocina marca las 6:30, pero el reloj de la cocina siempre va diez minutos adelantado. Diez minutos de adelanto no le bastan para ser más listo que yo. Ya me sé este pequeño truco. Es un reloj, no tiene mucho más que hacer que intentar colar sus chistes malos a gente que tiene que ir a algún sitio de verdad. Yo tengo que ir a un sitio. Tengo que salvar la vida de mi madre.

—Toma —digo, y le lamo la frente para despertarla. Le paso una taza de té—. Levántate y deslumbra.

Nos sentamos en el borde de la cama mientras nos tomamos el té, mirando fijamente el papel pintado.

—Si hay un cuerpo... —dice Tenaya, pero no termina la frase.

—Chsst —digo—. Solo sacaremos la cabeza y llamaremos a la policía.

—Podrías tocarle tú la cabeza.

—Vale, tocaré yo la cabeza.

Mi móvil vibra. Un mensaje de Ping. «Viens ta noche?»

Miro a Tenaya.

—¿Quieres ir a la colina esta noche? —le pregunto.

—No sé. No me apetece mucho.

—Vale.

Contesto «n puedo, lo siento. ocupdo». Miro la hora en el teléfono (6:40) y añado: «q acs levntao?». Un segundo después, Ping contesta: «no m e acstao».

Cuando Tenaya se acaba el té, cojo los pasamontañas y nos vamos en silencio. En la calle hace una de las claras mañanas típicas de las afueras. No queda muy lejos y solo nos cruzamos con un hombre con sobrepeso vestido con un polo que pasea un pitbull color castaña y una madre de esas que te molaría tirarte, rubia, corriendo con mallas de licra y una expresión seria y motivada. Tenaya me regaña por seguir el movimiento del culo de la mujer con la mirada. Dice que la mujer no es un objeto. Le contesto que la mujer no es un objeto, pero su ano sí.

18

Antes de la exhumación, dibujé un pene con típex en la parte de atrás del pasamontañas de Tenaya para que, si nos ven, la gente informe a la policía de un pasamontañas con un pene, lo encuentren en posesión de Tenaya, la arresten a ella y yo quede libre. Por desgracia, se da cuenta antes de ponérselo e insiste en que nos lo cambiemos, así que ahora voy a exhumar a la ex mujer de Keith con un grosero falo blanco dibujado en la parte de atrás de mi cabeza.

Llevamos media hora cavando en el montículo sospechoso con las manos. Tenaya no está haciendo mucho porque no quiere que se le llenen las uñas de tierra. Le he dicho que es cuestión de vida o muerte, pero no me ha creído. El sol ha salido del todo y el cielo es de un azul claro, tan claro como la piel de las mejillas de Georgia Treely. Para prepararme ante el horror que nos espera, me he estado imaginando a Georgia Treely con un bikini amarillo guiñándome el ojo. La familia que vive en la casa se despertará pronto. Aún no hemos encontrado nada.

—Me parece que deberíamos irnos —dice Tenaya.

—¿Quieres que mi madre muera?

—No creo que tu madre vaya a morir, Jasper.

—La gente tampoco creía que Martin Luther King fuera a morir —le explico.

Tenaya suspira profundamente.

Sigo sacando tierra con las manos. Solo encuentro un tazo con un dibujo de Taz, el Demonio de Tasmania. Me meto el tazo en el bolsillo y sigo cavando, se me están poniendo las manos del color del chow mein. Un par de minutos después, Tenaya tira de mí y nos quedamos los dos tumbados en la tierra.

—¿Qué coño pasa? —pregunto.

—He visto a alguien moverse en la casa.

—¿Por qué no hemos corrido? ¿De qué nos va a servir quedarnos aquí tumbados?

Noto una piedra presionándome la entrepierna y bajo la mano para quitarla.

—Jasper, ¿qué estás haciendo?

Una chica con un pijama de pequeños elefantes de dibujos sale de la casa al jardín. No nos ve enseguida. La piedra sigue aplastándome el pene y el testículo izquierdo. La chica se coge un cigarro de detrás de la oreja y lo enciende. La chica nos ve. Tenaya es la primera en ponerse de pie. Se quita el pasamontañas. Yo me dejo el mío.

—Gracias por no gritar —dice Tenaya.

—¿Qué coño estáis haciendo? —pregunta la chica, más tranquila de lo que cabría esperar. El cigarro sigue en su mano, transformándose rápidamente en un cilindro de ceniza. Ninguno de los dos decimos nada. Me duele la entrepierna, así que me recoloco el pene con la mano a través del pantalón—. ¿Puedes dejar de tocarte la polla, por favor? —dice la chica—. Y quítate el puto pasamontañas.

Me quito el puto pasamontañas.

—Lo siento —dice Tenaya—. Estamos buscando a nuestro gato.

—¿Con pasamontañas?

—A Rupert le dan miedo las caras. —La chica nos mira fijamente—. Nos marchamos ya.

La chica asiente. Tiene la cara roja, como si le hubiera explotado una lata de sopa de tomate.

Tenaya y yo nos damos la vuelta, corremos y volvemos a saltar la valla del fondo del jardín. Seguimos corriendo hasta que estamos a tres calles, y entonces nos paramos, jadeantes. Lío un cigarro y lo enciendo. Tenaya me coge el tabaco y hace lo mismo. Nos sentamos en un muro bajo.

—Rupert es un nombre de mierda para un gato —comento.

—Era una excusa mejor que tú tocándote la polla.

Un hombre calvo, que lleva a su hijo pelirrojo de la mano, pasa a nuestro lado con una peculiar expresión en la cara, como un extraño abanico oriental.

—¿Crees que se lo dirá a sus padres? —pregunto.

—No. —Tenaya niega con la cabeza—. Se ha despertado temprano y ha salido a fumar. Es más fácil no decir nada que intentar explicar la situación.

Cuando recuperamos el aliento y nos acabamos los cigarros, volvemos a mi casa a desayunar. Mamá y Keith ya se han ido a trabajar, así que no tenemos que inventarnos excusas. Nos sentamos a la mesa de la cocina con un bol de Cheerios y un té cada uno. Yo uso mi taza de Harry Potter y Tenaya usa la de Mamá que dice LA MEJOR MADRE DEL MUNDO. No le compré la taza a Mamá. Keith la compró, la envolvió y me la dio para que se la regalara por su cumpleaños. Lo hizo porque sabe que soy un egoísta pero no quiere que Mamá lo sepa porque eso la haría infeliz y si es infeliz tal vez le deje y entonces no podrá asesinarla. No quiere perder la oportunidad de asesinarla. Para Keith, el asesinato es mejor incluso que el sexo anal.

—No ha funcionado —dice Tenaya.

—Ya —comento. Un hilo de leche me cae por la barbilla tragándose los pequeños pelos como un tsunami se traga a los niños pobres—. Me siento mal.

—Deberíamos estudiar.

No quiero dejar sola a Tenaya, especialmente después de la exhumación fallida, y menos en compañía de libros de texto.

—Podríamos ir esta noche a la fiesta.

Sus brazos me lo agradecerán.

—No, tenemos que estudiar.

—¿Te acuerdas de la última vez que subimos a la colina?

Tenaya se ríe.

La última vez que subimos a la colina fue cuando nos gustaba quemar cosas. Recorríamos los barrios vacíos de las afueras en busca de cobertizos y casas viejas.

Los dos nos emocionamos mucho cuando encontramos el cobertizo en lo alto de la colina. Estaba cerrado, así que metimos bolas de papel de periódico en los agujeros y grietas, las prendimos con cerillas y nos sentamos a brindar con cerveza.

Es emocionante ver cómo el cobertizo se disuelve entre plumas naranja que inundan el verde moteado del bosque. Aún veo el naranja reflejado en los ojos de Tenaya. El fuego calienta el cristal de las botellas de cerveza.

Después, gritos.

Y arañazos.

Arañazos desesperados dentro del cobertizo.

Un hombre sale corriendo. Es difícil verlo bien porque partes de su cuerpo arden, como los pantalones o el pelo, por ejemplo. Tiene la boca abierta. Le veo los dientes, pequeños trozos de marfil combinados con agujeros negros y costras amarillas como las de los heroinómanos que salían en los DVD que la señora Thorne nos ponía en clase de Salud y Desarrollo Personal y Social.

—¡Joder! —grita Tenaya. Siento una oleada de gratitud porque no se ha aficionado, como su madre, a embellecer los tacos—. Mierda, Jasper, haz algo.

Miro a Tenaya, al suelo y al hombre en llamas que ahora está muy cerca de nosotros rodando como un queso largo y delgado. Miro a Tenaya. Miro al hombre. Debería hacer algo. Tengo miedo y me preocupa que el hombre intente apuñalarme con una de sus agujas, lo que me contagiaría el VIH que a su vez podría convertirse en sida que podría derivar en mi muerte. Miro la casa. Miro a Tenaya.

—¿A qué coño esperas? —grita, mirándome con expectación.

Siempre decepciono a la gente. Soy un egoísta. Me pongo encima del hombre, me saco el pene, pequeño y marchito, y lo riego con orina hasta que me da un fuerte golpe en la espinilla. Me dan ganas de devolvérselo. Se lo devuelvo. Tras mi acto instintivo de venganza aparece de inmediato una sensación de culpa porque él sigue ardiendo y yo no. Sus ojos son los más grandes que he visto jamás.

Sigo meando porque, como dice Mamá, algún día me lo agradecerá.

—Tuviste suerte de que no te diera en la polla —dice Tenaya.

Cojo las tazas y las llevo al fregadero.

—Pues sí —comento—. Entonces, ¿vamos a la fiesta?

Tenaya suspira de nuevo. Suspira a menudo.

—Vale.

Soy el salvador de los brazos adolescentes.

Dejo una nota en un post-it en la nevera.

NO VOLVERÉ ESTA NOCHE, MAMÁ. DIVIÉRTETE.

CON CARIÑO,

TU HIJO FAVORITO

(JASPER)

19

16:06. Estamos en casa de Ping llamando a la puerta blanca de plástico. Contesta su madre. Lleva una camiseta de Led Zeppelin y los labios pintados del color de las barras de neón rosas. La madre de Ping es muy atractiva sexualmente. Me planteo guiñarle un ojo. Decido no hacerlo. Le preguntamos si está Ping y nos dice que está en la cama, que subamos. Cuando pasamos a su lado, me aseguro de rozarle el pezón con el hombro. Le pido perdón y me sonríe. Me gustaría muchísimo follármela. Si la madre de Ping fuera prostituta, cometería una estafa con tarjetas de crédito para conseguir el dinero suficiente para pagar lo que costara acostarse con ella.

Arriba, entramos en la habitación de Ping uno detrás del otro y nos ponemos a saltar encima de él haciendo sonidos estridentes y sin sentido. No paramos hasta que se pone a gritar: «¡Idos a la mierda!», y a darnos bofetadas en nuestras sonrientes caras. Al final consigue sentarse en la cama.

—¿Qué hora es? —pregunta. Tiene la voz ronca por el sueño.

—Las cuatro.

—¿Las cuatro? —repite—. ¿Y por qué coño me habéis despertado?

Tras decir esto, se vuelve a tapar la cabeza con el edredón. Tenaya y yo le damos puñetazos hasta que se sienta otra vez.

—Tenemos que ir a por Jonah —dice Tenaya—. Y después subir a la colina.

—Tampoco tardaremos tanto.

—Jonah no quiere conducir de noche.

Ping se ríe.

—Menudo marica —dice mientras sale de la cama. Se pone de pie a nuestro lado, en calzoncillos, y se rasca la cabeza—. Vale, vale —dice—. Vale.

Le observamos mientras busca unos vaqueros, una camiseta y una sudadera con capucha y bajamos. Ping coge una tostada de la mano de su madre, le da un beso en la mejilla y nos vamos.

El camino hasta casa de Jonah no es muy largo pero Ping aprovecha el trayecto para probar varios chistes nuevos sobre Abby Hall que se le han ocurrido.

—Oye, Jasper, ¿qué tal estuvo follarte a una tía con una cara como Stonehenge? —me pregunta cuando llegamos a la calle de Jonah.

Hasta Tenaya se ríe.

Los padres de Jonah están en el trabajo, así que nos abre él. Nos sentamos con él en el sofá a ver *Celebrity Big Brother*.

Intentamos adivinar quiénes son los famosos. Le digo a Ping que su madre está lo suficientemente buena como para ser famosa y me da un puñetazo en el brazo. Tenaya pregunta si el negro es Will Smith. Ping la llama racista.

—¿Queréis cerveza? —pregunta Jonah.

Le decimos que sí y va a la cocina. Vuelve y seguimos allí sentados, bebiendo cerveza y viendo la tele. Vemos a otra gente sentada viendo a otra gente.

—Ojalá George Bush entrara en *Gran Hermano* —dice Ping.

—George Bush no iría a *Gran Hermano* —comenta Tenaya.

—¿Por qué no?

—Alguien le dispararía.

—¿No le han disparado ya? —pregunta Jonah.

—No —contesto—. Estoy seguro de que George Bush sigue vivo.

—Es normal pensar que alguien le haya disparado. En teoría, los estadounidenses están como putas cabras y de lo único que hablaban era de cuánto le odiaban.

—Tampoco han disparado a Obama —dice Ping.

—Todo el mundo quiere a Obama.

—Porque es negro. Ya no mola ser racista.

Pienso en mi camiseta del Klan y en Julia. Tengo que acordarme de sacar el tema de Obama con Julia. Keith una vez le llamó extranjero con aires de superioridad.

—¿Podemos dejar de hablar de Estados Unidos? —dice Tenaya.

—¿Conoces a la hermana pequeña de Ana?

—Sí.

—Ha visto tanta tele de Estados Unidos que tiene acento de allí.

Arrugo los labios.

—Qué gilipollez.

—Pues sí.

—Pero Hannah Montana está buena.

—Ya ves.

Después de *Gran Hermano* lo único que hay es un episodio repetido de *Friends* que todos hemos visto seis veces, así que nos vamos.

Tenemos que recoger a Ana. Su casa no queda lejos. Cuando llegamos a su calle, está fuera gritándole a una mujer mayor que lleva un gorro amarillo. La mujer tiene la cara llena de arrugas y lunares y los párpados medio cerrados.

—La casa está por allí —grita—. Vieja estúpida de mierda. Vuelve y deja de seguirme.

Ana es cruel.

Ping nos explica que la mujer es la abuela de Ana y también su única tutora legal. Ana es la niña de su abuela. En el coche, Ana nos cuenta que su abuelo murió hace seis años y que a veces su abuela se pone sus gafas y se queda sentada llorando. Le cuento lo que Mamá dijo sobre que las mujeres saben salir adelante cuando sus maridos mueren. Ana dice que eso es una estupidez. Se tarda media hora en coche hasta el claro de lo alto de la colina y tenemos que parar de camino para comprar alcohol y tabaco. Cuando llegamos, ha oscurecido y Jonah está cabreado.

20

En el claro de la colina arde una buena hoguera. Al lado, alguien ha colgado un tablón de madera de un árbol con una cuerda azul deshilachada para hacer un columpio. Una chica alta que nunca había visto antes está sentada en él con los ojos cerrados y baba en la barbilla. Ketamina. Ya han montado tres tiendas y la mayoría de la gente está sentada en mantas o troncos en grupos alrededor del fuego. Un chico del curso inferior al nuestro está sentado junto a un saco de leña lanzando ramas a las llamas. Crystal Castles suena en los altavoces portátiles de un iPod.

Saludamos a la gente que conocemos y nos fijamos en los que no. Hay una cantidad razonable de chicas guapas. Georgia Treely no está pero tampoco esperaba que viniera. No la habrían dejado y tampoco tendría demasiado interés en venir. Probablemente estará en casa, estudiando con el coño seco y escuchando a Mahler de fondo con el volumen bajo. A Georgia Treely le gusta mucho Mahler. A Georgia Treely no le cae bien Sam porque en clase de Economía dijo que en realidad no había ningún cambio climático.

Bebemos cerveza hasta que todo el mundo decide que está bastante borracho, y entonces nos sentamos. Un rato después, Jonah me mira con expresión confusa.

—Jasper —me dice—, ¿qué generación somos nosotros?

Me encojo de hombros.

—No lo sé. La Z o algo así.

—No, es la Y —afirma Ping.

—Pensaba que éramos la Generación X.

—No, gilipollas —digo—. La Generación X fueron Van Halen y esos.

—Deberíamos ser la Generación Culo.

—¿Por qué cojones deberíamos ser la Generación Culo?

—Porque somos la primera generación que se ha liberado del estigma asociado al sexo anal.

—No es verdad.

—Sí, yo no pienso acercarme al culo de nadie.

—Vale, entonces somos la Generación Capullo.

—Tú eres la Generación Capullo.

—Sea cual sea, me parece que no formamos parte de ella.

—¿Qué? ¿Por qué?

—¿Qué porcentaje de la población mundial crees que son chicos blancos de clase media?

—La generación la componen los ricos, imbécil, claro que formamos parte de ella.

—Claro. Si no, no se le habría puesto el nombre de un grupo punk. Habría sido la Generación Malaria o algo así.

—La Generación X no se llama así por un grupo, se llama así por el libro.

—Qué va, ese libro era una puta mierda. Se llama así por el grupo.

—Mi madre dice que somos la Generación Facebook —comenta Ping.

—Uf, me encantaría follarme a tu madre.

Ping levanta el dedo de en medio.

Todo el mundo se ríe.

Una hora más tarde, Jonah nos está contando no sé qué

cosa que hacen en Europa del Este en el solsticio de verano. Dice que encienden hogueras y las saltan por turnos y que cada vez que alguien la salta ponen un tronco más. Dice que deberíamos probarlo. Estamos todos borrachos. Nos parece bien.

Jonah dice que nos dirá el orden en que saltaremos con el generador de números aleatorio del móvil. Me siento a su lado. En realidad, ha escrito el orden que cree que será más divertido. Queda así:

Jonah
Yo
Ping
Tenaya
Ana

Me sonríe y lee el orden. Ping se queja del lugar de Ana, pero Jonah le contesta que Dios ha hablado.

Jonah y yo saltamos el fuego sin problemas. Antes de que salte Ping, Jonah vacía todo el saco de madera en la hoguera. Los del Baccant High nos miran. Ping empuja a Jonah. Están a punto de pelearse pero alguien se mete en medio moviéndose como loco.

—¡JODERJODERJODER, AYUDADME! —grita—. ¡AGUA! ¡CERVEZA! ¡ALGO FRÍO! ¡AYUDADME, JODER!

—¿Qué coño pasa? —pregunta Tenaya.

—¡PUTASORTIGASJODER! ¡ME HA EMPUJADO UN COLEGA! ¡AYUDADME, JODER! ¡AYUDADME!

Tiene la cara como un pan tigre. Me gusta el pan tigre. Largas cadenas montañosas de color rojo sobresalen de su piel.

Jonah le tira una lata de cerveza vacía a la cabeza. El chico se aleja dando tumbos intentando mitigar el dolor.

Tenaya chasquea la lengua.

—Teníamos que haberle ayudado.

—No —dice Jonah—. Es un capullo.

—No le conoces.

—Se le veía en la cara. Da igual, si no era un capullo, ¿por qué iban a empujarle a las ortigas?

—¿Porque eran unos capullos?

—Tú sí que eres capulla.

21

Cuando el cielo se tiñe de negro por completo, Tenaya se sienta mirándose las manos a la luz del fuego. Eso significa que se le estará nublando la mente. Necesita movimiento. Le pregunto si quiere andar. Asiente con la cabeza despacio y nos levantamos. Los demás están todos borrachos, hablando o partiéndose de risa, así que nadie se da cuenta.

Salimos del claro. La única luz es la que proyecta la hoguera. Se cuela en haces entre los árboles. Seguimos su estela por la tierra y las hojas. Cuando se vuelve tan débil que se desvanece, saco el teléfono del bolsillo y lo utilizo de linterna. Subimos un poco más hasta llegar al campo empinado con el roble ennegrecido por un rayo. Nos sentamos en las ramas bajas del árbol, desde allí vemos la luz de las farolas y las ventanas. Fumo y Tenaya balancea las piernas. Tira los zapatos y hunde los pies en la alta hierba.

—Tom tiene novia —dice Tenaya.

Se saca del abrigo una pequeña botella de vodka de marca de supermercado y bebe. Me la pasa. Sabe a hospital. Se la paso y nos quedamos en silencio un rato.

—¿Quién es? —pregunto.

—Lydia Jenkins.

—¿La que es un año más mayor y tiene nueve dedos?

Tenaya se ríe.

—No, la que tiene un año menos y siempre lleva un pañuelo en la cabeza.

—Ah —digo—. Ella.

—La verdad es que no lo he superado —dice.

—Lo sé —le respondo.

Me vuelve a pasar el vodka y me mira. Una de las ventanas se oscurece. Otras se iluminan. Me giro para mirar a Tenaya. Tiene los párpados medio cerrados y las mangas del abrigo estiradas hasta los nudillos.

—Pronto seremos viejos, yo tendré un bombín y tú tendrás un labrador —comento—. No te acordarás de su cara.

—Desde aquí arriba se ve todo —dice—. Pero aún no hemos llegado aquí.

Nos pasamos el vodka durante un rato, observando las luces de abajo y preguntándonos cuáles serán las nuestras algún día. Lío dos cigarros y lanzamos anillos de humo al aire helado. Un rato después, Tenaya dice que tiene frío y me pregunta si podemos irnos. Dice que podríamos volver andando. Tardaremos horas pero le digo que sí y saco el móvil para utilizarlo como linterna mientras volvemos entre los árboles hacia el camino principal.

El camino de bajada de la colina es empinado, difícil y lleno de baches. Nos vamos parando de vez en cuando para liar cigarros y tumbarnos de espaldas. De pie en medio del camino, Tenaya me coge de la mano y dice que no sabe.

Un coche que baja por el camino hace ruidos como un hombre asmático. Se para a nuestro lado. Es un viejo Citroën con el capó arqueado y los faros circulares. Un hombre saca la cabeza por la ventana abierta. Tiene el pelo blanco como una nube y lleva encajado un gorrito.

—Ei —pregunta la cabeza—. ¿Adónde vais?

Tenaya me mira y asiento. Sabemos que no deberíamos subir a coches como aquel pero estamos borrachos y además el coche huele a marihuana, lo que significa que el hombre no podrá moverse con rapidez y nosotros podríamos escapar corriendo si intentara matarnos o violarnos. Tenaya le da su dirección a la cabeza.

—Putamadre —dice la cabeza—. Subid.

Tengo que sentarme en el asiento del copiloto porque atrás lleva un motor de coche. Una vez dentro, el hombre se enciende un porro y se pone en marcha. Conduce en silencio durante unos minutos y después aparta la vista del camino para mirarme.

—¿Cómo te llamas? —pregunta.

—Jasper —respondo.

—¿Has celebrado el Bar Mitzvah, Jaz?

—Jasper —le corrijo—. Y no. Mis padres son cristianos.

—Qué suerte. No te ha tocado sentarte a leer ese puto libro gordísimo delante de todos esos niños. Te equivocas y tus padres te ponen esa puta cara, como si te hubieran pillado pelándotela con un calcetín una y otra vez. Un puto infierno. Nunca aceptes tener un Bar Mitzvah. Aunque yo no tuve elección.

—Joder —digo.

A Tenaya se le escapan unas risitas en la parte de atrás. El judío no se da cuenta.

—Sí, joder. Ser judío es una mierda.

Da una calada al porro. Mueve los dedos, nervioso. El judío no presta atención a la carretera sino a sus manos. El coche vira ligeramente y la rueda delantera izquierda choca con el bordillo, sacudiendo el coche. En el espejo veo a Tenaya con la boca abierta. El judío salta y levanta la cabeza. Se queda en silencio un momento.

—No soy judío, no de verdad. ¿Sabéis lo que soy? —Niego con la cabeza—. Soy un discípulo del coño.

No digo nada. Tenaya se ríe aún más.

—¿Has leído la Biblia, Jaz?

—No.

—Yo he leído la Torá, la Biblia y el Corán. No leas ninguno, ¿me oyes?

—Sí.

—No son más que la palabra de Dios tras años de jugar al teléfono roto. Al puto teléfono roto. ¿Has jugado al teléfono roto en la escuela alguna vez, Jaz?

—Claro, unas cuantas veces.

—El profesor empieza con una frase normal, ¿vale? Después hay algunos críos que entienden perfectamente lo que les dice el que tienen al lado, pero les parece que cambiar la frase sería la hostia de divertido, así que meten algún joder o polla o follar o zorra, ¿vale?

—Sí, me acuerdo.

—Lo hacen para molar más. «Tío, conoces al pavo ese que lanzó el bombazo en el corro, es la hostia.»

Asiento con la cabeza con todas mis ganas. Me pasa el porro.

—Eso es la Biblia, Jazzy. No es la palabra de Dios. Es la palabra de Dios con unos cuantos joderes y pollas y zorras en medio. Solo que la Biblia no dice ni joder ni polla ni zorra. ¿Sabes lo que dice?

No respondo. Masco el aire denso. El humo de la marihuana se acumula en pequeñas nubes entre nuestras cabezas.

—Dice «mujeres, cubríos la cabeza y gays, arded en el infierno y no os atreváis a usar un puto condón, niños, y ¿qué haces trabajando el domingo, Mamá?».

Observa el techo durante un momento. Le imito. El techo. Hay amplios círculos marrones dibujados por sus cigarros, como manchas de tazas de té gigantes.

El judío me hace un gesto para que sujete el volante mientras se lía otro porro y lo enciende.

—Fúmatelo como si fuera tu mujer —le oigo susurrar—. Oye, Jazzy.

—¿Qué?

—¿Quieres saber cuál fue la verdadera palabra de Dios?

—Sí.

—Dijo: «Fóllate a esa zorra por el agujero».

Cuando llegamos a casa de Tenaya, le damos las gracias al judío.

—Nada de Bar Mitzvah —murmura, y me pasa un porro.

Le da la mano a Tenaya e intenta besarla pero ella se aparta. Los ojos no le cambian de forma. Está acostumbrado a que le rechacen, imagino.

Bajamos directamente al sótano de casa de Tenaya y pone agua a hervir para preparar té. Su madre está sentada a la mesa con una botella de vino tinto. Tiene manchas rojas alrededor de la boca y en la blusa, muy juntas, como un archipiélago después de años de guerra.

Le dice a Tenaya que su padre es un chupapollas.

Me dice que soy un buen chico.

En la cama, Tenaya y yo nos colocamos espalda contra espalda. No encajan bien pero es una sensación agradable. Antes de dormirnos, me dice que *Waldeinsamkeit* es una palabra alemana que describe el sentimiento de soledad en un bosque.

22

Las paredes de la habitación son del color de la gasolina. Hay un chico en un rincón con un collar de madera acariciándole el pelo a una chica sin cara. Unos números verdes se desplazan por el suelo.

—Yo que tú tendría cuidado —dice el chico.

—¿Por qué?

—Matrix —contesta—. El puto Matrix.

Cojo un jarrón del suelo y lo estampo contra la pared. Se rompe. Los pedazos se esparcen por la habitación.

—Cuidado —me advierte el chico.

Cojo un candelabro de la repisa de la chimenea y se lo tiro al chico. Le da en la cabeza. La sangre le corre por la frente, por los valles de ambos lados de la nariz, hacia las comisuras de los labios.

—Estás loco —me dice.

Coge la mano de la chica y tira de ella hacia la chimenea. Corren hacia la oscuridad.

—¡No! —grito—. Parad.

Cojo marcos vacíos de la mesita y los tiro a la chimenea. Se encogen y desaparecen. Me quito los pantalones y los tiro también. Después tiro el jersey, la camiseta y los calcetines.

—No —digo. Me enrosco como un ovillo en la moqueta—. No.

Hay un pasamontañas negro en la repisa de la ventana. Le han pintado un crucifijo en la parte de atrás. Lo veo desde mi ovillo. Me levanto y me lo pongo.

Salgo de la casa.

Jonah está en el jardín. Un campo de trigo. Un sol color salmón tan ancho como el mundo. Está cortando troncos con un hacha del tamaño de su brazo. Hay una cabaña a medio construir detrás de él. No se detiene cuando me acerco.

—¿Qué coño es esa cosa? —me pregunta.

—¿Qué cosa?

—Esa cosa que llevas en la cabeza.

—Es una metáfora —digo—. Ilustra cómo puedo estar rodeado de gente y seguir sintiéndome solo y anónimo.

Un tronco se parte en dos. Las mitades vuelan al separarse, una en cada dirección, como imanes que se repelen.

—Quítatelo —dice Jonah—. Pareces gilipollas. Y vuelve dentro. Si te quedas aquí mucho más, tendré que construirte un ataúd.

—No me gusta estar en la casa.

—Entonces, levántate del suelo del salón.

Me doy la vuelta y entro. Las paredes de esta habitación son del color del tulipán. El suelo de esta habitación es de césped artificial.

En la cocina, Tenaya sale de un horno. Se arrastra hasta mis pies y se levanta. Su cara está cerca de la mía.

—Quítatelo, Jasper —me dice.

—No.

—Quítatelo.

—No.

Coge el pasamontañas con las dos manos y tira. Le lanzo la mano derecha a la mandíbula. Se parte. Cae de espaldas sobre el linóleo. Tiene la mitad de la cara roja, cubierta de sangre. Es un oso que ha estado atiborrándose a lo loco de pescado. Le dan ataques como a un epiléptico. Tiene los labios tan estirados que le tocan la barbilla y la nariz.

—¿Qué estás haciendo? —pregunta.

—Participo en la escena de un sueño —grito—. Para mi novela. Mi novela. Les dará a los lectores una idea de mis sentimientos más profundos. Alargará el libro.

—¿Qué estás haciendo, Jasper?

—La escena de un sueño —grito.

—¿Qué estás haciendo?

—Sueño —grito.

—¿Jasper?

—Sueño.

—¿Jasper?

Tenaya está sentada a un lado de la cama dándome en el hombro con el codo. Tiene la piel fría. Lleva un vestido blanco de verano y sujeta dos tazas de té.

—Buenos días —dice.

Me froto los ojos y le sonrío. Quiero llorar pero no lo hago.

—Buenos días.

Cojo el té y me siento.

—Mamá está borracha —me cuenta—. Me ha dicho que Papá se ha largado y que no va a volver.

—¿Estás bien?

—Quería que se marchara desde hace tiempo. Sin él, Mamá no tendrá con quién discutir.

—Podría discutir contigo.

—Intentaré mantenerme alejada.

—¿Crees que las cosas mejorarán?

—No lo sé.

—Vale.

23

Es importante aprobar los exámenes por varias razones:

- ✓ Para que Mamá no se ponga roja y no me grite y me siga dando dinero para comprar cerveza y drogas.
- ✓ Para poder terminar el bachillerato el año que viene y no tener que preocuparme por encontrar trabajo ni por tener que tomar parte activa en la vida durante un año más.
- ✓ Para poder entrar en la universidad y no tener que preocuparme por encontrar trabajo ni por tener que tomar parte activa en la vida durante tres años más.
- ✓ Para que Georgia Treely crea que soy un hombre que va a conseguir algo y que será trabajador y un buen padre para sus hijos.
- ✓ Para que Tenaya no me pegue.

Estoy en la bañera pensando en estas cosas. Tengo en las manos el libro de Filosofía y Religión. Leo que algunas personas creen en Dios porque han tenido visiones de la Virgen María. Hay una foto grande de la Virgen María con un vestido azul y una expresión tranquila, de alegría. Me aburro. El libro dice que las personas pueden alucinar como consecuencia de un estrés emocional extremo. Me pregunto si alucinaré por el estrés emocional que me provoca Keith con su incesante conspiración homicida. Espero alucinar con Georgia Treely masturbándose con un cepillo de dientes.

Doblo el libro para que la foto de la Virgen María quede a la vista y lo sujeto con una mano. Me sumerjo más en el agua y sujeto la foto justo a la altura de mi cabeza. Me la acerco a la cara hasta que la nariz de la Virgen María casi toca la mía. La foto tiembla mientras me masturbo. Después, me recuesto y observo el semen flotar tristemente formando islas en la superficie.

El siguiente tema que trata el libro es la Trinidad. No hay nada pajeable en estas páginas, así que leo un poco. Representan la Trinidad con un gráfico de un triángulo con el Padre, el Hijo y el Espíritu Santo escritos en los tres vértices y la frase ¡TODOS SON UNO! escrita en el centro. Haile Selassie es el nombre de un emperador etíope, significa «el poder de la Trinidad». Los rastafaris creen que era Jesús. Se ponen a ambos lados de Copson Lane y se gritan su nombre los unos a los otros. Mamá no quiere pasar a su lado porque cree que si respira el humo de su marihuana se volverá adicta a las drogas y morirá de sobredosis de heroína en una casa con las paredes llenas de ratones muertos.

Me lavo el pelo púbico con champú y me pongo acondicionador, después repito la operación con el pelo de la cabeza antes de salir de la bañera. Me enrollo una toalla a la cintura y la remeto para que se aguante sola. Mamá me espera fuera del baño con las manos en las caderas.

—Jasper —dice—. Has estado en la bañera casi una hora.

—Mamá —le respondo—, es ilegal interrogar a gente que no lleva nada de ropa.

—¿Qué estabas haciendo?

Muevo el libro de Filosofía y Religión delante de su cara.

—Estaba estudiando —digo—. Voy a hacer que estés muy orgullosa de mí, Mamá.

Lanza una exclamación del tipo «hummm» y me aparta para entrar al baño.

En mi habitación, descargo y veo una película serbia sobre un hombre que cree que su mujer es un fantasma.

—Para ser un fantasma, has estado muy bien, cariño —le dice en una escena después de follar.

Ella le da una bofetada y sale de la habitación.

Cuando las nubes se han tragado todo el azul del cielo, me siento ante mi escritorio y retomo el trabajo en mi novela. Tomo notas sobre un hombre que construye una cabaña en el bosque y la utiliza para violar chicas. Después de violarlas, con un cuchillo de untar corta sus cuerpos en pequeños trozos con los que hace rollitos de salchicha que luego le da a su madre esquizofrénica. Creo que es importante escribir sobre cosas así. Es importante porque estas cosas pasan a menudo, sobre todo en Estados Unidos. Suelen ser hombres con bigote quienes las hacen, como Keith.

Posibles títulos para la novela:

Y los árboles callan
Sube al coche y te harás famosa
Desflorada en el bosque
Clavar el tronco
Ramera

Me miro fijamente las manos durante un rato. Pienso en las cosas malas que la gente hace. Me doy cuenta de que tendré que llamar a la policía y dar un chivatazo anónimo para contar lo que Keith ha hecho. Seguro que el cuerpo de Margaret Clamwell está enterrado profundamente y por eso no lo encontré cavando con las manos. Cuando la policía sepa el paradero del cuerpo, excavarán todo el jardín, dos veces. Tendré que dar el chivatazo justo antes de irme a la fiesta de fin de exámenes en la casa de campo porque, si Mamá se entera, no me dejará ir.

Carrie Waterman da una fiesta en su casa mañana. Tenaya ya ha dicho que no irá porque tiene que estudiar. Decido llamar a Jonah para preguntarle si va.

Responde tras dos timbrazos.

—¿Qué pasa? —dice.

—No mucho. Me aburro. ¿Irás a la fiesta mañana?

—¿A la de Carrie?

—Sí.

—No, mi madre dice que me tengo que quedar.

—¿Qué? ¿Por qué?

—No estoy seguro. El Papa sale en la tele, creo.

—¿El Papa? ¿Por qué te importa todavía? ¿No había violado a unos niños o algo así?

—No, eso fueron unos curas irlandeses.

—¿Católicos?

—Sí.

—Mamá dice que eres la gente con la que vas.

—Ha pedido perdón.

—Las disculpas no arreglarán el culo desgarrado de nadie.

—Supongo que no.

—Entonces, ¿no vienes?

—No puedo, tío. Lo siento.

—No pasa nada.

—Buenas noches.

—Sí.

Cuelgo.

Miro el calendario de exámenes clavado en el corcho sobre el escritorio. No es muy apasionante.

Veo viejos episodios de *QI* en el reproductor de la BBC. Ojalá Stephen Fry no fuera gay y mi madre pudiera casarse con él. Me enseñaría cosas como que se hace más daño al pegar a una persona si llevas guantes de boxeo que si no. Lo único que Keith me ha enseñado es la vigilancia constante.

Como medida para evitar estudiar, relleno un cuestionario larguísimo en Facebook. Esto se llama procrastinar.

1. Tu ex está en el arcén de la carretera ardiendo. ¿Qué haces?
   se puede hacer eso de cuando cortas con alguien pero después vuelves a follar una o dos veces, por favor?
2. Tu mejor amiga te dice que está embarazada, ¿cuál es tu reacción?
   vas a ser una muy buena madre, creo en ti
3. ¿Cuál fue la última vez que te dieron ganas de dar un puñetazo en la cara a alguien?
   menuda mariconada
4. ¡Enhorabuena! Acabas de tener un hijo, ¿cómo se llama?
   martin luther king
5. ¡Enhorabuena! Acabas de tener una hija, ¿cómo se llama?
   simone olive zorrón
6. ¿Qué deseas ahora mismo?
   el fin del racismo institucionalizado
7. ¿Cuál es tu posición sexual favorita?
   la posición de la «polla en el coño»
8. ¿Te gustan los pepinillos?
   no
9. ¿De qué color tienes la entrepierna?
   color avellana
10. ¿Qué tienes en el bolsillo?
    humus
11. Digamos que te dan un test de embarazo ahora mismo, ¿aprobarías o suspenderías?
    ya me gustaría
12. ¿Has bloqueado a alguien de Facebook?
    no deberías haberlo hecho

13. ¿Conoces a alguien en la cárcel?
sí. qué vergüenza. menuda chorrada infantil. no quiero seguir haciendo esto.

* * *

Las posibles repercusiones de implicar a Keith en la desaparición de la chica me estresan y me provocan insomnio. Son las 3:46. Una de las cosas que hago cuando no puedo dormir es investigar sobre el insomnio y la privación del sueño. Algunos datos sobre el insomnio:

✓ No hay prácticamente ningún aumento en la mortalidad relacionado con el insomnio. De hecho, parece haber un aumento de la esperanza de vida.
✓ Somnifobia es el miedo al sueño.
✓ Thai Ngoc es un insomne vietnamita que afirma no haber dormido en treinta y tres años.
✓ La privación del sueño ha demostrado ser efectiva como tratamiento de la depresión. El tratamiento se llama «Terapia de la Vigilia».

Probé la Terapia de la Vigilia cuando pensaba que tenía meningitis pero me quedé dormido.

Son las 3:51. Si sigo sin dormirme a las cinco, me sentaré afuera sobre el rocío, beberé tazas de té fuerte y dulce y observaré el alba. Me gusta estar fuera al amanecer y al atardecer porque creo que el cielo es mucho más creativo con el uso del color en esos momentos. Por ejemplo, el gris deja espacio al fucsia, al azafrán, al salmón o a otros tonos de rojo con nombres románticos.

Entro en www.girlsoncam.com, me pongo LARGATRANCANEGRA y le doy a ENTRAR.

Tú: hola guapa
Mujercitadulce: hola cielo como estas?
Tú: cachondo guapa. tu?
Mujercitadulce: cachonda tambien. vamos al privado?

No.

Tú: me enseñas un poco tu cuerpo antes de ir al privado guapa?

Se estira sobre la cama para que pueda ver su cuerpo mediocre de mediana edad. Los muslos con la piel picada se tocan y el estómago le cuelga como un grueso pedazo de pollo sobre la cintura. Es un espécimen típico de la categoría de «madre follable».

Tú: mmm
Mujercitadulce: ;)
Mujercitadulce: privado?

Decido que me aburro y que voy a utilizar la Wikipedia para descolocarla. Voy a inyectar confusión en su extraña y distante vida.

Tú: que harias en privado?
Mujercitadulce: todo lo que quieras cariño
Tú: te lavaras los dientes?

Pausa.

Mujercitadulce: claro cielo. en privado
Tú: puedes hacerlo ahora por favor? no quiero acabar en una fiesta de sarro!
Mujercitadulce: en privado cielo

Tú: una vez pague para ir al privado con una chica y luego no quiso lavarse los dientes
Mujercitadulce: yo no soy asi cielo
Tú: eso no lo se, por favor
Mujercitadulce: vale vale
Mujercitadulce: seria mejor ir al privado

Mujercitadulce se baja de la cama de mala gana. Lleva bragas lila y un sujetador marrón manchado. Al moverse, veo que no ha domado su pelo púbico, que se extiende por el interior de los muslos y por el valle arrugado en forma de media luna de entre las nalgas.

Dos minutos después, vuelve y enseña los dientes pixelados a la webcam. Mujercitadulce cree que es una loba vestida de cordero. Cree que soy su presa.

Tú: guapa tienes que cepillarte los dientes durante tres minutos
Mujercitadulce: que?
Tú: un minuto en la parte de abajo, otro en la de arriba y el que queda se puede dedicar a atacar la placa de la parte de dentro, o para cepillar las encías o la lengua

Pausa.

Pienso en que tal vez su padre le pegará si no gana dinero. Pienso en que tal vez su voz suene como un monzón de grava y vodka. Porque no sabe qué otra cosa hacer. No sé qué otra cosa hacer. Hoy no estoy demasiado receptivo.

Mujercitadulce: al privado
Tú: no te has lavado bien los dientes
Mujercitadulce: he hecho lo que me has dicho
Tú: solo me preocupo por ti

Tú: la descomposicion en los dientes es una de las causas de la caries. si no se evita, se infectara el tejido de la camara pulpar, lo que derivara en necrosis y la necrosis, si no se detiene, puede afectar la mandibula
Tú: es verdad, lo estoy leyendo ahora mismo
Tú: en la wikipedia
Tú: es verdad de verdad de verdad
Tú: si tienes la mandibula torcida nadie ira al privado contigo

Pausa.

Mujercitadulce: por favor privado

Fascinado, observo en la pantalla cómo le cae una lágrima por la mejilla. Agacha la cabeza. Mujercitadulce se ha aclarado el pelo y se le ven unas tenues raíces cobrizas. Me pregunto si sabe que el sonido de un llanto puede desencadenar el «reflejo de eyección de leche» en las madres de los recién nacidos. Cuando lo pienso, me imagino a Mamá, después de tenerme, viendo una película con Papá. En la película, un bebé llora porque unos duendes han rodeado la cuna y están bailando. A Mamá empieza a salirle leche de los pezones y se le moja la camiseta. Eso pone cachondo a Papá, pero entonces me pongo a llorar y no pueden hacerlo. Lo siento, Papá.

Tú: toc toc
Mujercitadulce: que
Tú: toc toc
Mujercitadulce: quien es?
Tú: medes
Mujercitadulce: medes quien?
Tú: me desconecto

Me desconecto.

Son las 4:06. Cincuenta y cuatro minutos hasta el punto de no retorno.

Sería mejor trabajar en mi novela en el cobertizo. En el cobertizo, podría sentir mejor las motivaciones del violador.

Me encamino despacio al jardín vestido solo con los bóxers y un edredón. Me preocupa que Keith se despierte y me mate con una pala u otra herramienta de jardín contundente y después me entierre bajo el manzano junto a Margaret Clamwell y otras víctimas que aún no he descubierto. Margaret Clamwell se estará pudriendo. Es la segunda etapa de la descomposición caracterizada porque el abdomen se vuelve verde debido a la actividad bacteriana y una acumulación de gases provoca que los líquidos y las heces salgan del cuerpo. Todavía no estoy preparado para que me pase esto. Si veo a Keith, le plantaré cara. Le apuñalaré en el ojo con el boli y le daré al pulsador sin parar una vez haya conseguido clavárselo. Esto se llama «rematar la jugada». Mi e-mail a Abby Hall también entra en esta categoría.

Sentado bajo el edredón en el cobertizo, con el teléfono como linterna, muerdo el extremo del boli hasta que parece una víctima de un atropello. No puedo escribir. Intento recordar y dibujo todos los muñequitos de los Dones que puedo. Resultado final: cuatro. Me quedo dormido.

24

Durante el periodo de exámenes, Mamá me hace escribir programas de estudio cada día y colgarlos en la nevera. La mayoría de veces, me levanto a la hora de comer, me quedo un rato en la cama mirando el techo y luego bajo. Desayuno Weetabix, fumo y escribo el programa para hacer feliz a Mamá. Normalmente, a esas horas aún estoy demasiado cansado, así que solo escribo:

7:00 Levantarme
Todo el día – Estudiar
23:00 Dormir

Después, muevo los imanes de palabras por la nevera para formar frases de tono positivo que harán que Mamá se sienta optimista ante el futuro de su único hijo.

yo soy feliz amor hombre árbol y rojo
hombre amor
árbol feliz hombre y yo
soy yo hombre

Todos los exámenes son a primera hora de la mañana o a media tarde. Para los exámenes de la tarde, me levanto a la hora de comer, como y voy al instituto. Para los exámenes de por la mañana, me levanto a las siete, voy andando al instituto y luego voy a casa de Tenaya a tomar el té. A veces, mientras estoy en su casa, intenta hacerme estudiar delante de ella. Arruga la cara en una expresión extraña y me dice que quiere que me salgan bien. Algún día, Tenaya será una muy buena madre.

En el instituto, mi mesa es la número 86. Resulta que está cerca de las primeras filas. Oscar Chao se sienta a mi lado. Cada vez que le he visto hacer un examen los últimos dos meses llevaba los mismos calcetines. Son lilas con rayos amarillos. Son sus calcetines de la suerte, creo. No sé por qué. Quizá perdió la virginidad con una modelo de revista cuando los llevaba puestos.

No tengo calcetines de la suerte. Tengo la insoportable sensación de un fracaso inminente.

* * *

Mi rutina relajada y libre de exámenes solo se ve alterada una vez. Recibo una llamada de teléfono y tengo la siguiente conversación:

—¿Jasper?

—¿Quién es?

—Abby.

—Oh. Hola, Abby.

—Tengo un retraso de dos semanas.

Pausa.

—Tengo un retraso de dos semanas, Jasper.

—¡PUES MÉTELE PRISA, JODER!

Lágrimas (mías, no).

—Creo que estoy embarazada, Jasper.

—Lo siento, creo que te has equivocado de número.

—Jasper, por favor.

—¿Qué?

—Creo que estoy embarazada, Jasper.

—¡PUES ABORTA PERO YA!

Cuelgo.

Soy insensible y cruel.

Tengo miedo.

Abby Hall no me va a estropear el Plan Georgia con su asqueroso bebé, ni de coña.

Joder. Joder. Joder.

25

15:29. Estoy sentado en la consulta de Julia pensando en cómo acabé viniendo a verla por primera vez. Intentando no pensar en bebés ni en la paternidad. En mi mente, es el verano de 2009. El recuerdo es una vía de escape. Tenaya y yo estamos en un muro bajo de ladrillos al final de mi calle. Liamos cigarros. Deberíamos estar estudiando para el examen del certificado de secundaria.

A un lado del muro, se extiende el jardín delantero del número 46 de Chestnut Crescent. Al otro, un río de asfalto que desemboca en Ivythorne Road.

Observamos el sol.

—¿Jasper? —me pregunta Tenaya.

—¿Qué?

—Algún día seremos viejos.

Observamos el sol un poco más. Se derrite y forma lagos sobre el cemento, la hierba y los ladrillos.

—Sí, supongo que sí. A no ser que nos asesinen o pillemos el sida o nos atropelle un autobús o decidamos acabar con nuestra vida por una confusión emocional insoportable.

—Pero, estadísticamente, es probable que nos hagamos viejos.

—Sí —digo—. Es verdad.

—Eso significa casarse y tener hijos.

—Estadísticamente.

—Sí, pero yo no quiero hijos.

—¿Y?

—Bueno, que probablemente los quiera cuando sea mayor, ¿no?

—Supongo.

Tira el cigarro al jardín y apoya la cabeza en una cuna que ha formado con las manos.

—¿Significa eso que seré una persona diferente?

—No.

—Sí.

—No.

—Pero pensaré de forma diferente.

—La gente es inconstante.

—No quiero ser una persona diferente.

—¿Por qué no?

—No lo sé.

La pellizco.

—Toma —digo—. Ahora eres una...

Mamá aparece por la esquina, paseando y hablando enfadada con el manos libres de plástico azul. No nos ve porque está mirando el chapucero camino de entrada del número 32. Tenaya me tira del cuello de la camiseta y caigo del muro al jardín del número 46.

Es entonces cuando aterrizo encima del gato.

Tardamos un rato en darnos cuenta de lo que ha pasado. El animal ha lanzado una especie de grito ahogado. Está aplastado debajo de mí, como si formáramos parte de una escena de *Tom y Jerry*.

Tengo que quedarme tumbado encima del animal hasta que Mamá desaparece tras la esquina. Durante ese tiempo, al gato le quedan pocos músculos intactos para oponer resistencia. Tenaya y yo nos levantamos y lo miramos, un par de dioses jóvenes e inexpertos y con el estómago ligeramente revuelto.

—Mátalo, anda —dice Tenaya.

Siempre espera que tome la iniciativa porque soy un chico.

—No quiero matarlo, mátalo tú.

—Lo has aplastado tú.

—A ti te gustan los gatos —respondo, no del todo convencido de mi defensa.

—¡¿Qué?!

Miro al gato. Se le han salido los ojos fuera de las órbitas. Convulsiona como un epiléptico. Me pregunto hasta qué punto es consciente.

—¡Mátalo, joder! —grita Tenaya.

Debido al pánico y a un agresivo sentido de la responsabilidad, aplico una lamentable y cruda forma de eutanasia. Estampo la cabeza del gato contra el muro, con fuerza. El resultado es una explosión de fuegos artificiales de terciopelo compuestos de cerebro y sangre. Mi pie derecho en particular tiene una nueva y recargada decoración.

El Tiempo lleva mucho tiempo en danza, así que suele aburrirse. Para liberarse por un instante de su aburrimiento, al Tiempo le gusta recrear una serie de sucesos altamente improbables. Si estos eventos son románticos, se llaman Destino, pero si son del tipo negativo, los llamamos Coincidencia Desafortunada.

Acto seguido se da una Coincidencia Desafortunada porque el hombre calvo con manchas marrones en la piel del número 46 sale de su casa inmediatamente después de darle el golpe mortal a su gato con la bota. Aún está cubierta de trocitos de cerebro.

Nos da un ataque de pánico.

Corremos aunque es inútil porque conoce a mi madre. Creo que queríamos evitar la confrontación. Aun así, me tocó enfrentarme con Mamá, pero no con Keith. Keith tiende a evitar los enfrentamientos. Si alguna vez surge la posibilidad de un debate, dice: «Estamos de acuerdo en que no lo estamos». Me pregunto cómo defenderá su caso ante el tribunal. Usará una escopeta que dispare lágrimas de cocodrilo y una corbata que grite «buen cristiano».

Al final, Mamá dijo: «Eres un psicópata cruel», y yo dije: «Fue un accidente», y Keith dijo: «Estamos de acuerdo en que no lo estamos», y después me tocó ir a ver a Julia. Que es donde estoy ahora.

Julia está radiante hoy. Quizá alguien ha decidido que la quiere. Quizá tiene un novio que corre maratones y la llama July.

Quizá se sientan juntos por las noches bebiendo vino barato y viendo películas de Hugh Grant.

Pienso en pedirle consejo a Julia por lo del niño de Abby Hall. Julia probablemente intentará convencerme de que sea padre. Veré al hijo feo de Abby cada fin de semana en un McDonald's de carretera porque me dará demasiada vergüenza llevarlo a un McDonald's de la ciudad. El niño intentará que le dé dinero. Le diré que me deje en paz.

La luz de la consulta de Julia hoy es como el mar por la mañana visto por unos marineros tristes. Es una mala metáfora que significa que hay luz pero que no es cálida. Es grisácea y cae en formas estiradas sobre la moqueta. Julia le da al botón del boli sin parar mirándome con impaciencia. Acaba de preguntarme por Tabitha Mowai.

—Me sentí triste —digo.

Recuerdo que Julia cree que soy racista. A veces, si cuentas las mentiras suficientes, estas hacen piña y se ponen en plan abusonas. Una se agacha detrás de ti mientras otra te empuja para que te caigas. Eso es lo que me están haciendo ahora mis mentiras.

—¿Sí? —pregunta Julia.

—Sí —respondo—. En realidad, no soy racista.

Julia sonríe.

—Lo sé.

—¿Qué?

—Sé que no eres racista, Jasper. Eres un buen chico, solo que de vez en cuando te dejas llevar demasiado por tu imaginación.

A esto se le llama cliché.

Me quedo mirando a Julia un rato con la boca abierta. Me pregunto si fingir durante todo este tiempo que era imbécil era solo un truco psicológico inteligente. Quizá sea una mujer extremadamente lista que podría darme un arsenal infalible de técnicas de seducción.

—Am —murmuro.

—Lo que importa —continúa Julia— es que estás madurando. Esperaba que lo hicieras y estaba en lo cierto. Tu madre solo quería que vinieras para asegurarnos.

—Pero sí que soy gay —afirmo—. Y Sebastian es real.

Julia vuelve a sonreír.

Se pone de pie, rodea la mesa y se agacha para envolverme en un ligero abrazo. Su pelo me roza la cara. Huele a mango.

—Creo que hoy es la última vez que nos vemos —dice Julia.

Así es.

Tercera parte

Lluvia y ganado

26

00:52. En la cama. Suena Radio 4. Escucho el pronóstico marítimo. El pronóstico marítimo es un edredón comodísimo. Si hubieran puesto el pronóstico marítimo durante la batalla del Somme todo el mundo habría tirado las armas y se habría metido en los sacos de dormir para hablar del maquillaje de las estrellas hasta el amanecer.

> Viking Norte Utshire Sur Utshire Sureste

Antes del pronóstico marítimo ponen «Sailing By»; después, el himno nacional. A veces, cuando estoy borracho, me gusta sentarme en la cama y cantar el himno nacional intentando imaginarme cómo sería creer de verdad que nacer en un lugar concreto es algo de lo que estar orgulloso. Follar con una chica durante más de siete minutos es algo por lo que estar orgulloso. Ser británico, no.

> Cuatro o cinco, aumentado a cinco o seis, virando al sur cuatro o cinco después

Los británicos ven programas benéficos en la tele para huérfanos con sida de Etiopía y se dicen los unos a los otros que eso les pone tristes. Dicen que es una pena que algunas personas mueran de hambre. A veces, cogen el teléfono y mandan que les quiten tres libras de sus cuentas todos los meses.

Precipitaciones ocasionales, favorable

Pero nadie pide que los huérfanos etíopes con sida puedan venir a Gran Bretaña. El país es nuestro. Y las televisiones. Y los zapatos. Y los asados para cenar. No nos comportaríamos así si fuéramos etíopes. No diríamos: «No puede venir nadie a este país. Es nuestro. Y el agua sucia. Y las barrigas hinchadas. Y el sida».

Bancos de niebla, con tendencia a ser moderados o débiles

Miro al techo. Tengo la cabeza llena de marineros en un enorme petrolero, apiñados alrededor de la radio, bebiendo ron Captain Morgan. Están solos en medio de un océano negro. Bancos de niebla avanzan sobre el reflejo de la luna que parece un diente de león. Más tarde, en sus hamacas, comentarán que echan de menos a sus mujeres e hijos. Se balancearán hasta dormirse mecidos por el viento de fuerza seis o siete.

Tengo sueño. Intento pensar solo en los marineros y no en el feto de Abby. He decidido no contarle a nadie lo del bebé. He decidido no pensar en el bebé. He decidido que, si es necesario, la chantajearé para que aborte.

Abby, aborta o envenenaré a tu perro.

Duérmete. No pienses en el bebé de Abby Hall. Si no piensas en ello, desaparecerá. Abby Hall es una zorra. El bebé no es tuyo. ¿Qué bebé? Exacto.

Mi móvil vibra. Tenaya. «Jasper, estoy borracha y sola y

quiero hablar contigo.» Pienso en Tenaya, de pie en la cocina con el vapor del té elevándose entre sus manos y una pila de paracetamol sobre la mesa. Le contesto: «puente, 15 min». Sacrificaré mi sueño por sus brazos.

Mamá y Keith se fueron a dormir a las diez. Ya estarán perdidos en los aburridos bosques suburbanos de sus sueños. Me pongo unos vaqueros y una sudadera con capucha gris. Cojo dinero de la hucha de Doctor Who que tengo junto a mi cama, me lo meto en el bolsillo y bajo de puntillas por las escaleras como un ninja. La puerta está de mi parte. Se cierra en silencio detrás de mí.

La noche fuera es fría y distante. Es una manta enorme. Nos cubre a mí, y a Tenaya, y a Abby Hall, y a su feto, y a los marineros en sus hamacas, y a las mujeres que echan de menos, y al mar que empiezan a odiar. Camino rápido por nuestra calle, junto a los plataneros plantados en agujeros en el asfalto y ocultos en la noche. Silueta sexual en ventana.

En el Happy Shopper, me aplasto el pelo, cojo aire y entro. Una mujer de ojos tristes lee un periódico rosa en el mostrador. Me acerco con pasos largos a la caja. La confianza es la clave del éxito.

—Dos botellas del vino blanco más barato —pido.

Me mira de arriba abajo. Coge dos botellas de la estantería que tiene detrás y las coloca en el mostrador.

—¿Carné?

—¿Carné? —grito—. ¿Carné? —Más fuerte—. Tengo veinticinco años, joder. Tengo hasta un puto hijo de cinco años.

Me entran náuseas. Dentro de cinco años, puede que eso sea verdad. También me siento culpable pero necesito salvar a Tenaya.

Suspira.

—Vale —dice al coger el dinero—. ¿No tendrás algo que ver con la poli?

—Claro que no —digo al coger una botella con cada mano—. Siento mucho haber gritado.

Corro con las botellas por el puente que cruza la autopista. Tenaya está sentada en la parte más alta, con las piernas cruzadas, dándole la espalda a la ciudad. Me dejo caer a su lado y le paso una botella. Lanza un chorro de humo a la noche.

—Gracias, Jasper —dice.

Enciendo un cigarro.

—De nada. ¿Estás bien?

—No lo sé.

—No durará para siempre.

—Lo sé.

Miro abajo, a las tiras de faros y de luces traseras, ríos rojos y blancos. La farola que tenemos encima nos tiñe las piernas con su luz naranja. Estamos fuera de la corriente. Me siento como si estuviera hombro con hombro con Tenaya en el límite del mundo, mirándolo todo desde arriba.

—Entonces —digo—, ¿de qué querías hablar?

—No quería hablar de nada.

—Me dijiste que querías hablar conmigo.

Tenaya apoya la cabeza en mi hombro. Le doy un trago al vino. No la entiendo. Entiendo que se siente mal y que quiero ayudarla. No tengo las herramientas necesarias para arreglar el desequilibrio emocional.

—No tienes que decir nada —comenta—. Me vale con que nos quedemos aquí sentados.

No le voy a contar a Tenaya lo de la cosa en el útero de Abby Hall. No quiero cargarla con mi bebé. Mi bebé. Bebé. No pienso ser padre.

Aborta, Abby, o hablaré con la revista *Hello!* y les contaré que eres la hija secreta de Michael Jackson.

Un hombre para en el arcén. Baja del coche. Sostiene un móvil junto a la oreja. Lo aguanta ahí, aplastado entre el hombro y la mejilla, se pone un cigarro en la boca y lo enciende. Tenaya eructa para dentro. El hombre camina de un lado a otro y gesticula con la mano como loco mientras habla por teléfono. Es Tony Blair. Sus manos son armas.

—Está hablando con su mujer —comenta Tenaya—. Le está diciendo que ya está harto y que no va a volver.

—Está hablando con su jefe —digo yo—. Le ha dicho que es un cabrón y que se puede ir a tomar por culo.

—Está respondiendo a un anuncio gay del periódico para echar un polvo.

—Le está diciendo a su hija que se la quiere follar.

—Muy bonito, Jasper.

—Lo siento.

Nos ponemos de pie y nos apoyamos en la reja. El hombre sujeta el teléfono en la mano extendida. Lo mira como si fuera un ano desgarrado.

—Parece como si le hubieran dicho que alguien ha muerto —comenta Tenaya.

—Sí.

—Se le ve triste.

—Si te murieras, incendiaría algo muy grande. El instituto, o la catedral.

—Gracias, Jasper.

Me siento. Tenaya hace lo mismo. Nos encendemos otros dos cigarros.

—Voy a ligarme a Georgia Treely en Devon —digo.

—¿Con qué?

—Con Rohypnol, no.

—Qué bonito.

—Con mis pintas de golfo y mi ingenio.

Tenaya se ríe.

—¿Qué? —pregunto.

—Nada.

Unas pequeñas colinas claras aparecen en los brazos de Tenaya. Tiene frío. El viento se está despertando. Es un corredor nocturno.

—¿Estás bien?

—Mejor, gracias.

Nos terminamos las botellas de vino, las estampamos, y volvemos al barrio.

27

Mi último examen es el segundo parcial de Psicología, que empezó a las 9:15. Son las 10:30. Ya he terminado, miro a mi alrededor, al resto de la clase. Georgia Treely terminó hace diez minutos pero no para de repasar el examen. Espero que le haya salido muy bien. Seguro que le ha salido bien. Al final, acabará teniendo una granja rehabilitada en alguna zona de las Midlands donde las adolescentes cuelgan pósteres de David Cameron en la pared. Jonah paró de escribir hace media hora y está dibujando penes con caras en la parte de atrás del examen.

Por fin nos dicen que dejemos los bolis y salgamos. Todo el mundo grita de alegría menos Oscar Chao porque todavía le queda el examen de chino por la tarde. La persona que vigila la clase se pone roja y grita que seguimos bajo las normas del examen y que no podemos hacer ruido hasta que hayamos salido. Volvemos a gritar y salimos corriendo.

Tenaya me espera fuera del recinto del instituto. Sujeta dos cigarros. Uno para mí, otro para ella. Su último examen era Historia, hace dos días.

—¿Qué tal ha ido? —me pregunta.

Vamos al Yellow Pony. Es un pub frecuentado sobre todo por viejos pero vamos allí porque no nos piden el carné.

—Normal —le digo—. Parecía fácil.

—Más te vale haber aprobado, Jasper.

—Lo sé.

—Porque, como suspendas, te corto la polla.

Sonrío.

—Vale.

Me da un puñetazo en el brazo.

Me pregunto cómo me castigará por haber dejado embarazada a Abby Hall.

No está embarazada.

No está embarazada, no.

Jonah ya está en el Yellow Pony, sentado tras una cerveza y una novela de Murakami. No entiendo mucho a Jonah pero sí por qué lee a Murakami. Murakami me hace sentir seguro y optimista. Ojalá Murakami fuera mi padrastro. Murakami nunca asesinaría a mi madre.

—Buenos días —dice Jonah. Tenaya va a la barra a pedirnos algo—. ¿Ha ido bien?

—Genial —contesto—. ¿A qué hora nos vamos mañana?

Me imagino levantándome por la mañana y encontrándome a Haruki Murakami tomando café y leyendo *The Guardian* en nuestra mesa de la cocina.

—No lo sé. Sobre las cuatro, imagino, ven a esa hora.

Papá, ¿en qué has estado trabajando últimamente?

—¿A quién más vas a llevar? Tenaya va con Ping y Ana porque tiene que quedarse hasta más tarde en casa por no sé qué cosa familiar.

Murakami no me llamaría con apodos condescendientes.

—Joder, es verdad. Se me había olvidado contártelo. He pillado dos chicas para nosotros. Se vienen.

—¿Qué? ¿Quiénes?

—Susan Pilkington y Jenna Slater —dice.

Conozco los nombres. Son chicas del curso inferior. Pienso en sus caras. No están mal.

—Están bastante buenas —digo.

—Sí —comenta—. Ya te digo.

Tenaya vuelve con una Newcastle para mí y una Carling para ella. Señala con la cabeza el libro sobre la mesa.

—¿Es en el que se folla a su hermana y después a su madre? —pregunta.

—A la hermana solo se la folla en un sueño —comento.

—Vale ya —dice Jonah—. No me lo jodáis.

Murakami sería un padrastro de repuesto de puta madre.

28

Me despierto a las doce y bajo. Mamá y Keith están trabajando. Quito todos los programas de estudio de la nevera y los tiro a la basura. En bóxers y con el sol dándome en las mejillas, me siento optimista, me siento bien. La fiesta de esta noche será la leche. Georgia Treely estará allí. Prepárate para ser seducida, Georgia Treely.

Pero, primero, tengo que hacer una cosa.

Sentado en el sofá de cuero blanco del salón, cojo el móvil. Marco 1-4-1 para ocultar mi número y después marco el teléfono de la comisaría de policía. Responde una mujer.

—Policía de West Midlands. Dígame, ¿en qué puedo ayudarle? —pregunta.

—Hola —digo—. Me gustaría dar un chivatazo anónimo, por favor.

—De acuerdo. ¿De qué se trata?

La mujer pronuncia el «de acuerdo» estirando la «o» hasta que tiene la forma de un balón de rugby.

—De un asesinato.

—¿Un asesinato?

—Sí —respondo—. Sé quién mató a aquella chica que murió la semana pasada y el mismo hombre también mató a una mujer llamada Margaret Clamwell. Planea volver a matar.

—De acuerdo —dice la mujer. Vuelve a estirar la «o»—. ¿Qué pruebas tiene de todo esto?

—Muchas pruebas —le aseguro. Entonces, le digo rápidamente mi dirección y cuelgo.

Subo.

Me miro en el espejo del baño, preparándome para seducir a Georgia Treely. El Plan Georgia. ¿Me pongo gel en el pelo? ¿El gel es de gays?

Gente que se pone gel en el pelo:

Robert Pattinson en *Crepúsculo*
Hugh Grant en *El diario de Bridget Jones*
Neo en *Matrix*

Sí, me pongo gel.

Le doy forma de brillantes ondas al pelo y me acerco al espejo.

—Qué cara más guapa —me digo.

Me acerco más al espejo.

—Qué cara más guapa —me repito, más fuerte.

Sigo sin creérmelo.

Me paso la mano por la mandíbula. Pincha. Rutina de afeitado: una vez cada dos semanas. ¿Me afeito los pinchos antes? Decido dejármelos. Me darán un aspecto más maduro. Georgia Treely pensará que soy un hombre de verdad. Aunque lo que soy en realidad es astuto.

Tengo un grano en la ceja izquierda. Es perfectamente circular y amarillo. Se acurruca entre los pelos como un niño pequeño en el bosque. Aprieto para sacar el pus y llevo el trofeo hasta mi habitación en la punta del índice derecho. Me lo limpio en el pequeño espejo en forma de estrella. Siempre que puedo, desde los quince años, dejo esos trofeos expuestos en el espejo. Vuelan en largas manchas, emborronando el espejo con extrañas formas, como apagados fuegos artificiales reflejados en un lago de metal. Es una obra de arte contemporáneo. Pronto Charles Saatchi querrá comprarme el espejo. Me hará una oferta que no podré rechazar.

* * *

Cuando voy a casa de Jonah a las cuatro, sigue durmiendo. La puerta está abierta, así que entro. Arriba, tiro del edredón y le doy una palmada en el culo.

—Levántate ya, capullo —le grito.

—Vete a la mierda —me grita, pero al final se levanta.

Nos sentamos al borde de la cama, él no para de restregarse las legañas de los ojos y quejarse.

Cuando se ha aclarado los ojos, Jonah enciende el portátil y pone Leftover Crack. Se viste deprisa y lía un porro. Nos lo fumamos en su invernadero tomando un té. Le cuesta mucho despertarse del todo. En el invernadero hace mucho calor y hay bastante luz. El cielo es amarillo y empieza a oscurecer.

—¿Dónde las recogemos? —pregunto.

—Delante del Argos, en el centro, a y media.

—Deberíamos irnos.

—Sí —dice Jonah.

Apaga el porro en un cenicero.

—¿Jonah?

—Sí.

—¿Qué te pasa?

—¿Qué quieres decir?

Le da un golpecito al teléfono. Imagino que solo mira la agenda para no tener que mirarme a mí.

—Es que pareces... —digo. Me paro un instante—. No lo sé, estás como en otro mundo. Aún no has dicho nada desagradable.

—No es nada —comenta—. Hablamos luego. Vamos a por los chochos.

Me río.

—Vale.

Susan Pilkington y Jenna Slater nos están esperando frente al Argos. Susan es rubia y tiene las tetas grandes y redondas. Lleva una falda de flores y leggings blancos. Jenna tiene el pelo muy corto y oscuro y unas tetas más pequeñas y de aspecto más cercano. Lleva unos vaqueros ceñidos y una parka verde oliva. Las dos sonríen, inquietas, y así, en general, ambas parecen personas simpáticas y enteras.

Jonah sonríe y se estira para abrir la puerta del copiloto. Susan Pilkington se sienta a su lado. Eso significa que me ha endiñado a Jenna Slater a mí. Me parece bien porque las tetas grandes me asustan.

Jenna Slater se sienta a mi lado.

—Hola —dice, sonriendo ampliamente. No sabe que voy a ser padre.

—Hola —le digo.

Intento sonreír con todas mis fuerzas. Seguro que parezco retrasado. Me pregunto si esto va a ser como la última vez que me lié a una tía con Jonah. No. No puede ser así. Estas chicas son jóvenes, simpáticas y sexualmente atractivas.

—¿Qué tal? —me pregunta.

Escucho a Jonah hablando tranquilamente con Susan. Se le da bien entender qué es lo que quieren oír las chicas. Antes a mí también se me daba bien pero creo que se me ha olvidado cómo se hacía.

Es hora de esforzarse. Mamá dice que mientras haga todo lo que pueda, nadie podrá exigirme nada más.

—Mmm —digo—. Bien. Estoy muy, muy bien. —Miro a mi alrededor. Por la ventana veo a un niño mordisqueando el dobladillo de la falda de su madre—. ¿Tú qué tal?

Vuelve a sonreír. Más aún.

—Genial —contesta—. La fiesta estará bien.

—La fiesta estará bien —repito como un tonto.

Soy imbécil. Debería fingir que duermo durante todo el viaje.

Se tarda una hora y media en llegar a Devon. Jonah le da a Susan un mapa que ha impreso de Google Maps para que le guíe. No parece demasiado segura cuando habla. Jonah dijo que no iba a beber y conducir pero enseguida se frustra e insiste en que le pase una cerveza, cosa que hago porque soy un buen amigo.

Hablar con Jenna es cada vez más fácil después de varias cervezas y algunos porros. A Jenna le gusta hablar así que no tengo que hacer mucho. Jonah conduce cada vez peor y casi choca contra una caravana que lleva una pegatina de LOVE LIFE; Susan le hace parar en una estación de servicio para que se tome un café. Jenna no para de hablar en todo ese tiempo. No me molesta, en realidad. La mayoría de palabras no las entiendo y me resulta relajante escucharla. Es como escuchar Radio 4.

Algunas de las cosas de las que habla Jenna:

✓ Jesús es sin duda un tío genial y, aunque todo el mundo ande jodiéndolo todo, él aún los ama porque él es así.
✓ Tocar en la Joven Orquesta Nacional de Jazz es muy divertido porque conoces a mucha gente nueva muy guay que cuenta historias geniales que después puedes contarle a Jasper Wolf porque está atrapado en un coche y no puede escapar.
✓ Sería genial mudarse a París en un futuro porque París es romántico.
✓ Todos los países del mundo deberían dejar de comprar armas y empezar a comprar bolas de espejo.
✓ Ludovico Einaudi es, como, un genio.
✓ *Amélie* es, como, la mejor película del mundo mundial.

✓ El pelo rubio le quedaría mejor pero también igual menos sofisticado pero igual podría probarlo con, no sé, un tinte casero de Boots o algo así. No sé. ¿Tú qué piensas, Jasper?

Me la quedo mirando un rato.

—Ah —digo—. Sí, sí. Estás muy guapa.

De vuelta en el coche, me bebo una lata de cerveza y me fumo un cigarro con la cabeza fuera de la ventanilla. Miro abajo, a la autopista llena de coches impacientes y al cielo rojo fuego con el sol que se va escondiendo lentamente tras las colinas. Jenna se queda dormida sobre mi hombro. Yo me quedo dormido con la mejilla pegada en el cristal.

29

Como estamos dormidos, Jenna y yo nos perdemos la acalorada discusión entre Jonah y Susan sobre «¿Dónde coño estamos? Esto no parece Devon», y, cuando nos despertamos, el coche está aparcado en un claro embarrado al borde de un enorme campo de amapolas. Jonah está de pie, fumando bajo la poca luz del sol que queda, con Susan a su lado. Se han reconciliado. Han dejado atrás el pasado.

Hemos tenido que aparcar lejos de la casa porque Amanda cree que si la gente aparca cerca estropeará el césped y los padres de Amanda se enfadarán. Seguramente, la gente aparcará cerca de la casa de todas formas.

Le doy con el codo a Jenna para despertarla. Entreabre los ojos y sonríe. Se levanta y me da un beso en la mejilla. Intento sonreírle otra vez. Me alegra que no haya se haya puesto a hablar. Cuando nos besemos, no pasará nada porque puedo usar mi boca como un arma para callarla.

Jonah dice que tenemos que cruzar el campo hasta el bosque y que en el bosque encontraremos una cascada con un pequeño lago al lado, que es donde Polly nos espera. Polly nos llevará a la casa. Pregunto por qué es Polly quien nos va a llevar pero Jonah se encoge de hombros.

Polly es un chico polaco de cara afeminada. Su nombre real

es Krasicki o algo así. Probablemente es algo racista llamarle Polly pero no parece que le importe.

Sacamos las abultadas mochilas del maletero y nos ponemos a cruzar el campo con la tenue luz. Susan se quita la camiseta y Jonah y yo hacemos lo mismo, dejando que el sol se deslice por nuestros hombros, bajando por la espalda, para formar pequeños charcos de luz entre las amapolas. Jonah carga el equipo más pesado porque lleva el hornillo de la keta y las latas de cerveza; yo llevo la mochila de las drogas y el humus.

Jenna y yo nos quedamos atrás enseguida porque se para cada dos por tres para mirar a su alrededor con la boca abierta.

—Esto es precioso —dice.

—Sí —respondo—. Todo verde, bonito y eso.

Muy convincente.

—A la gente parece que ya no le importa. Dejan que se destruya la naturaleza.

—Ya —afirmo. Me enciendo un cigarro—. En vez de toda esta hierba tan bonita hay gente y casas con más gente dentro. Horrible.

—Y ya nadie da nada a la beneficencia.

—Todo el mundo debería donar a la beneficencia —digo.

Creo que la beneficencia es como escayolar a una persona que no tiene piel.

—Deberían venir aquí para empaparse de la belleza de la naturaleza. Entonces lo entenderían.

Respiro sonoramente por la nariz y cierro los ojos.

—Precioso —digo.

Joder, qué estoy haciendo. Voy a necesitar drogas.

Jonah se detiene y nos mira.

—Vamos a parar —dice—. Estoy cansado y quiero un porro.

Susan y él se sientan donde están. Jenna y yo los alcanzamos y nos dejamos caer también, aplastando amapolas con el culo.

Nos sentamos formando un cuadrado. Jonah manosea el King Rizla encima de la mochila. La luz se evapora. El cielo es color miel y el aire va cargado de polen.

—¿A que es precioso? —le dice Susan a Jenna.

—Es impresionante —responde Jenna.

Jonah me mira, molesto, y yo intento no reírme. Ya habrá tiempo de reírnos después, cuando se la haya metido a Jenna. Me imagino su pelo púbico todo revuelto, como el campo de amapolas en el que estamos sentados. Igual la dejo embarazada también. Para de dejar embarazadas a las chicas, Jasper. No tienes madera de padre.

Aborta, Abby, o me pondré una cabeza de caballo y entraré en tu habitación por la noche.

Le trastornaré la vida y le enseñaré a no cargar a gente inocente con bebés feos.

Tengo una chispa brutal.

No tengo a Georgia Treely.

Me pregunto si la policía ha detenido ya a Keith, si le han dado descargas eléctricas en los genitales para conseguir que confiese, si Mamá se siente aliviada porque se ha dado cuenta de la que se ha escapado. Soy un muy buen hijo por haber evitado su asesinato. Seguramente me comprará un Mini Cooper.

Cabeceamos un rato mientras nos pasamos el porro. Jonah está tumbado de espaldas con la cabeza en la mochila. Susan apoya la cabeza en sus piernas mientras se hace nudos en el pelo rubio. Jenna me sonríe y yo intento devolverle la sonrisa pero no se me ocurre nada que decir. Parece expectante.

Cojo una amapola.

—La heroína se hace con amapolas —digo—. Sherlock Holmes fumaba opio.

Pienso en que es ilegal vender droga hecha de flores que crecen en todas partes pero no es ilegal producirla en un laboratorio y venderla por Internet. Al menos, la gente sabe cuáles son los efectos a largo plazo de la heroína sobre la salud y cómo tratarlos. Sabes que si empiezas a meterte heroína al final se te harán rastas en el pelo y morirás. No se sabe qué son las drogas de diseño. Cuando nuestra generación crezca, puede que todos tengamos Parkinson o algo así.

Jonah se sienta y rebusca en la mochila. Saca cuatro cervezas baratas polacas y las tira al centro del cuadrado.

—Bebéoslas —dice—. Estoy cansado de cargar todo el rato con esta mierda.

Abrimos las cervezas y nos las bebemos. Apenas distingo ya el borde del sol en el horizonte. Una tenue luna de pergamino ya ha aparecido en el cielo entre insinuaciones de pequeñas estrellas.

—La luna —comenta Jenna con alegría.

—Anda —digo—. La luna.

Jonah se ríe y escupe la cerveza de la boca en una ducha. A Susan le caen gotitas sobre la piel, pero no dice nada.

Jenna se tumba y se le levanta la camiseta dejando a la vista gran parte del estómago. Me enciendo un Richmond y dejo que se consuma entre mis labios mientras le quito los pétalos a una amapola y los coloco sobre el ombligo de Jenna. Eso se llama flirtear. Flirtear es la puerta tras la que espera el sexo. El sexo es la puerta tras la que esperan los bebés. Putas puertas. Nadie debería abrirlas.

—Deberíamos irnos. Polly estará esperando —dice Jonah.

Jenna se levanta y los pétalos se le caen del estómago. Nos levantamos todos y cargamos las mochilas.

Solo quedan unos metros hasta donde termina el campo y empieza el bosque. Al cruzar los primeros árboles, la luz queda reducida a colores pálidos que se cuelan entre las ramas altas. Jonah dice que tenemos que seguir el camino hasta llegar al lago.

Pasa media hora hasta que encontramos la cascada y el lago

en la pegajosa penumbra del bosque. Polly está subido a una roca, con un cigarro entre los labios, esperando. Dejo caer mi mochila. Jonah se acerca y habla brevemente con Polly. Polly casi nunca sonríe. Vuelve hasta donde estamos.

—Vamos a bañarnos —dice con una sonrisa en la cara.

Observamos la cascada. Es alta y fina, de la anchura de un perro labrador tumbado de lado, y cae a una larga charca rodeada en intervalos irregulares por rocas cubiertas de musgo. Al caer, el agua es de un blanco revuelto, confuso, pero al asentarse en la charca se tiñe de un tono triste de verde.

—¿En serio? —pregunta Susan.

—Sí, en serio. ¿Por qué no?

—¿No está un poco verde? —dice Jenna.

—No —explica Jonah—. Imagínatelo más bien como una esmeralda.

Para convertir el verde triste en esmeralda, nos metemos unas rayas de mefedrona colocadas sobre el espejo compacto de Susan. Jenna duda pero le explico que es una droga legal que se compra por Internet. Eso la convence. Fácil.

El agua no tarda en parecer más atractiva. El verde enfermizo se transforma en el verde del césped recién cortado en verano. Miro bien a Jenna. Ha pasado de ser un objetivo aceptable a ser una estatua griega. Estoy cautivado por la forma en que su ligero cuerpo se hunde sin esfuerzo formando un arco de caderas, muslos esculpidos y espinillas color salmón hasta los perfectos pies diminutos y las tenues uñas de melocotón.

Después, llegan las sonrisas. Nos tiran de las mejillas a uno detrás de otro. Hacemos una ola de sonrisas torcidas. Nos desnudamos mientras nuestros miembros se agitan felizmente y nuestras bocas se aceleran.

—Os quiero a todos —dice Jonah.

—A la gente solo le importa el dinero y la guerra —digo.

—Deberían quererse más. Te quiero.

Jenna se da la vuelta y me abraza fuerte. Le meto la lengua en la boca y la muevo.

—La guerra y el dinero me la chupan.

—¡Vamos a casarnos todos!

—¡Sí, joder!

La tierra me hace cosquillas en la cabeza. Jenna está tirando montones al aire.

—También quiero a Polly.

—Yo también quiero a Pollyloly.

—¡Deberíamos decírselo!

—¡Cásate con él!

Más tierra en la cabeza, por el cuello.

—Que se bañe, debería bañarse con nosotros.

—O nosotros deberíamos bañarnos con él.

Todo se mezcla en una mancha de sonido y color. Soy la explosión de una supernova de buen rollo.

Formamos un círculo alrededor de Polly, que sigue sentado en la roca, fumando. Somos leones del amor rodeando a una gacela herida. Parece resignado y ligeramente divertido. Tal vez tenga miedo, no lo sé. Todo me parece maravilloso.

—Polly, eres increíble —dice Susan.

—Báñate, por favor.

—Báñate.

—Con nosotros.

—Lo siento mucho por todo.

—Eres un superhombre.

—Superhombre.

—Oh, gracias —dice Polly al moverse sobre la roca.

—Me acostaré contigo. Quiero follarte.

Veo una mano que se acerca a la entrepierna de Polly. Nos lanzamos para rodearlo en un feroz abrazo de oso que le provoca un sonido extraño antes de salir corriendo entre los árboles. Aullamos de risa y nos tiramos a la fría charca esmeralda.

Al meternos en el agua nos sentimos como si hubiéramos ganado un gran premio en metálico. Se nos filtra en la piel y nos convierte en velas. Todo brilla, todo es maravilloso.

—¡No somos la Generación de Internet!

—¡A la mierda la generación!

—¡A la mierda!

—¡A la mierda la televisión!

—Y Twitter.

—Y Formspring.

—¿Qué es Formspring?

—Da igual.

—Te quiero, Jonah.

—Te quiero, Jasper.

—Te quiero, Jenna.

—Te quiero, Susan.

El lago no es muy profundo y podemos estar de pie pero nos dedicamos a hacer volteretas. Levantamos paredes de agua que caen enseguida y se me cuelan entre el pelo y en la boca. Se nos mancha la lengua de verde. Nos reímos sin parar.

Me pego a Jenna. Sus ojos entran en los míos. Sus tetas aplastadas contra mi pecho me hacen darme cuenta de que son la única parte de su cuerpo que no encajará con el mío. Ojalá tuviera unos huecos en el pecho del tamaño de sus tetas para que pudiéramos estar más juntos.

Nuestras narices se tocan.

—Esquimales —susurra.

Grito.

Se ríe.

Nos dejamos caer hacia atrás en el agua, yo encima de ella, hasta que está en el fondo de la charca retorciéndose. Cuando salimos de nuevo a la superficie, se nos llenan las mejillas de más risas. Jenna está preciosa. Tiene el pelo aplastado y oscuro por el agua sucia. Parece chocolate derretido.

Jonah y Susan están encajando sus cuerpos al otro lado de la charca. Ella gime como un caballo moribundo y tiene los ojos muy abiertos, como si acabara de ver a su abuelo muerto vestido de mujer haciéndole un baile erótico a la Reina entre los árboles.

Pongo una mano a cada lado de la cintura de Jenna y le acerco la pelvis por el agua como Tiburón. Hunde la cara en la curva de mi cuello y después se desliza hacia arriba, hacia el lóbulo, y muerde. Sangre. Grito y me aparto.

—Lo siento —dice—. No puedo.

Chapoteo hacia el paisaje de ropa tirada y me pongo los bóxers. Así es como debe de sentirse Ping. Agachado sobre la piedra de Polly, enciendo el porro que se había olvidado Jonah. Los observo mientras follan. La mefedrona aún me lo pinta todo de rosa así que todo me parece bonito. Pienso en que lo que en realidad busca la gente es penetrar a los demás. No estar rodeado de otras personas, sino estar dentro de otras personas. Someter a otras personas. Entregarse, desnudos y sinceros, a otra persona. Dejar que la boca emita sonidos animales en la cara de otra persona. Escuchar a esa otra persona emitir sonidos animales.

Cinco minutos después, Polly aparece de entre los árboles y se pone a mi lado, con un cigarro colgando en los labios. Se pasa la mano por el pelo.

—¿Casi acabado? —pregunta.

—Sí, casi.

—¿Qué dice?

—Que sí.

—¿Sí?

—Sí.

Sé que se me está pasando el efecto porque me empieza a molestar su acento.

Polly tira la colilla a la charca y se cruza de brazos.

—Vamos, ahora —dice en voz alta pero sin gritar.

Jenna chapotea y Jonah y Susan están abrazados, gastan las últimas risas de la droga y salen del agua. Mientras se visten y buscan tabaco, intento sacarle información al polaco sobre la fiesta.

—¿Qué tal están las chicas de la fiesta? —pregunto, señalando los árboles con la cabeza.

—¿Qué dice?

—¿Chicas?

Señala el culo desnudo de Jenna, del color del pollo cocido.

—Sí.

—Mmm. —Mira a su alrededor como si buscara respuestas—. Volv... Vuel... Vol... Volve.

—¿Qué?

—Vol... Volve.

Me rindo y voy a robarle un cigarro a Jonah. A mí se me han acabado. Espero que haya muchas chicas, me da igual lo de Jenna. Tampoco era tan guapa. Era extraña y alegre y aburrida.

—Vamosvamos —ordena Krasicki.

Se adentra entre los árboles y le seguimos.

30

La casa de campo de los padres de Amanda Forthwart se llama Chinkapin Farm. Es grande, achaparrada y está pintada de un color entre el rosa y el naranja. La hiedra cubre la parte delantera.

La gente está en corros, fumando y bebiendo latas de cerveza. Las puertas y ventanas de la casa están abiertas. No conozco a mucha gente. No veo a Georgia Treely.

Dentro, las alfombras ya se han llenado de barro, manchas de cerveza y colillas de cigarro. Hay gente en los sofás y sentada por el suelo.

—Vamos arriba —le digo a Jonah.

Lo aparto de Susan y Jenna. Si no puedo follármela, tampoco quiero estar cerca de ella.

Arriba, encontramos una habitación de invitados con papel pintado de flores. Dentro solo está una rubia que se ha desmayado en la cama. Nos sentamos en la moqueta y encendemos el hornillo para cocinar la ketamina.

Cuando el líquido se ha vuelto polvo, hacemos rayas en un libro de Danielle Steel de tapa dura que había en una estantería de la habitación. Nos metemos dos por cada lado de la nariz y nos tumbamos. Noto la droga como orugas por la garganta.

—Jasper —dice Jonah.

—¿Qué?
—Antes estaba raro porque me he puesto a pensar.
—Sí.
Oigo su voz pero no llego a entender las palabras. Me enciendo un cigarro y me miro las líneas de las manos.
—Pensaba en que el año que viene es nuestro último año, ¿no? Después, nos iremos de aquí. Odio esta puta ciudad pero es que hemos estado aquí siempre.
—Jonah.
Se aprieta los ojos con las manos.
—¿Qué?
—¿Tienes miedo?
—No —responde mirando a la chica de la cama—. Vete a la mierda.
—Sí que tienes —le confirmo. Todo el mundo tiene miedo.
—No seas marica.
—Yo también tengo miedo —le digo. Soy sincero.
—¿Sí?
—Sí. A la mierda el ejército. Vámonos a Francia. Podemos robar comida y follarnos a las chicas de los pueblos. O podemos ir a Canadá y encontrar una cabaña en un lago y llenarla de vino y putas.
—Jasper —dice—. Me voy a alistar en el ejército. El ahora es para hacer el capullo, el mañana es para hacer algo. No puedes hacer el capullo para siempre.
—¿Por qué no?
—Porque, si lo haces, acabarás como los padres de Tenaya.
Me miro las manos. Las líneas bailan.
—Vale —digo.
—¿Quieres otra raya?
—Vale.
—Después, deberíamos bajar.
—Vale. Voy a ligarme a Georgia Treely.

Jonah se ríe.

Después de las rayas, no bajamos. Nos tumbamos y nos quedamos mirando el techo. El yeso tiene unas líneas que forman pequeñas olas. Una modesta lámpara de araña cuelga sobre nuestras cabezas pateando la poca luz que aún entra por la única ventana.

La rubia se despierta, se revuelve el pelo y se levanta de la cama. Nos mira con unos ojos vidriosos y lejanos, vacíos.

—¿Quieres una raya? —le pregunta Jonah.

Asiente con la cabeza.

Me pregunto quién será, si alguna vez se tumba en la cama dándose bofetadas solo para asegurarse de que aún puede, qué ve en su imaginación cuando intenta pensar en qué viene después.

Le hago una raya y se la mete. Se desmaya otra vez, ahora encima del regazo de Jonah. La empuja para quitársela de encima y ella cae al suelo.

—Vamos abajo —dice Jonah.

Ping, Tenaya y Ana ya han llegado. Ping está sentado junto a la televisión con Tenaya, Ana y otros seis o siete más sentados alrededor. Tiene un sifón para la nata de metal negro y vacía pequeñas bombonas plateadas en forma de balas en globos brillantes de colores.

Los globos de óxido nitroso son experiencias religiosas. Te sacan del lugar en el que estés y te dejan en mitad de la nada. Dejas de tener manos, pies y cabeza. Todo es un eco. Todo es un eco. Todo pasa extremadamente despacio pero de forma brusca, como ver un vídeo de YouTube con una conexión de acceso telefónico. Solo duran medio minuto o así.

Se puede comprar un cargador de óxido de nitrógeno y recambios en Internet por poco dinero. A veces, lo llaman «crack hippie». Me siento junto a Tenaya. Tiene los ojos húmedos otra vez. Quizá haya muerto alguien más. Quizá alguien se haya caído por el borde del planeta. Tenaya es una persona muy emotiva. Todas las personas son emotivas. Yo soy muy emotivo pero no lo muestro porque, si lo hiciera a menudo, pensarían que soy débil y me atracarían, emocionalmente.

—Hola —dice Tenaya.

—¿Qué te pasa? —le pregunto.

—No me había puesto de nitrógeno en mucho tiempo.

—¿Qué te pasa? —repito.

Tenaya señala por encima del hombro. A través de la puerta abierta, veo a Tom fumando fuera junto a una chica con un vestido morado. Están cogidos de la mano. La chica no lleva zapatos.

—Ese vestido es mío —dice.

—Gilipollas —digo yo.

—Sí.

Le pongo una mano en el pelo y se lo revuelvo, con cariño. Estoy haciendo que se sienta mejor.

—Para, Jasper.

—Vale.

Ping nos pasa dos globos. Alguien pone la canción «Grow Up and Blow Away», de Metric. La música es una parte muy importante del nitrógeno. Te coloca en un pedestal desde el que observar lo que te rodea. La música suena a todo volumen.

Si esto es vida,
¿por qué morir hoy me hace sentir tan bien?
De azul a gris
crece y desaparece.

Ping cuenta hasta tres. A la de tres, todos soplamos y nos metemos el cuello del globo en la boca para inhalar y exhalar el gas de sabor agradable. Veo a Tenaya a mi izquierda. Tiene los ojos cerrados. Enseguida dejo de ver.

Todo lo que mis ojos y oídos perciben se reduce a una serie de círculos borrosos que no paran de girar. La música se convierte en un fuerte sonido ambiental. Otros sonidos oscilan, se repiten y se separan.

La letra de la canción se ralentiza hasta detenerse y se sienta delante de mí, flotando en el aire. Crece y desaparece. Estoy sentado en la C de Crece. Me cuelgan las piernas. Subo por las palabras del estribillo.

Tenaya se ríe pero sigue teniendo los ojos rojos. Todo se enfoca. Hay risas por todas partes. Todo el mundo salta, se abraza y grita de alegría, como si hubiéramos luchado en una guerra y hubiéramos ganado.

31

Me siento bien. Es la 1:30. Estoy en la cocina hablando con una chica que cree en los ángeles. Dice que mi aura es azul. Yo le digo que ella parece que no tiene. Llega Ping. Me coge del brazo y me dice que vaya con él a la despensa de debajo de las escaleras y que necesitaré una cerveza.

La despensa huele a humedad. Está totalmente a oscuras porque Ping ha cerrado la puerta. Les doy a los botones del móvil para que dé luz.

—¿No pensarás darme un beso? —digo.

—Vete a la mierda.

—¿Entonces?

—Es por Abby Hall —dice Ping. Da un trago a la cerveza—. Por lo del bebé.

Escupo la cerveza como un mal actor.

—¿Cómo coño sabes eso?

—Abby se lo contó a Ana.

—¿Y por qué coño se lo contó a Ana?

—Ana no les cae muy bien a las chicas. No puede permitirse no ser amiga de alguien. Da igual. ¿Quieres que te lo cuente o no?

Algo muere en mi estómago.

—No lo sé.

—Sí lo sabes.

Me bebo la cerveza de un trago.

—Vale.

—Es de Ben McKay.

Grito de alegría. De puta madre. Esto es genial. Es lo mejor que podría haber pasado. Me tranquilizo.

—¿Qué? ¿Cuándo?

—En la fiesta de Carrie Waterman.

—Pero Abby está castigada —digo—. ¿Cómo fue?

—Sí —contesta Ping—. Pero Ben McKay le dijo que la quería así que se escapó para verle.

Me río con todas mis ganas, otra vez.

—¿Por qué le dijo eso?

—Le habían contado que Abby es fácil.

—Es verdad.

—Jasper.

—¿Qué?

—¿Por qué no nos dijiste nada?

—No lo sé. No quería pensar en el tema.

—Vale.

—¿Te has follado ya a Ana?

—No.

—Ah.

—Ya casi ni me importa.

—¿En serio?

—Sí.

—Qué raro.

—Ya.

—Vamos fuera.

—Vale.

32

Me están entrando ganas de vomitar. ¿Dónde está Georgia Treely? Estoy muy borracho. El Plan Georgia. No voy a ser padre. 2:35. No he visto a Tenaya desde hace una o dos horas. Decido ir a buscarla.

No está en la cocina, ni en los armarios de la cocina, ni bajo los cojines del sofá, ni en la televisión, ni en ninguna de las habitaciones de arriba. La gente aún no está de bajón, ni se ha tumbado en el suelo a dormir. La gente sigue bebiendo y follando. La casa sigue llena de mucho ruido.

Seguramente, Tenaya estará fuera.

Voy al baño a sentarme. Me siento en el váter y me miro fijamente las manos. Las líneas bailan. Los pliegues de los dedos sufren espasmos.

Un ruido desde el otro lado del baño.

El armario del calentador.

Abro la puerta y me encuentro a Tenaya agachada junto al aislamiento del calentador. Queda el espacio justo para meterme a su lado. Es como si estuviéramos en una caja llena de aire de la selva. Lleva el iPod puesto. Le quito el auricular del oído derecho y me lo pongo en el izquierdo. Bon Iver. Sus ojos son estuarios pero, al menos, no se ha autolesionado. Durante un rato, no hacemos nada, nos quedamos sentados. Sé por qué llora. Me siento comprensivo. Llora por Tom pero también por lo que Tom representa: fracaso. Todos fracasamos a menudo. Nos fallamos los unos a los otros y nos fallamos a nosotros mismos. Mamá le falló a Papá, Keith le falló a Margaret, Tabitha le falló a la vida, Tom le falló a Tenaya, Jonah les ha fallado a unas treinta chicas. Supongo que yo le he fallado a Abby. Lo siento, Abby.

A la media hora o así, empieza a llover. El agua repiquetea en la pared de detrás de nuestras cabezas como si tuviera una vejiga del tamaño de una moneda y estuviéramos metidos en el único baño. Lluvia persistente, de acero. El sonido del agua al caer no encaja con el ambiente de sauna que nos rodea. Es como una niña gritando porque se ha cortado en la rodilla mientras estás calentito en la cama leyendo *Harry Potter*.

Cuando te sientes triste y llueve se llama «falacia patética». Como en *Macbeth*, cuando Duncan muere y hay una tormenta. La falacia patética en la vida real es como si la Naturaleza se mostrara insensible y empeorara las cosas. Por eso, ahora mismo no creo que la Madre Naturaleza deba llamarse así. Debería llamarse Naturaleza Keith o Naturaleza Tom o Naturaleza Hijadeputa. Mi cabeza de cristal se ha roto y Tenaya está triste. Las madres no se mean sobre las personas cuando se sienten así, las abrazan y maldicen a sus enemigos.

Saco la papelina de mefedrona y preparo dos esquinas de la tarjeta de crédito para sentirnos mejor.

Enciendo un cigarro.

Tenaya apoya la cabeza en mi pecho y siento la humedad de sus mejillas empapando mi camiseta.

—¿Estás bien? —pregunto.

—No lo sé. —Me quita el cigarro de la mano y le da una calada—. Me siento rara.

—Ya —le digo—. Lo sé.

Tenaya levanta la cabeza. Me mira directamente a los ojos.

Intenta subir por mi cuerpo como sea. Va a subir y a esconderse allí.

Se acerca más y me besa.

Resulta extraño que estemos haciendo esto pero tampoco tanto porque no parece Tenaya, sino una imagen borrosa y aguada. No pienso en quién es o en qué pretende, solo pienso en estar cerca de otro cuerpo.

Nos seguimos besando. Besa con seguridad.

Abre la puerta del armario del calentador. Salimos y vamos a la bañera vacía. Se mete dentro. Es un feto enorme en un útero blanco de plástico. Se baja los pantalones y saca su precioso pie izquierdo.

No debería.

Me tumbo entre sus piernas. Muevo la pelvis de forma sencilla pero agradable. Abre la boca. Levanta la cabeza y se da con el grifo. Lo hago lo mejor que sé.

Después, me siento y ella se queda tumbada, con la cabeza sobre mi pecho. Me doy cuenta de que hay charquitos en el fondo de la bañera. Mapas de agua se dibujan en la tela de mi pantalón. Tiene el pelo mojado. Como una niña que se ha ahogado en el océano. Una niña diminuta. Por accidente. Solo una vez.

Tengo lágrimas en los ojos porque, no sé por qué. Siento que me tiemblan las manos. Se me acelera el corazón. Ella sigue con la cara hundida en mi pecho.

Me doy cuenta de que lo he hecho.

Me he mordido las uñas hasta sangrar.

Me he ahorcado con una media de rugby.

He asesinado a mi ex mujer.

Al menos, ya no voy a ser padre.

Me arrastro debajo de ella para salir de la bañera y me voy.

33

Miro la hora en el móvil. Las 3:11. Me quedo mirando a la pared. Vuelvo a sacar el móvil para ver la hora. Las 3:12. Hay una lata medio llena de cerveza sobre el televisor, así que la cojo. He dado tres vueltas a la casa y no he encontrado a Georgia Treely. Mi cabeza no para. No retengo nada. Un chico y una chica que no conozco están acurrucados en el sofá. La chica emite grititos agudos.

No quiero ver más gente follando, así que salgo. El aire es frío y negro. Me hace daño en la garganta. Hay gente dormida en los coches, envueltos en mantas, acurrucados.

Sigo el camino bordeado de arbustos que se dirige al campo. La luna ilumina lo suficiente.

Avanzo un poco y me detengo. Oigo ruidos detrás de unos arbustos. Hay ropa y zapatos al borde del camino.

Meto la cabeza entre las hojas. Toma ya. Tom y su nueva novia están follando sobre la hierba. Deben de tener mucho frío porque tiene la piel del culo de porcelana erizada.

Saco la cabeza de entre los arbustos y me bajo la bragueta. Apunto con la polla a uno de los zapatos de Tom y disparo un chorro de pis amarillo neón. Siento que estoy haciendo justicia, más o menos. A Tenaya le parecerá bien, seguro.

¿Dónde estás, Georgia?

Vamos, Jasper.

Soy un chico extremadamente asqueroso.

Siguiendo por el camino, oigo más ruidos procedentes de un campo al otro lado de los arbustos. Son ruidos de otro tipo. Aullidos, tacos y mugidos. Interesante.

Atravieso el arbusto. Al otro lado, Ping, Jonah y Ana corren desnudos alrededor de tres vacas. ¿Por qué todo el mundo se desnuda? Ping tiene un palo enorme en la mano y una vaca le persigue. Me río.

Cuando Jonah me ve, corre hacia mí y me anima para que me quite la ropa. Le digo que se vaya a la mierda. No acepta irse a la mierda como respuesta. Jonah, Ana y Ping me tiran al suelo y me quitan la ropa. Me resisto pero no paro de reírme. Grito que no voy a ser padre. Qué se habrán tomado. Jonah y Ping me tiran de los pantalones y Ana me quita la camiseta. Poco después, estoy en el suelo en bóxers con la hierba rozándome las piernas. Jonah intenta quitármelos pero entonces una vaca color caoba viene hacia nosotros.

Me levanto y corro.

Corremos por el campo, alejándonos de la casa.

Jonah se para.

—¿Qué? —pregunto.

Señala a la distancia. Apenas puedo distinguir una luz suspendida en el aire. No tengo buena vista. No podría ser piloto ni cazador profesional.

—Es el puto granjero —dice. Su voz suena asustada pero sonríe.

—Escuchad —dice Ping.

Escuchamos.

Ladridos.

—Trae perros.

Nos damos la vuelta inmediatamente y corremos hacia las

vacas, en dirección a la casa. Las vacas dan mucho menos miedo que un granjero enfadado con perros enormes.

Corremos a ciegas en dirección contraria a los perros que ladran. Solo me detengo para sacar mi jersey de la boca de una vaca. No me paro a buscar el resto de mi ropa.

No dejo de correr hasta que estoy cerca de la casa y apenas puedo respirar.

Ana, Ping y Jonah no están conmigo pero no me preocupo. Seguro que han escapado, seguro que nadie ha sido devorado. Meto las piernas por los brazos del jersey. Los bóxers asoman por el agujero de la cabeza.

En el salón de la casa, me paro en seco.

Georgia Treely.

Hora del Plan Georgia. Muéstrate sexy. Seguro. Está sentada en el sofá, sola, sujetándose la cabeza. Lleva el pelo lleno de horquillas brillantes y pasadores. Parece un nido de luciérnagas. Quiero llevar sus luciérnagas sobre los hombros. Quiero permiso para tocarle la piel y abrazarla fuerte y no pensar en Keith ni en Tenaya ni en Tabitha Mowai ni en Abby Hall durante unos minutos. Me quedo mirándole los pies sin decir nada. La luz tenue de la lámpara hace que los huesos de sus pies proyecten sombras. En la tele están echando la segunda película de *Jackass*.

Cojo una cerveza medio vacía del suelo y me la bebo de un trago para armarme de valor. Esto se llama «valor holandés». Es ofensivo para los holandeses porque implica que no son capaces de hacer nada sin beber antes.

—Hola, Georgia Treely —digo al colocarme delante de ella.

—Ah, Jasper. Hola. —Me mira de arriba abajo—. Jasper —dice—, ¿por qué llevas un jersey en las piernas?

—Por nada —digo, y me siento a su lado—. ¿Estás bien?

—Sí. No. No lo sé. Me encuentro un poco mal. Creo que he bebido demasiado. No suelo beber.

—Ah —digo—. Lo siento.

Le pongo la mano en la espalda y la muevo de arriba abajo. Le muestro comprensión. La comprensión atrae.

—¿Quieres hacer algo para sentirte mejor?

—Nada de drogas, no tomo drogas.

—No, drogas, no. Bueno, sí, drogas, pero de las legales. Me refería a un café.

—Mi madre bebe café.

—Genial. Vamos arriba a por un café.

La cojo de la mano y la llevo arriba.

Una vez en la habitación de invitados, Georgia Treely y yo nos tomamos un café enorme. Le aseguro que la gente siempre toma cafés así de grandes.

Georgia Treely se queda un rato mirando a la pared. Imagino que la cabeza le burbujea porque es la primera vez que toma algo.

Le confieso que siempre la miro en clase de Psicología y que intenté hablar con ella por el chat de Facebook pero que no estaba. Asiente. Me toca la mano. Es la primera vez que se droga. Pensará que está enamorada de mí.

—Te quiero, Jasper —me dice.

¿Esto está bien? Me parece algo retorcido. Ligeramente inmoral. Un poco estilo violador, tal vez.

Celebro un breve juicio moral en mi cabeza. Utilizo los personajes de *Rebelión en la granja*.

Cerdo: ¡Protesto rotundamente! Qué espanto. Sería como mear en un jarrón de porcelana fina de la dinastía Ming.

Perro: Protesto. Está victimizando al acusado.

Cerdo: Protesto, solo una víctima puede ser victimizada.

Rata: ¡Desconfusión gramatical!

Juez: Irrelevante.

Vaca: ¿El qué?

Perro: Está bastante buena.

Cerdo: Muy buena, sí.

Juez: Entonces, adelante.

Jasper J. Wolf: Muchas gracias a todos.

—Yo también te quiero —le digo.

Me levanto y voy a la cama. La chica desmayada sigue ahí. La levanto y la dejo en el suelo. Georgia Treely se tumba en la cama. Me tumbo sobre Georgia Treely. Quiero un holocausto nuclear que acabe con todo y nos deje intactos a Georgia Treely y a mí.

Creo que lo que pasa a continuación y lo tremendamente bien que me siento es bastante obvio.

34

7:32. Tengo la cabeza ardiendo y me duele. Una débil luz llena la habitación y el ambiente está cargado, pesa como el cristal. Me giro a la izquierda. La cabeza de Georgia Treely está junto a la mía. Es la cabeza más bonita del mundo. Parece un poco muerta. Espero que no esté muerta. Igual es una broma. Igual alguien ha puesto una cabeza falsa de Georgia Treely en la cama a mi lado para que me sienta muy feliz al despertarme hasta que vaya a besarla y me dé cuenta de que es de plástico. Toco la cabeza. No es de plástico. Le doy un beso en la frente.

Algunas mujeres solo les parecen guapas a ciertos hombres a ciertas horas de la mañana con cierta luz. Georgia Treely no es una de ellas.

Entonces recuerdo lo que pasó anoche.

Todo indica que igual la he violado. A ver, ella quería pero probablemente no quería querer. Fueron las drogas las que la hicieron querer. En el juicio, afirmaré que no tenía ni idea. En el juicio, lloraré hasta que me dejen marcharme. Me deslizo fuera de la cama. Me siento muy mareado. Alguien se ha dejado la ropa en el suelo. Me la pongo y salgo rápidamente. Escapo de la escena del crimen. Una chica pasa corriendo por delante de la puerta cuando salgo. Desaparece escaleras abajo y sale de la casa. Su cara era la de alguien que ha escapado por los pelos de la muerte. Jonah sale despacio de la habitación con un edredón sobre los hombros.

—¿Qué coño ha sido eso?

Jonah mueve un envoltorio vacío delante de mi cara.

Condón católico.

Me río con todas mis ganas.

—Me pareció gracioso —comenta—. No sé.

—La gracia no dura tanto —le digo—. Y un bebé dura siglos.

—Lo sé. Ha sido una gilipollez. —Se aprieta los ojos con los dedos—. Voy a dormir un poco. Buenas noches, Jasper.

—Buenas noches.

Se tapa la cara con el edredón y entra tambaleándose en la habitación.

Hay gente durmiendo en los pasillos y en la escalera y en el suelo de abajo. Dos chicos del Baccant High siguen despiertos fumándose un porro en la cocina. Uno de ellos me saluda con la cabeza. Salgo fuera a sentarme.

El cielo es amplio, blanco, con una capa del verde menta de las primeras horas de la mañana. Las nubes rosas se apretujan y se aparean. Avanzan en pequeños grupos por el borde de los campos. Todo está en silencio. El silencio más silencioso siempre llega después del estruendo más estruendoso. Eso pasa porque el silencio puede rodearte con el brazo, señalar al ruido que lo precede y decirte: «Mira todo ese ruido y compáralo conmigo».

Rodeo la casa y, a un lado, encuentro a Tenaya sentada con las piernas cruzadas en el capó del coche de Ping. Está fumando y sostiene una taza de té junto al pecho. Me subo a su lado.

—Buenos días —dice.

—Hola —respondo. Me pasa la taza de té, le doy un trago y se la devuelvo—. Anoche fue... —Es todo lo que consigo decir.

—Lo sé —comenta—. Los dos teníamos miedo y estábamos tristes y borrachos. Ya lo hablaremos.

Me sonríe.

—No pasa nada —me dice.

—Vale.

—¿Qué pasó después?

Trago saliva.

—Mmm —balbuceo—. Nada.

—Venga ya.

—Vale. —Tenaya es capaz de hacerme admitirlo todo, siempre—. Puede que haya violado a Georgia Treely.

Tenaya se ríe.

—No creo que hayas violado a nadie, Jasper.

—Pues la drogué un montón y después me la follé.

Tenaya se ríe otra vez.

—Eso me suena a lo que les pasa a la mayoría de chicas.

—No estoy seguro, a mí no me suena nada bien.

—No seas tonto. —Tenaya se termina el té de un largo trago—. ¿Podemos ir ya a buscar a Ping y largarnos de aquí? —me pregunta.

—Sí —digo—. Me muero de hambre.

Pateamos la casa durante un buen rato antes de encontrar a Ping y a Ana dormidos en un armario enorme lleno de calcetines. Despertamos a Ping para que nos lleve porque no queremos tener que andar hasta el coche de Jonah. Ping se caga en todo durante un rato cuando lo despertamos pero después se da cuenta de que también tiene hambre y accede a llevarnos.

Para en una cafetería que parece una cocina de plástico, con manteles llenos de manchas moradas y menús en los que el plastificado empieza a abrirse. Todas las camareras son extranjeras. Hablan en acelerados desprendimientos de palabras duras. Es sexy que chicas guapas hablen idiomas feos.

—Quiero el Desayuno Madrugador —le digo a la camarera.

—¿Qué cosa?

—Esto, el Desayuno Madrugador...

—¿Qué?

—MA-DRU-GA-DORRR.

Rodeo las palabras con los labios como si les estuviera haciendo una mamada.

—¿Eh? No entiende.

Ya no es tan sexy.

Estiro los brazos como si me estuviera desperezando y me llevo una mano a la boca. Sonríe. Jonah y Tenaya se ríen.

Al final, le señalo el menú.

Comemos rápido y en silencio. Cuando Ping me deja en casa, solo pienso en dormir. Mamá no piensa en dormir. Mamá está de pie en la puerta con las manos en la cadera.

35

La sala de interrogatorios de la policía en la que estoy sentado huele a café y a madera vieja. Huele como una sala en la que la gente no quiere entrar. Incluso la pintura de las paredes intenta irse. Quiero irme.

—Quiero irme —digo—. Estoy muy cansado.

Enfrente de mí hay un hombre que dice llamarse P. C. Holloway. P. C. Holloway tiene un bigote apenas visible y unos enormes ojos azules. Junta las manos encima de la mesa. Me está mirando. La mirada es neutral. Me cuesta leer su lenguaje corporal.

—Tienes que entender que esto ha sido una grave pérdida de tiempo para la policía —me dice.

Habla de Keith. De que Keith en realidad no es un asesino y me he equivocado porque a veces pienso demasiado, con demasiadas ganas y durante demasiado tiempo. Una manera de explicarlo sería decir que mi imaginación es como un río de aguas rápidas y que mi cuerpo es un barco en el río que la corriente se lleva pero que debe aprender a no dejarse arrastrar. Me duele la cabeza.

—Lo entiendo —digo—. Lo siento mucho, muchísimo.

Se pone de pie. Me pongo de pie.

—Siéntate —me dice.

Me siento.

—Es broma —me dice.

P. C. Holloway tiene un gran sentido del humor. Algunas de las personas más divertidas del mundo son hombres. Su mujer tiene mucha suerte.

Me acompaña hasta la puerta de la comisaría y me revuelve el pelo.

—Pórtate bien —me dice.

Ojalá P. C. Holloway fuera el marido de Mamá.

Encuentro a Mamá sentada en los escalones que llevan hasta la puerta de la comisaría. Se está fumando un cigarro. Me siento a su lado.

—Mamá —digo.

—Sí, Jasper.

—Los cigarros contienen alquitrán que te dejará los pulmones negros y te los destrozará —la informo.

—Sí, Jasper —dice mientras apaga el cigarro—. Gracias.

—No deberías volver a fumar. Sé que estás estresada pero el cáncer es más estresante aún, supongo.

—Lo sé.

—Vale —digo, y me levanto—. ¿Podemos irnos a casa ya?

—Sí.

Mamá está enfadada conmigo por hacer que detengan a su marido pero todavía me quiere porque soy su hijo.

36

8:30. Me despierto. Radio 4 sigue sonando. Un hombre y una mujer discuten sobre el futuro del cine en 3D. Salgo de la cama y voy al baño. En la ducha, toso y tiemblo. La tinta del tabaco extranjero barato me ha jodido los pulmones. El agua se calienta. Mi cabeza se despeja.

Me siento muy confuso.

Me siento vacío.

Me siento frustrado.

Pero me follé a Georgia Treely.

Vale.

Georgia Treely es guapa. Georgia Treely es sexualmente atractiva. Un tribunal de animales antropomorfizados dictaminó que debía follarme a Georgia Treely. Me he follado a Georgia Treely. El sexo lo es todo. El sexo es para las vallas publicitarias y las revistas. No sirve para tomar decisiones vitales. El sexo debería ser una consecuencia de algo más. Georgia Treely es una vaca y la he matado por el cuero. Solo se deberían matar vacas para comer.

¿Qué coño significa eso? No importa, por lo menos, no voy a ser padre.

Me seco, me visto y bajo. Keith está sentado en la cocina, leyendo *The Sun*. Levanta la vista.

—Hola —digo.

—Buenos días.

Cuando volvimos de la comisaría de policía, Keith me dijo que me había perdonado. Es un hombre de una moralidad excepcional. Sin embargo, ha dejado de utilizar sus apodos condescendientes y simpáticos. Tendré que esforzarme para volver a ganarme su confianza, para que vuelva a llamarme «colega».

Me sirvo un vaso de leche y lo llevo al cobertizo del fondo del jardín. Saco mi cuaderno de detrás de una pala y empiezo a trabajar en mi novela de nuevo. La novela está casi terminada. Es la historia de un joven dotado de un gran carisma e ingenio que intenta averiguar qué hacer y cómo hacerlo. Tiene todo lo que quería: una escena con una especie de violación (lo siento otra vez, Georgia), una especie de revelación (lo siento otra vez, Keith) y una especie de lección. Aún no sé cuál es la lección pero está claro que habrá una.

Soy Holden Caulfield solo que menos temerario y más atractivo.

37

15:28. Estoy con Tenaya en su jardín. El sol parece muy cercano, es enorme. Las gallinas cantan. Hay una tetera entre los dos.

Su madre sale por las puertas acristaladas. Lleva una camiseta que dice BOYCOTT ISRAELI GOODS. Trae un plato de galletas Custard Cream.

—Gracias, Mamá —dice Tenaya.

Está igual de confusa que yo.

—Gracias, señora Enright.

—Papá se ha marchado, Ten —le dice su madre.

—Ya lo sé.

—Se va a quedar un tiempo con un amigo.

—Tengo diecisiete, Mamá. Papá y tú os vais a divorciar.

Su madre entrecierra los ojos. Se le llenan de lágrimas, rebosan y le caen por las mejillas.

—Lo siento —dice Tenaya.

Se levanta y abraza a su madre. Me levanto y abrazo a la madre de Tenaya por detrás. Su culo presiona mi entrepierna. Somos un bocadillo de madre de Tenaya. No es momento de erecciones. Pienso en Terry Wogan, desnudo, practicando judo, con Louis Walsh.

Tras un par de minutos, se separa de nosotros. Me revuelve el pelo.

—Está mucho mejor sin él, señora Enright —le digo.

La madre de Tenaya vuelve tranquilamente a la cocina. Nos sentamos y la observamos descolgar unas ollas de los ganchos de la pared embaldosada. El olor a cebolla frita se escapa al jardín.

Pongo una mano sobre la mano de Tenaya, en un gesto sexy.

—Jasper —dice—, ¿qué estás haciendo?

—Es para mi novela —respondo—. Le falta el desarrollo del personaje y la resolución.

—Ah.

—¿Puedo escribir que nos besamos?

—Si quieres —responde.

—Vale.

Nos besamos.